DOLLARS AND DREAMS
The Changing American Income Distribution

THE POPULATION OF THE UNITED STATES IN THE 1980s

A Census Monograph Series

DOLLARS AND DREAMS
The Changing American Income Distribution

Frank Levy

for the
National Committee for Research
on the 1980 Census

RUSSELL SAGE FOUNDATION / NEW YORK

The Russell Sage Foundation

Library of Congress Cataloging-in-Publication Data

Levy, Frank, 1941–
    Dollars and dreams.

    (The population of the United States in the 1980s)
    Bibliography: p.
    Includes index.
    1. Income distribution—United States. 2. Income—United States. 3. United States—Economic conditions—1945– I. National Committee for Research on the 1980 Census. II. Title. III. Series.
HC110.I5L47 1987   339.2'0973   86-42952
ISBN 0-8-7154-523-3

Cover and text design: HUGUETTE FRANCO

10 9 8 7 6 5 4 3 2 1

The National Committee for Research on the 1980 Census

The committee is sponsored by the Social Science Research Council, the Russell Sage Foundation, and the Alfred P. Sloan Foundation, in collaboration with the U.S. Bureau of the Census. The opinions, findings, and conclusions or recommendations expressed in the monographs supported by the committee are those of the author(s) and do not necessarily reflect the views of the committee or its sponsors.

Foreword

Dollars and Dreams is one of an ambitious series of volumes aimed at converting the vast statistical yield of the 1980 census into authoritative analyses of major changes and trends in American life. This series, "The Population of the United States in the 1980s," represents an important episode in social science research and revives a long tradition of independent census analysis. First in 1930, and then again in 1950 and 1960, teams of social scientists worked with the U.S. Bureau of the Census to investigate significant social, economic, and demographic developments revealed by the decennial censuses. These census projects produced three landmark series of studies, providing a firm foundation and setting a high standard for our present undertaking.

There is, in fact, more than a theoretical continuity between those earlier census projects and the present one. Like those previous efforts, this new census project has benefited from close cooperation between the Census Bureau and a distinguished, interdisciplinary group of scholars. Like the 1950 and 1960 research projects, research on the 1980 census was initiated by the Social Science Research Council and the Russell Sage Foundation. In deciding once again to promote a coordinated program of census analysis, Russell Sage and the Council were mindful not only of the severe budgetary restrictions imposed on the Census Bureau's own publishing and dissemination activities in the 1980s, but also of the extraordinary changes that have occurred in so many dimensions of American life over the past two decades.

The studies constituting "The Population of the United States in the 1980s" were planned, commissioned, and monitored by the National Committee for Research on the 1980 Census, a special committee appointed by the Social Science Research Council and sponsored by the Council, the Russell Sage Foundation, and the Alfred P. Sloan Foundation, with the collaboration of the U.S. Bureau of the Census. This committee includes leading social scientists from a broad range of fields—

demography, economics, education, geography, history, political science, sociology, and statistics. It has been the committee's task to select the main topics for research, obtain highly qualified specialists to carry out that research, and provide the structure necessary to facilitate coordination among researchers and with the Census Bureau.

The topics treated in this series span virtually all the major features of American society—ethnic groups (blacks, Hispanics, foreign-born,); spatial dimensions (migration, neighborhoods, housing, regional and metropolitan growth and decline); and status groups (income levels, families and households, women). Authors were encouraged to draw not only on the 1980 Census but also on previous censuses and on subsequent national data. Each individual research project was assigned a special advisory panel made up of one committee member, one member nominated by the Census Bureau, one nominated by the National Science Foundation, and one or two other experts. These advisory panels were responsible for project liaison and review and for recommendations to the National Committee regarding the readiness of each manuscript for publication. With the final approval of the chairman of the National Committee, each report was released to the Russell Sage Foundation for publication and distribution.

The debts of gratitude incurred by a project of such scope and organizational complexity are necessarily large and numerous. The committee must thank, first, its sponsors—the Social Science Research Council, headed until recently by Kenneth Prewitt; the Russell Sage Foundation, under the direction of president Marshall Robinson; and the Alfred P. Sloan Foundation, led by Albert Rees. The long-range vision and day-to-day persistence of these organizations and individuals sustained this research program over many years. The active and willing cooperation of the Bureau of the Census was clearly invaluable at all stages of this project, and the extra commitment of time and effort made by Bureau economist James R. Wetzel must be singled out for special recognition. A special tribute is also due to David L. Sills of the Social Science Research Council, staff member of the committee, whose organizational, administrative, and diplomatic skills kept this complicated project running smoothly.

The committee also wishes to thank those organizations that contributed additional funding to the 1980 Census project—the Ford Foundation and its deputy vice president, Louis Winnick, the National Science Foundation, the National Institute on Aging, and the National Institute of Child Health and Human Development. Their support of the research program in general and of several particular studies is gratefully acknowledged.

The ultimate goal of the National Committee and its sponsors has been to produce a definitive, accurate, and comprehensive picture of the U.S. population in the 1980s, a picture that would be primarily descriptive but also enriched by a historical perspective and a sense of the challenges for the future inherent in the trends of today. We hope our readers will agree that the present volume takes a significant step toward achieving that goal.

CHARLES F. WESTOFF

Chairman and Executive Director
National Committee for Research
on the 1980 Census

For Ray and Floss, David and Marin,
and most of all,
for Kathy

Acknowledgments

This short book has taken a long time to write. In the process, I have acquired many debts.

My greatest debt is to my family. My wife Kathy and my children David and Marin have seen me through three years of writing. They put up with enormous aggravations. I owe them a great deal.

Major financial support came from the Alfred P. Sloan Foundation and the Russell Sage Foundation, through the National Committee for Research on the 1980 Census. Their generosity gave me the time to explore the income distribution at my own leisurely pace. Along with their funding came a superb group of reviewers—Victor Fuchs, Gordon Green, Jim Morgan, David Sills, and Charles Westoff—whose comments on an earlier draft made my job much easier. The Russell Sage Foundation also provided Priscilla Lewis, an editor with the patience of Job.

Moral support came from my colleagues at the University of Maryland's School of Public Affairs. In-kind support came from several other university units: The Computer Science Center, the Computer Center of the Division of Behavioral and Social Sciences, and the Provost's Office of the Division of Behavioral and Social Sciences. Other support came from the U.S. Bureau of the Census and a Ford Foundation grant to the Urban Institute.

Three people were indispensable. Richard Michel of the Urban Institute is the origin of some of the ideas in this book, and all of the book's ideas were discussed with him at great length. Joung-Young Lee, now at the University of Inchon, provided research and programming assistance with an enormous can-do spirit. Rosemary Blunck of the University of Maryland's School of Public Affairs kept her sanity and mine through revision after revision as I was learning about my subject.

Equally indispensable were two libraries: the McKeldin Social Science Library at the University of Maryland and the Urban Institute library. In those rare instances where I could not find what I needed on their shelves, the library staff would quickly get it for me.

After I finished the first draft, a number of friends and colleagues commented on all or part of the manuscript. Still others took the time to educate me on particular topics where my understanding was weak. After all the writing—surely one of the loneliest vocations—all the comments and conversation proved a very welcome change. Thanks go to Henry Aaron, Jodie Allen, Gordon Berlin, Suzanne Bianchi, David Bloom, Barry Bosworth, Gary Burtless, Sam Erenhalt, Frank Furstenberg, Boyd Gibbons, Charles Hulten, Florence and Raphael Levy, Larry Long, Maureen McLaughlin, Tom Mueller, Patricia Ruggles, Paul Ryscavage, Allen Schick, Eugene Smolensky, Barbara and Clifford Swartz, Kathy Swartz, David Truman, Bruce Vavrichek, and Ed Welniak.

Michael Cohen and Jose Garcia provided technical assistance when it was needed. Sheldon Danziger provided both technical assistance and insight.

Final thanks go to Gene Bardach, Richard Easterlin, Marty Levin, Sandy Muir, Jim Tobin, and Aaron Wildavsky who, in different ways, expanded my sense of what an economist can do.

FRANK LEVY

Contents

List of Tables

List of Figures

The heart of man is not so much caught
by the undisturbed possession of anything valuable
as by the desire, as yet imperfectly satisfied,
of possessing it,
and by the incessant dread of losing it.

Alexis de Tocqueville, *Democracy in America*

DOLLARS AND DREAMS
The Changing American Income Distribution

TRENDS AND EPISODES

W HEN INCOMES are big news, it is a bad sign. The *New York Times* of June 8, 1986, is a case in point. A front page story discussed the rapid growth of U.S. employment since 1980. The number of new jobs was an achievement, but the article warned that many of the jobs may pay too little to support a decent living. In the *Times* magazine section the New York City Council President described the 40 percent of New York City's children who now live below the poverty line, 700,000 children in all. A second part of the magazine entitled "The Business World" featured portraits of wealthy executives, including Laurence Tisch of the Loews Corporation and CBS.[1]

By accident or design, these articles in the same day's newspaper added to a sense that American income inequality is growing. This sense has been building for at least a decade and has generated a list of fears:

- American families are splitting apart into the rich and the poor while the middle class vanishes.

---

[1] William Serrin, "Growth in Jobs Since '80 is Sharp, But Pay and Quality are Debated," *New York Times*, June 8, 1986 sect. 1, p. 1; Andrew Stein, "Children of Poverty— Crisis in New York," *New York Times*, June 8, 1986, sect. 6, pt. 1, pp. 38ff; "The Business World," *New York Times*, June 8, 1986, sect. 6, pt. 2.

- The American job market is developing two tiers in which middle-income manufacturing jobs are lost and replaced by a few high-paying jobs and many low-paying jobs in the service sector.

- Young workers—the baby boomers—are worried that they will not live as well as their parents. They are concerned about making money. The "youthful idealism" of the 1960s seems lost.

- A growing proportion of children are being raised in poverty, and it is arguable that welfare programs themselves are responsible for this poverty through the creation of a growing, dependent underclass.[2]

These fears describe an increasingly polarized income distribution with growing concentrations of families at high and low incomes. Paradoxically, official U.S. census statistics show something different: Family income inequality is very large, but it has remained relatively constant since World War II. There have been some trends: a drift toward equality through the late 1960s; a drift away from equality through the 1970s; a slightly sharper move from equality since 1979. But these movements have been modest. The richest one fifth of families received 43 percent of all family income in 1947, 41 percent in 1969, and 43 percent today.

The paradox continues, for the fears describe a society of declining mobility and falling living standards. Yet Department of Commerce statistics show that since 1970 consumption spending per person, adjusted for inflation, has risen by 1.8 percent per year, a faster rate than in Dwight Eisenhower's 1950s.

In the chapters that follow, we describe the evolution of the American income distribution since World War II. The subject is rich because the income distribution mirrors economic life. The

[2] On the vanishing middle class, see, for example, Bob Kuttner, "The Declining Middle," *Atlantic*, July 1983, pp. 60–72; and Lester C. Thurow, "The Disappearance of the Middle Class," *New York Times*, February 5, 1984, sect. 5, p. 2. On the two-tier job market, see Barry Bluestone and Bennett Harrison, *The Deindustrialization of America* (New York: Basic Books, 1982); and Bruce Steinberg, "The Mass Market is Splitting Apart," *Fortune*, November 28, 1983, pp. 76–82. On the baby boomers, see Phillip Longman, "Justice Between Generations," *Atlantic*, June 1985, pp. 73–81; and Frank Levy and Richard C. Michel, "Are Baby Boomers Selfish?" *American Demographics* 17, (April 1985): 38–41. On children in poverty, see U.S. House of Representatives, Committee on Ways and Means, *Children in Poverty*, Committee Print (Washington, DC: U.S. Government Printing Office, 1985). On the possible relationship between the underclass and welfare, see Charles Murray, *Losing Ground* (New York: Basic Books, 1984).

baby boom, the baby bust, the growth of the suburbs, big city riots, the rise and fall of big steel, expanding Social Security, oil price increases, more college graduates, children born out of wedlock, two-earner families, the flood of imports: They have all affected our total income and its distribution. By exploring this history, we can reconcile the America of the statistics and the America we see around us.

We also need history to understand our current situation. Each of the fears in the list above contains some truth. But to deal with them, we need to know their source. How many come from irreversible, long-term trends? How many come from a bad episode? Separating trends from episodes is subtle work. Think of how the economy looked in 1935. The Great Depression was five years old, unemployment stood at 20.1 percent, and it was easy to believe that mass unemployment was here to stay:

> The majority of people were hit and hit hard. They were mentally disturbed you're bound to know 'cause they didn't know when the end of all this was comin'. There was a lot of suicides that I know of. From nothin' else but just they couldn't see any hope for a better tomorrow. I absolutely know some who did. Part of 'em were farmers and part of 'em were businessmen, even. They went flat broke and they committed suicide on the strength of it, nothing else. [Mary Owsley, a resident of Oklahoma in the early 1930s][3]

The recovery was slow in coming. It required enormous government intervention culminating in the expenditures for World War II. When the recovery came, it was uneven and many people and places never regained what they had lost. But in the end the Great Depression was a very bad episode, not part of some structural trend.

A Failure of Growth

A similar conclusion runs through the chapters of this book. It begins with the fact that post–World War II life divides into two distinct economic periods. The first ran from the end of World War II through 1973. During this time inflation-adjusted wages—for example, the average weekly earnings of all 40-year-old men—grew by

---

[3] As quoted in Studs Terkel, *Hard Times* (New York: Pantheon Books, 1970), p. 44.

2.5 to 3.0 percent per year. It was a twenty-seven-year boom. The second period extended from 1973 through at least 1985. Over this period inflation-adjusted wages have stagnated and, in many cases, declined. This stagnation has led to a kind of quiet depression that is responsible for many of our current problems.

The reader may be surprised to see the terms "depression" and "boom" used to describe a period's wage growth rather than its unemployment. The point is not that unemployment is unimportant—clearly it is very important—but over the long run rising living standards are a better index of the nation's progress. During Dwight Eisenhower's two terms in office (1952–60), the economy experienced one mild and one quite serious recession, but the average family's income, adjusted for inflation (hereafter, real income), still rose by 30 percent. The full employment of the Kennedy-Johnson years drew more people into the labor force and so distributed growing incomes more equally, but the average family's real income again grew by 30 percent.

Today such growth seems remarkable. In the eight years following Richard Nixon's first term (1973–80), the average family's real income *declined* by 7 percent. During Ronald Reagan's first four years in office it grew by only 5 percent.

What went wrong? Like people in the middle of the Great Depression, we are not quite sure. The large OPEC oil price increases of 1973–74 and 1979–80 each cut purchasing power by 5 percent. More important was the way in which worker productivity suddenly stopped growing after 1973. Productivity measures the value of output per worker and rising productivity is the ultimate source of rising living standards. In a simple world we could explain its sudden halt with a single, neat theory. But the real world yields few simple answers and when we examine the productivity slowdown in Chapter 4, we will have only pieces of an explanation: large increases in energy prices, a fast-growing labor force, a ten-year inflation which developed its own momentum, and a corporate structure which had problems adapting to slow-growing markets. As this book is being finished (in 1986), some of these problems have improved dramatically only to be replaced by others, including a mountain of financial debt and an addictive reliance on imports and foreign capital. But if the earlier problems were largely beyond our control, our current problems are not. If we can exploit our situation, the economy should return to more normal growth rates and the 1973–85 period will be seen as a twelve-year episode of stagnation, much as the Great Depression was a far more serious episode five decades ago.

Mobility and the Safety Net

This book, then, will argue that many of our current troubles have come from cyclical and episodic events—what used to be called bad times—rather than from irreversible structural trends. Does this make sense? Are twelve years of stagnant wages enough to account for the kinds of fears that opened this chapter? Almost surely they are. From the end of World War II through 1973 rising real wages had been so automatic that we took them for granted. Only when wage growth stopped did we understand its role as a giant safety net for economic change.

Thirty-five years ago, Joseph Schumpeter coined the term "creative destruction" to describe how even a healthy economy is full of dislocation and chaos.[4] A healthy American economy in the 1970s would have been no exception. Supply and demand tells us that the huge baby boom cohorts, born after 1950, would have progressed more slowly than earlier cohorts. From Schumpeter's logic we know that our smokestack industries would have undergone wrenching adjustments as they faced international competition. Better interstate highways and the civil rights revolution would have enabled the Southeast and Southwest to compete aggressively with other regions. For reasons no less complex than the productivity slowdown, the black community would have developed a visible split between a middle class and an increasingly isolated underclass. In the best of times, each of these developments would have caused pain, but in many cases it could have been the pain of relative decline. In the 1970s stagnation, relative decline became absolute decline. Mass mobility evaporated.

An Inequality of Prospects

The link between wage growth and mobility comes as no surprise. The link between slow wage growth and inequality is more

[4] Joseph A. Schumpeter, *Capitalism, Socialism and Democracy* (New York: Harper, 1942), chap. 7.

5

subtle. It involves the way the economy and political process have divided a slow-growing pie. As we noted, census measures of family income inequality have remained roughly constant throughout the postwar period, including the period after 1973. But *within* this constant shape, substantial rearrangements have taken place. Incomes of the elderly have moved up while incomes of younger families have moved down. Fewer families have at least one worker while more rely on government benefits. Regional income gaps have closed but city-suburban income gaps have grown larger, a reflection of the growing number of city families headed by single women.

These rearrangements have not dramatically increased the inequality of *current* income. But when coupled with stagnation, they have increased the inequality of what economists call permanent or life cycle incomes. Put simply, there is a rapidly increasing *inequality of prospects*, an inequality in the chance that a family will enjoy the "middle-class dream."

Over a century ago Alexis de Tocqueville noted the importance of material possessions in American life: "In America the passion for physical well-being is not always exclusive, but it is general; and if all do not feel it in the same manner, yet it is felt by all."[5] His observation still holds. While today's middle-class dream does not carry a precise price tag, it exists in popular consciousness and has come to include a single-family home, one or two cars (including one new car), a washing machine and dryer, a dishwasher, a color TV, raising and educating children, providing for a period of retirement, and so on.[6] When times are good, the dream easily expands to include new items—long distance phone calls, a certain amount of travel—but the dream is much slower to contract when times are bad.

Precisely because the economy is in constant flux there are always large numbers of people trying to achieve the dream (or achieve it again): young workers just starting out, older persons who can no longer work, workers who have lost jobs in declining industries, and workers who have lost jobs in successful industries through technological change.

In the early postwar period real wages rose so fast that many of these people were quickly absorbed. Incomes grew faster than

---

[5] Alexis de Tocqueville, *Democracy in America* (New York: Appleton, 1899), vol. 2, p. 615.

[6] For a good discussion of conceptions of living standards, see Lee Rainwater, *What Money Buys* (New York: Basic Books, 1974).

dreams and a growing part of the population found middle-class life within reach. Rising incomes also helped to fund a larger welfare state to assist people at the bottom of the distribution.

In the 1973–85 stagnation this all changed, but it changed in uneven ways. People who had already attained the dream found that they had certain protections: job seniority and a fixed payment mortgage that kept housing costs under control.[7] If they owned physical assets, they could prosper from inflation. If they were retired, they found that their Social Security benefits were regularly adjusted for inflation. But families that had not yet reached the dream saw its price escalate rapidly. Now its attainment required a reliance on two earners, taking on large amounts of debt, and postponing or reducing the number of children. And of course, many people failed to achieve the dream at all. Census family income statistics are not adjusted for mortgage payments or the number of earners or the number of children, and so this kind of inequality—the varying gap between expectation and achievement—went largely unmeasured.

Given the sheer number of new baby boom workers and the increase in families headed by women, prospects would have grown less equal even in a healthy economy. But inequality was made much larger by a bad economy, albeit an economy that was bad in subtle ways. Low productivity growth is less visible than mass unemployment. Unemployment statistics appear regularly on the *CBS Evening News*. Productivity statistics are buried on the twelfth page of the *New York Times* business section.[8] For this reason it is difficult to see the 1973–85 period as a whole, and so we have paid too much attention to individual trees and not enough to the forest. In our story, the forest and the trees get equal billing.

The Plan of the Book

Discussions of the income distribution typically focus on changes in income inequality—on changes in the "shape" of the distribution. But over the 40 years since World War II family income inequality has not changed much, and our story will focus more on

---

[7] Even established middle-aged families did not have protection against rising college costs for their children, but they were helped by the rapid escalation in the value of their homes against which they could borrow.

[8] See for example, the article reporting productivity growth for the fourth quarter of 1985 in the *New York Times*, January 30, 1986 sect. D, p. 12.

two other dimensions which have changed substantially. One is the *level* of the distribution, the average income around which the distribution is centered. The other is the *content* of income distribution: the declining number of persons who work in agriculture, the growing number of persons who work in services, the growing number of families with two earners and families who retire early, the growing reliance on government benefits as an income source, and so on.

To put these pieces together, think of the income distribution as a circus tent. The modest changes in income equality mean that since World War II the tent has maintained a fairly constant shape. From 1947 through 1973 (when incomes were growing) we kept moving the tent to higher ground. From 1973 through 1985 the tent slid back a little. And in *every* year the acts and audience inside kept changing.

Chapters 2 and 3 set the scene. Chapter 2 describes the years since World War II as they appear in summary census statistics. These statistics serve as a framework for the details that follow. They show that throughout the postwar period income inequality among families has moved within narrow limits but income levels have passed through two distinct phases: steady growth from 1947 through 1973 and general stagnation thereafter. Chapter 2 also describes the income distribution for unrelated individuals—persons who live outside families. That distribution shows a modest trend toward greater equality and reflects the growing number of prime-age workers who now live alone.

Chapter 3 describes the economy of the late 1940s. To many of us 1947 is not so long ago, but the country then was quite different. Incomes were about half of what they are today. Ownership of cars and houses was low. In most other ways the economy was what we now call traditional. Manufacturing was the dominant sector (though services were already important). White men accounted for two thirds of the labor force. The largest geographic income distinctions were between the Southeast (which was poor) and the rest of the country. City-suburban income distinctions did not exist. Few families were headed by a single woman or someone who was retired, and few families had two earners. Ninety-five percent of all families had at least one member in the labor force, and this went hand in hand with a welfare state and tax burdens that were less than half of what they are today. We summarize this picture by describing the income distribution as it appeared in the late 1940s: the kinds of families in each income range, the kinds of jobs they held, where they lived, and how much they relied on government benefits.

The remaining chapters trace the income distribution as it has evolved through the mid-1980s. In Chapter 4 we describe the growth and subsequent stagnation of average incomes (the distribution's level). We discuss how much money we made, how we purchased the middle-class dream, the growth of government spending, and the way all of this changed as wages stagnated. As we tell this part of the story we explore how much of the growth (and subsequent stagnation) was due to specific government policy and how much was due to less controllable forces.

The next four chapters trace income inequality by examining the potential sources of that inequality:

- The industrial structure of the economy
- Geographic differences in income
- Labor force composition and occupations
- Family and household structure and the welfare state

In Chapter 5 we follow the economy's industrial structure as we became a service society. In reality this transition has been going on for some time and only recently has it been seen as something dangerous. We examine the fear that the rising service economy will lead to America's deindustrialization and a two-tier wage structure in which there are few middle-income jobs. While both fears have some merit, they owe more to demographics, the post-1973 stagnation, and subsequent macroeconomic problems than to the shift to services itself.

In Chapter 6 we look at the changing geography of income. Geographic income differences reflect migration of jobs and people and, like the economy's shift to services, the major trends were under way by the end of World War II. Whites were leaving the northern states for the Far West and Florida. Blacks were leaving southern states for northern central cities. Within regions, middle-income families and manufacturing jobs were migrating out of the cities. In the 1940s and 1950s these migrations were overwhelmed by high birthrates and rapid wage growth, and one region's gain did not necessarily mean another's loss. But by the mid-1970s the birthrate was low and wages had stagnated. Now the migration of people and jobs became a crucial determinant of an area's economic health.

Chapter 7 builds on the two previous chapters to examine occupation and earnings trends in the labor force. The postwar period
contained substantial upward mobility with people going to college
and people moving into white collar jobs, but the process of mobility
faced two limits. One was imposed by the macroeconomy. When
wages became stagnant, no occupation would pay as well as people
had expected. The other was a limit imposed by supply and demand.
When too many people tried to enter an occupation—lawyers in the
late 1970s—their average earnings were invariably forced lower.
These limits worked most clearly for white men. For white women,
black men, and black women there were additional limits of custom
and, in some cases, legal segregation which concentrated persons in
a few occupations. We trace how each of these four groups progressed, how the labor force became increasingly white collar, how
black working women made enormous occupational strides, and
how black men began to divide, with many doing very well and others dropping out of the labor force altogether, a behavior that in part
reflected a developing underclass.

Chapter 8 examines the interlocking topics of the American
family and the welfare state. Here, as with earlier topics, some "postwar" trends have a much longer history—most notably the shrinkage
of the extended family to a nuclear family. But in the postwar period
the nuclear family itself went through big fluctuations. From the end
of World War II through the mid-1960s it grew dramatically. Marriage occurred at increasingly younger ages, and there were large
numbers of children (the baby boom again). By the late 1960s the
birthrate was declining sharply, and by the mid-1970s marriage ages
were rising (creating a new class of young, apparently prosperous,
singles). Other changes in family arrangements were occurring as
well. A growing number of black families were headed by women—
a second aspect of an underclass. A growing number of older families
were formally retired. A growing proportion of all children were
being born in poor families.

As we describe these family changes, we simultaneously describe the growth of the welfare state. The connections between the
two topics are obvious. We cannot discuss retirement without discussing Social Security, and we cannot discuss the increasing number of female-headed households without assessing the role played
by welfare and government antipoverty programs. In recent years the
American welfare state has been criticized for encouraging depen-

dency, for favoring the elderly, for ignoring children, and for simply costing too much. All of these criticisms have some truth, but each owes a great deal to the conditions of the post-1973 economy. It follows that translating these criticisms into policy depends on our outlook for the economic future.

In Chapter 9 we describe the income distribution as it stands today and assess our prospects for the future. By the mid-1980s inflation was down, oil prices were falling, and the labor force was growing slowly. By themselves, these developments should have returned us to productivity growth of 2–3 percent per year. But the world has changed since 1973. We now face intense international competition, and we do not compete with a clean slate. Over the last five years, we have borrowed heavily from abroad to keep consumption growing. Servicing this debt and keeping it from growing larger requires a show of national will.

We have also built up a demographic debt in which rapidly declining birthrates among the middle class (black and white) and a growing number of families headed by women mean that one fifth of all children—one fifth of the next generation—are now being raised in poverty.

Navigating these problems will not be easy, and success will not bring nirvana. Some scars of the last twelve years will never heal, and we will still have to accommodate the turmoil that is part of any healthy economy: the movement of firms from one place to another, the rise and decline of industries, and the need to put new workers and low-skilled workers into jobs. But all of this is far easier in a growing economy than in the period just past.[9]

---

[9] A final note: Our strategy in this book is to place contemporary economic issues in the perspective of post–World War II trends. For two contemporary issues, this has proven impossible. Until recently, income data for racial groups other than whites and blacks—in particular, Asians and Hispanics—have been too sparse to permit separate discussion. The current position of these groups is summarized in Appendix A, but they are omitted from the body of the text. Readers interested in more detail on Asians and Hispanics are referred to other volumes in the census monograph series.

Similarly, most economists agree that the underground economy—unreported transactions that do not appear in official statistics—now equals 10–15 percent of recorded gross national product. At the same time the sparse available data suggest that the underground economy has been growing quite slowly, and so we underestimated the economy in the booming 1960s just as we did in the stagnant 1970s and 1980s. It follows that even perfect data on the underground economy would be unlikely to change our basic conclusions. We summarize such data as exist in Appendix B.

2

WHAT THE NUMBERS SAY

IN ITS purest form the income distribution is a set of five or six numbers that hides more than it reveals.[1] In 1984 the poorest one fifth of families received 4.7 percent of all income going to families. What does this mean? Were they young people (whose incomes might improve over time) or were they elderly? Did they work in manufacturing or in services or did they work at all? And whatever their percentage share of all income, were their actual dollar incomes growing or declining over time? The simplest of distribution statistics are mute on these points.

What income statistics do provide is a framework around which we can organize post–World War II (hereafter postwar) economic history. To use the statistics in this way, we must first understand what the numbers say.

---

[1] The family income distribution is formed by listing all families in order of increasing income. It is then described by referring to the share of all family income that goes to the poorest one fifth (quintile) of families, the second quintile, the middle quintile, and so on. These five quintile shares are typically accompanied by a Gini coefficient, a statistical measure of inequality. Construction of the Gini coefficient is described in Appendix E.

Trends in Inequality

In 1984 a panel of the Conference of Catholic Bishops issued a "First Draft Pastoral Letter on Catholic Social Teaching and the U.S. Economy," a document which noted that the top 20 percent of families today receive more income than the bottom 70 percent. The panel wrote: "In our judgment, the distribution of income and wealth in the United States is so inequitable that it violates [a] minimum standard of distributive justice."[2]

Media discussion of the Bishops' letter implied that the inequality is something new. In fact it is not: Inequality among family incomes is about as great today as it was at the end of World War II. (See Table 2.1.) In 1947 the poorest one fifth (quintile) of America's families received 5.0 percent of all family income while the richest quintile received 43.0 percent.

How do we judge this inequality? In absolute terms it is very large. The top quintile of families now receives about $9.15 of income for every $1.00 received by the bottom quintile. It is also large when compared with the income inequality of our major industrial competitors, West Germany and Japan.[3] By historical American standards, however, inequality has moderated to a degree. In 1929, the top one fifth of families received over half of all income. The Great Depression and World War II leveled the distribution significantly, but since the war, family income inequality has changed much more slowly.

The income share of the poorest quintile gradually increased from 5.0 percent in 1947 to 5.6 percent of all family income in 1968–69. It then declined slowly to 5.3 percent in 1979 and more sharply to 4.7 percent in 1984. The income share of the richest quintile de-

---

[2] National Conference of Catholic Bishops, Ad Hoc Committee on Catholic Social Teaching in the United States Economy, "First Draft Pastoral Letter on Catholic Social Teaching and the U.S. Economy," *National Catholic Reporter*, November 23, 1984, p. 22.

[3] For example, Gary Burtless shows that in West Germany, the bottom one fifth of households (families and unrelated individuals) receive about 13 percent of all household income while the comparable one fifth of households in the United States receive 6 percent of all household income. See Gary Burtless, "Public Spending for the Poor: Trends, Prospects, and Economic Limits," paper prepared for the Institute for Research on Poverty Conference on Poverty and Policy: Retrospect and Prospects, Williamsburg, Virginia, December 6–8, 1984. All international comparisons must be treated with some caution because other countries have different and, in some cases, much weaker distributional statistics.

TABLE 2.1

Shape of the Family Income Distribution Over the Postwar Period

From 1947 to 1969 income inequality across families declined modestly; from 1970 to 1979 it increased modestly; and from 1980 to 1984 it increased more sharply. But the most obvious feature of the postwar family income distribution was its stability.

	Percentage of All Family Income Going to					Richest 5 Percent (Included in Top Quintile)	Gini Coefficient of Income Inequality
	1st Quintile (poorest)	2nd Quintile	3rd Quintile	4th Quintile	5th Quintile (richest)		
1947	5.0%	11.9%	17.0%	23.1%	43.0%	17.5%	.376
1949	4.5	11.9	17.3	23.5	42.7	16.9	.378
1954	4.5	12.1	17.7	23.9	41.8	16.3	.371
1959	4.9	12.3	17.9	23.8	41.1	15.9	.361
1964	5.1	12.0	17.7	24.0	41.2	15.9	.362
1969	5.6	12.4	17.7	23.7	40.6	15.6	.349
1973	5.5	11.9	17.5	24.0	41.1	15.5	.356
1974	5.5	12.0	17.5	24.0	41.0	15.5	.356
1979	5.2	11.6	17.5	24.1	41.7	15.8	.365
1984	4.7	11.0	17.0	24.4	42.9	16.0	.385

NOTES: The Gini coefficient is detailed in Appendix E; a larger Gini coefficient means greater inequality. The years of greatest income equality were 1967–69; 1967 and 1968 had Gini coefficients of .348, slightly lower than 1969 (.349). The last year before the first major OPEC price increase was 1973. The year of the greatest income inequality (census definition) was 1984.

SOURCES: U.S. Bureau of the Census, *Current Population Reports*, series P-60, no. 146, table 17; no. 149, table 4.

clined from 43.0 percent in 1947 to 40.6 percent in 1969 and then began to rise, reaching 42.9 percent in 1984.[4]

---

[4] Data for 1984 are the most recent available at this writing. In judging these trends it is important to note that between 1947 and 1957 the census was forced to estimate the shape of the income distribution from grouped data—that is, the number of families with incomes between $0 and $1,000, $1,000 and $2,000, and so on. After 1957 the census was able to base its estimates on computerized files of individual families which, presumably, gave the estimates greater accuracy. A separate issue is the extent to which the census understates income inequality because high-income individuals refuse to report their incomes. We know with certainty that significant proportions of doctors, lawyers, dentists, and others in high-income occupations refuse to give income numbers to the census. We also know that census methods for estimating these nonreported incomes are weak. This means that published estimates of, for example, lawyers' average income are probably too low. The effect of this underreporting on overall income inequality is less clear. Low-income families also underreport income and as long as unreported income occurs in no greater a ratio than reported income ($9 at the top for every $1 at the bottom), our overall estimate of inequality will not be changed. On the issue of underreporting by occupation, see Lee Lillard, James P. Smith, and Finis Welch, "What Do We Really Know About Wages?" *Journal of Political Economy* 94 (June 1986): 489–506.

These changes in inequality are larger than they appear. In thirty-seven years the share of income going to the poorest quintile varied within a range of .9 percent. But the range refers to .9 percent of *all family income* for a group that receives only about 5 percent of all family income to begin with. In 1984 an income share of 5.6 percent rather than 4.7 percent would have translated into a family income of $8,695 versus $7,297 in the poorest quintile, a big difference to the persons involved. But over almost four decades these are fairly moderate swings, and by standard measures family income inequality in the postwar period has remained relatively stable.

This stability is surprising because the economy itself has undergone enormous changes. In the late 1940s, only one wife in five worked. Today over half of all wives work. In the late 1940s, food stamps and medical insurance for the elderly (Medicare) were nonexistent. Today these programs cost $83 billion per year. In the late 1940s, only 6 percent of all families had no member who worked. Today 15 percent have no working member.

In some cases standard statistics miss these changes. Census income statistics measure pretax money income, and so changes in taxes and in such "nonmoney" income as food stamps and employer-provided health insurance are not recorded. But when we adjust for these accounting problems (as we will in Chapters 3 and 9), the relative stability of the distribution remains because most of the biggest economic and demographic changes have worked in offsetting ways. Social Security benefits helped many older families to move up in the income distribution, but a growing number of female-headed families took the vacated places at the bottom. Young baby boom workers faced particularly stagnant wages, but young families came to rely on two earners. The constant shape of family income distribution should not be mistaken for tranquillity. Rather it reflects a number of rearrangements that, to this point, have largely canceled each other out.

The family distribution is only one of two income distributions. The other is the income distribution for unrelated individuals, 29 million persons who live outside families. Today two thirds of this group live alone, while the rest share units with people to whom they are not related.[5] In terms of population, unrelated individuals

---

[5] This includes the roughly 2 million persons who are cohabiting with persons of the opposite sex but who are not married. See U.S. Bureau of the Census, "Marital Status and Living Arrangements: March 1984," *Current Population Reports,* series P-20, no. 399 (Washington, DC: U.S. Government Printing Office, 1985), table G.

are relatively unimportant: seven persons in eight still live in families. But these individuals account for one household unit in three, which reflects the nation's changing marital patterns. Forty years ago unrelated individuals as a group were heavily skewed toward the elderly and the disabled. Today they contain many more prime-age workers, including young persons who do not feel ready for marriage as well as divorced middle-aged men. This infusion of workers into the group of unrelated individuals has caused the group's income distribution to become moderately more equal over time (Table 2.2). Here, too, the trend is not earthshaking and the most obvious characteristic of the distribution is stability.

TABLE 2.2

Shape of the Income Distribution for Unrelated Individuals

Unlike the stability of the family income distribution, the income distribution of unrelated individuals shows a modest trend toward greater equality throughout the postwar period. This reflects the growing number of prime-age workers who live as unrelated individuals.

	Percentage of All Unrelated Individual Income Going to					Richest 5 Percent (Included in 5th Quintile)	Gini Coefficient of Income Inequality
	1st Quintile (poorest)	2nd Quintile	3rd Quintile	4th Quintile	5th Quintile (richest)		
1947	2.0%	6.2%	12.7%	22.5%	56.6%	29.3%	.552
1949	2.4	7.5	14.3	26.0	49.8	19.4	.483
1954	2.4	7.1	13.1	24.8	52.6	22.2	.508
1959	1.4	7.2	13.2	24.8	53.4	22.1	.522
1964	2.5	7.1	12.8	24.4	53.2	22.9	.512
1969	3.3	7.8	13.8	24.3	50.9	20.7	.481
1973	3.7	8.6	14.4	23.9	49.5	20.0	.460
1974	4.2	8.9	14.6	24.1	48.3	19.5	.444
1979	4.0	9.2	15.3	24.3	47.2	18.5	.435
1984	3.8	8.9	15.2	24.1	48.1	19.1	.448

NOTES: The Gini coefficient is detailed in Appendix E. The year of greatest income inequality for unrelated individuals was 1947. The last year before the first major OPEC price increase was 1973. The years of greatest income equality among unrelated individuals were 1979 and 1980, with a Gini coefficient of .435 in both years.

SOURCES: U.S. Bureau of the Census, *Current Population Reports*, series P-60, no. 146, table 17; no. 149, table 4.

Trends in Income Levels

It is possible to discuss income inequality without talking about actual incomes (as we have just done). These discussions suggest that the income distribution is a disembodied shape, floating freely in space, which becomes more or less equal over time.

The picture is misleading. The family income distribution is centered on an explicit dollar figure, median family income. And where postwar income inequality has moved within moderate limits, median family income has moved dramatically.

In a healthy economy, median family income steadily increases through economic growth. The postwar economy saw such growth from 1947 through 1973, during which time the census measure of median family income (adjusted for inflation) set new records every one to three years. In 1947 it stood at $14,100 (in 1984 dollars). By 1959 it had increased to $19,300 (+37 percent), and by 1973 it had increased to $28,200. This was a virtual doubling in twenty-six years, and steady income growth was assumed to be automatic (Figure 2.1). Income inequality during this time remained roughly constant, but the *whole income distribution* kept moving to higher levels as most people improved their situation (Figure 2.2).[6]

Then the growth ended. By 1975 median family income had fallen by $1,700. It gained most of this back by the end of 1979, but fell sharply in the 1980–82 recession and stood at $26,433 in 1984. Preliminary data for 1985 indicate little additional improvement. This sudden break in trend—twenty-six years of income growth followed by twelve years of income stagnation—is the major economic story of the postwar period.

In discussions of data, income inequality and income growth can be examined separately. In actual life they blur with one another. Consider a man who loses a job in a steel mill and has to take a job with lower pay. If incomes are rising throughout the economy, he can imagine regaining his former standard of living in a few years. When incomes are stagnant, he knows that such thoughts are fanci-

---

[6] Admittedly, Figure 2.2 does not look like the previous description of a circus tent that maintains its shape over the years (Chapter 1). When incomes are rising, some families retain their low incomes, and so families tend to spread out across income levels. Nonetheless, the three distributions in Figure 2.2 have the same shape in the sense that the first quintile of families within each of the distributions has about 5 percent of all income, the second quintile has 12 percent, and so on.

FIGURE 2.1

Median Income of Families and Unrelated Individuals, 1947–1984 (in 1984 dollars)

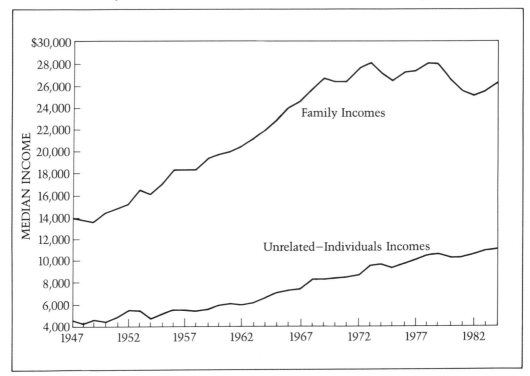

SOURCE: U.S. Bureau of the Census, *Current Population Reports,* series P-60, no. 151, table 11.

ful and it is a short mental leap to the idea that the middle class is vanishing.

Similarly, the Catholic Bishops' 1984 critique of today's income distribution—that the top 20 percent of families get more than the bottom 70 percent—applied with equal force in 1947 and all years in between. But before 1973 incomes were rising and most families were seeing steady economic progress. In 1984, after twelve years of stagnation, redistribution could seem like the only way for the poor to advance.[7]

---

[7] Because of the greater number of poor families headed by women, the Bishops may have also been afraid of a weakening connection between economic growth and reduced poverty. We examine this connection in Chapter 8.

FIGURE 2.2

The Family Income Distribution for 1947, 1973, and 1984
(in 1984 dollars)

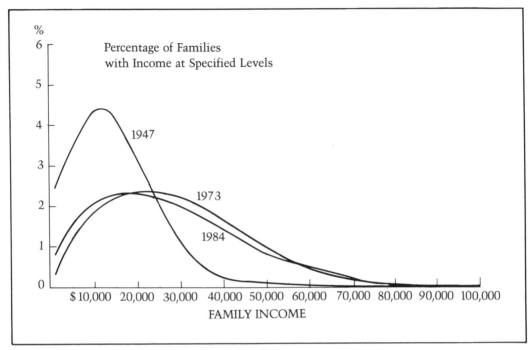

SOURCE: U.S. Bureau of the Census, *Current Population Reports*, various issues.

Fitting Yourself In

Before leaving the numbers, it will be useful for you, the reader, to place yourself in the income distribution. Table 2.3 contains the income levels that demarcated the 1984 income distributions for families and unrelated individuals. These numbers may come as a surprise. Most likely, you picture yourself in the middle of the income distribution, while you are actually near the top. This often leads to the following reaction: "According to your numbers, I'm in the top 20 percent. But I certainly don't feel as if I'm in the top 20 percent. First of all, where are the millionaires? Second of all, I see a lot of Mercedes around. If I'm in the top quintile, I should be able to afford one, but I can't."

This has several explanations, all of them instructive. The first involves the distinction between income and assets. The term "mil-

TABLE 2.3

Income Levels Defining the 1984 Income Distributions (in 1984 dollars)

In 1984 the top quintile of families had incomes beginning at $45,300, while the top quintile of unrelated individuals had incomes beginning at $22,066. Both numbers are lower than most people suspect.

	1st Quintile Ends at	2nd Quintile Ends at	3rd Quintile Ends at	4th Quintile Ends at	Top 5 Percent Begins at
Family Income	$12,489	$21,709	$31,500	$45,300	$73,230

lionaire" refers to people whose assets (wealth) total $1 million or more. Wealth is distributed far less equally than income. Today there are about 900,000 households (including unrelated individuals) in the United States with assets over $1 million, but only about 10,000 households—.0001 of all households—have annual *incomes* over $1 million.[8]

---

[8] Recently, the census has begun to collect wealth data on a scale comparable to its collection of income data. These statistics show that the richest 2 percent of households (families and unrelated individuals) have an *average* net worth of $1.1 million and together hold 26 percent of all assets owned by households. The top quintile of households together hold 75 percent of all assets owned by households. See U.S. Bureau of the Census, "Household Wealth and Asset Ownership: 1984," *Household Economic Studies*, series P-70, no. 7 (Washington, DC: U.S. Government Printing Office, 1986). Because of problems of confidentiality, data on both very high-income and very high-wealth individuals are very speculative. The estimates of the number of households with over $1 million in wealth comes from marketing specialists quoted in *U.S. News & World Report*. The estimate of households with $1 million or more in gross income comes from discussions with federal income tax researchers. See "Ordinary Millionaires," *U.S. News & World Report*, January 13, 1986, pp. 43ff.

TABLE 2.3 *(continued)*

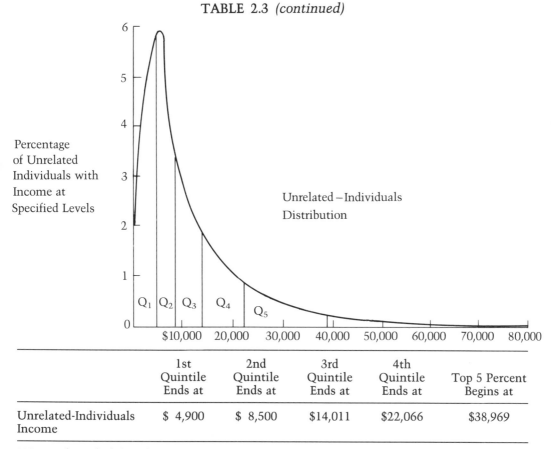

	1st Quintile Ends at	2nd Quintile Ends at	3rd Quintile Ends at	4th Quintile Ends at	Top 5 Percent Begins at
Unrelated-Individuals Income	$ 4,900	$ 8,500	$14,011	$22,066	$38,969

NOTE: The end of the 4th quintile is, of course, the beginning of the 5th (richest) quintile. The top 5 percent is included in the top quintile (top 20 percent).

SOURCE: U.S. Bureau of the Census, *Current Population Reports*, series P-60, no. 149, table 4.

A second explanation involves scale. Our country has today about 62 million families. Even the top 5 percent of this group represents 3.1 million families, a group large enough to contain many buyers of Mercedes cars (of which 90,000 are sold each year)[9] as well as many families who are "merely comfortable."

[9] See Richard Reeves, "Heartbreaker on Wheels," *New York Times*, December 29, 1985, sect. 6, p. 20.

A third explanation involves reference groups. The figure of 62 million includes families headed by a variety of people: a 75-year-old retiree on Social Security; a 43-year-old bank loan officer; a 30-year-old computer repairman; a 19-year-old unwed mother. When we judge our own status, we typically ignore most of these families to concentrate on our immediate peers and, occasionally, people in the news. Thus, many readers of this book will have a college education, will hold professional jobs, and will measure their progress against people just like themselves. Such people are relatively well off and the top quintile of this reference group—say, college-educated couples in their late 30s—begins at something over $62,000 rather than the $45,300 for all American families (Table 2.3).

A final explanation is that being in the top quintile isn't what it used to be. Prior to 1973 it meant two things: You were living well vis-à-vis most other families, and you were seeing your goals come increasingly within reach. The first condition still holds but the second is more problematic. In 1973 the top quintile of families had a mean average income of $68,278 (in 1984 dollars). In 1984 the top quintile of families had a mean income of $66,607. Average purchasing power had not improved.[10]

The point is not to shed tears for the well off: Over the same period average income in the lowest quintile declined from $9,136 to $7,297. But because stagnation affected most families, even the "well off" could feel that the middle-class dream was becoming more expensive.

Put differently, families can be in the upper half of the income distribution (above about $27,000) and still feel that they are not living as well as their parents did. But this is selective remembrance because it sees parents as they lived in the 1950s and 1960s—not as they lived in the 1930s. The 1930s, of course, were a much harder time, and they are where our story begins.

[10] This statement oversimplifies because it ignores the fact that most families in this quintile owned their own houses in 1973. Over the 1970s their earnings typically increased with inflation (though not necessarily as fast), but their mortgage payments remained fixed, which helped increase their purchasing power.

3

THE ECONOMY IN THE LATE 1940s

To many of us 1947 is not so long ago. World War II had ended, wartime rationing had been lifted, FDR had died, and Harry Truman was President. It is a time that merges in memory with the 1950s and even the early 1960s. But by the early 1960s we had covered enormous ground and we have covered more ground since. In this chapter we describe the economy and the income distribution as they looked in the late 1940s, a description that will serve as the base line for the rest of our story.

Income and Consumption

Beyond what is necessary for subsistence, incomes take on meaning in relation to other incomes.[1] In this sense the incomes of

---

[1] For example, during much of the postwar period, public opinion polls showed that a relatively constant proportion of the U.S. population described themselves as happy, even though real incomes rose steadily. In an ingenious article, Richard Easterlin explained this stability through the application of economist James Dussenburry's relative income hypothesis. In this hypothesis, one views one's income in relation to the incomes of others, rather than in absolute terms. See Richard A. Easterlin, "Does Economic Growth Improve the Human Lot? Some Empirical Evidence," in Paul David and Melvin Reder, eds., *Essays in Honor of Moses Abramovitz* (New York: Academic Press, 1974).

the early postwar years were defined by the Great Depression and World War II. On the eve of the Great Depression, in 1929, the typical family had an income of $11,260 (here and in the remaining chapters, all dollar figures will be in 1984 dollars unless otherwise noted).[2] By 1935–36 this income had declined by almost one third, and unemployment was running at almost 25 percent. The economy slowly moved into recovery, and by 1940 incomes had almost regained their 1929 levels.

America's entrance into World War II completed the return to full employment, but financing the war required high taxes and rationing of output so income could not be spent. In 1946 the typical family earned about one third more than it had in 1929, but spent no more on consumption. With this as a backdrop, the 1947 economy looked good. Median family income stood at $14,100, and the economy was quickly coverting to peacetime production.[3]

In one sense $14,100 overstated actual well-being. Normally a family consumes newly purchased goods such as food and a vacation, but it also consumes a portion of previously purchased durable goods like homes, cars, and appliances. The depression and the war together had caused production of these durable goods to stagnate, and so consumption of durables was low.

Consider automobiles. During the 1920s the number of automobiles on the road had increased by 14 million, but through all of the 1930s they increased by only 3 million more. What should have been a booming market held steady at a little under one car for every three adults.[4] (Today the figure is a little less than one car for one adult.)

Housing showed similar stagnation. Over the 1930s population had grown by 9 million (to 131 million), but the number of owner-occupied homes had increased by only 1 million. The proportion of households that owned their own homes had declined from 48 to 44

[2] All adjustments from earlier year dollars to 1984 dollars will be made using the Consumer Price Index. We will occasionally point out places where alternative inflation adjustments—for example, the Personal Consumption Expenditure Index—would lead to different conclusions.

[3] For pre-1947 incomes and consumption, see U.S. Bureau of the Census, *Historical Statistics of the United States: Colonial Times to 1970*, (Washington, DC: U.S. Government Printing Office, 1975), series G319-336 and G416-469 (hereafter *Historical Statistics*).

[4] *Historical Statistics* (1975), series Z148-162.

percent (compared with 77 percent today),[5] and within these units there was substantial doubling up:

- One family in fourteen lived in a household headed by another family or person, usually a relative.

- Seven unmarried adults in ten lived with other adults or families.

- About one quarter of the over-65 population (2.8 million persons) lived in households headed by their children.[6]

By today's standards these arrangements were very cramped. They were more normal by prewar standards but, as with automobiles, a potentially flourishing market for living space and privacy was held in suspension for sixteen years.

Because few new homes had been built, the nation's housing stock was slow to modernize and the average house of the mid-1940s offered far fewer amenities than we now take for granted. One third had no running water, two fifths had no flush toilets, three fifths had no central heat, and four fifths were heated by coal or wood. About half did not have electrical refrigerators while one seventh did not have radios. Television and air conditioning were largely unknown.[7]

Diets also fell below today's standards, particularly in the consumption of meat. At the end of the war we were eating 62 pounds of beef and veal per person per year, about half of what we eat today. Our consumption of chicken and turkey was about one third (17 pounds per person per year) of what it is today.[8] There were, however, some favorable comparisons. Fruit and vegetable consumption was about what it is today, and in the case of butter, margarine, and lard we were eating less then and probably living better. But on the whole, the 1947 diet is what we would now call stark.

The Great Depression and World War II were over, but for many families the middle class was not yet within reach. Public opinion

---

[5] *Historical Statistics* (1975), series N156-159.

[6] See Robert J. Lampman and Timothy M. Smeeding, "Interfamily Transfers as Alternatives to Government Transfers to Persons," *Review of Income and Wealth,* series 29, no. 1 (March 1983), pp. 45–66.

[7] See Stanley Lebergott, *The American Economy: Income, Wealth and Want* (Princeton, NJ: Princeton University Press, 1976); and Alan S. Blinder, "The Level and Distribution of Economic Well-Being," in Martin Feldstein, ed., *The American Economy in Transition* (Chicago: University of Chicago Press, 1980), chap. 6.

[8] Blinder, "The Level and Distribution of Economic Well-Being."

polls underlined the point. In the early 1950s only 37 percent of the public described itself as middle class while 59 percent described itself as working class.[9]

The Industrial Structure

With the enormous demands of war production, it is natural to think of the 1940s as a time when manufacturing was king. To a certain extent it was, but a healthy economy is always changing and

TABLE 3.1
Industrial Base, 1947

In terms of both output and employment, we were already a service economy in 1947. This fact reflects both the relatively common nature of most services and the way in which majority of services are consumed not only by individuals but also in the production of other goods and services.

Industry	Percentage of All National Output Produced in the Industry		Percentage of All Hours of Employment Generated in the Industry	
Agriculture	9%		12%	
Goods-Producing				
Mining	3		2	
Construction	4	36%	5	35%
Manufacturing	29		28	
Service-Producing				
Transportation, Communication, and Public Utilities	9		7	
Wholesale Trade	7		5	
Retail Trade	12	55%	15	53%
Finance, Insurance, and Real Estate	10		3	
Services	9		13	
Government	8		12	
	100%		100%	

NOTE: National Output equals Gross Domestic Product.

SOURCE: U.S. Department of Commerce, Bureau of Economic Analysis, *National Income and Product Accounts of the United States: 1929–76* (1981), tables 6.1 and 6.11B.

[9] See Philip E. Converse et al., *American Social Attitudes Data Sourcebook, 1947-78* (Cambridge, MA: Harvard University Press, 1980), table 1.24.

agriculture was still an important employer while services were growing rapidly.

The distribution of output and employment by industry is given in Table 3.1, which shows surprising strength in the service sector. By the end of World War II service-producing industries (including the government) accounted for more than half of both total output and total hours of employment. A look at the list of service industries explains why. Most service professions have been with us for some time: doctors, teachers, auto mechanics, utility workers, sales clerks, warehousemen, and so on. While some of these services are directly consumed by individuals, many others are consumed by business in the manufacture of goods. The fact that services often "follow" goods production will be important later in our story.

If the industrial base had one foot in the future, it was also tied to the past. The year 1880 is the last one in which more than half the labor force worked in agriculture. Over time, the rapid growth in output per agricultural worker (agricultural productivity) meant that the entire population could be fed through the efforts of a declining share of the labor force. But in 1947 agriculture still accounted for 12 percent of all hours of employment in the economy.

Between the past and the future were the traditional goods-producing industries: manufacturing, mining, and construction. Together they accounted for about one third of all hours of employment.

Economic Geography

In 1947 a monument marking the economy's center of activity would have been some place in central Indiana.[10] Three regions— New England, the Mid Atlantic (which stretches from New York through Washington, DC), and the Great Lakes—accounted for fully one half of the U.S. population (Figure 3.1). The Far West (including California) had doubled its population since 1920, and its rate of growth was much faster than the rest of the country, but growth had begun from a relatively small base and it was still home to only one person in ten.

Had population been the only consideration, the monument

[10] The location is the author's educated guess.

FIGURE 3.1

Median Family Income (1984 dollars) Within Regions, 1949

ROCKY MOUNTAINS	GREAT PLAINS	GREAT LAKES	MID–ATLANTIC	NEW ENGLAND
Idaho	Iowa	Wisconsin	New York	Maine
Montana	Kansas	Illinois	Pennsylvania	Vermont
Utah	Minnesota	Michigan	New Jersey	New Hampshire
Colorado	Missouri	Indiana	Delaware	Massachusetts
Wyoming	Nebraska	Ohio	Maryland	Rhode Island
	North Dakota		District of	Connecticut
	South Dakota		Columbia	
$13,857	**$12,635**	**$14,997**	**$15,122**	**$13,238**

FAR WEST

Washington
Oregon
California
Nevada

$15,416

SOUTHWEST

Arizona
New Mexico
Oklahoma
Texas

$11,656

SOUTHEAST

Virginia	Mississippi
West Virginia	Alabama
Kentucky	Georgia
Tennessee	South Carolina
Arkansas	North Carolina
Louisiana	Florida

$8,856

SOURCE: Income figures developed from 1950 U.S. Census of Population.

would have been further west and south—somewhere in southern Illinois.[11] But the northern tilt of population was reinforced by the geography of family income. The Southeast—the tier of states running from Virginia and Florida through Arkansas and Louisiana—was still a poor, heavily agricultural region. Median family income in, say, North Carolina averaged $8,700, far below the national average ($14,100). A portion of this gap reflected a lower southern cost of living.[12] More important were the extremely low incomes of southern black families locked by segregation into agriculture and other low-wage work. But these were pieces of a larger whole in which the Southeast was a depressed economy, separate from the rest of the country. White family incomes in Georgia averaged only $9,000, while in New York and California *all* families averaged $15,500. These low southern incomes further pushed the national economic balance toward the North. (See Figure 3.1.)

The gap between the Southeast and the rest of the country was the main distinction in the geography of income. By contrast, city-suburban income differences were modest. It was not so much that suburbs were poor, but that suburbs were small. The Great Depression and World War II had undermined the market for new housing and new cars and in geographical terms this was equivalent to depressing suburban growth. The war had also strengthened central cities through emergency production needs. Because time was so short, much war production took place in converted, existing facilities located in cities.[13]

In 1947, then, central cities were economically viable. They contained one third of the nation's population (suburbs contained one fifth). The ten largest cities contained 2.5 million manufacturing production jobs, 20 percent of all such jobs in the country.[14] And because suburbs were small, cities still contained much of the urban

[11] See U.S. Bureau of the Census, *Statistical Abstract of the United States: 1982–83* (Washington, DC: U.S. Government Printing Office, 1982), p. 7.

[12] See Jeffrey G. Williamson, "Unbalanced Growth, Inequality, and Regional Development: Some Lessons from U.S. History," in Victor L. Arnold, ed., *Alternatives to Confrontation* (Lexington, MA: Lexington Books, 1980), chap. 1.

[13] See John F. Kain, "The Distribution and Movement of Jobs and Industry," in James Q. Wilson, ed., *The Metropolitan Enigma* (Cambridge, MA: Harvard University Press, 1968), chap. 1.

[14] Author's tabulations from U.S. Bureau of the Census, *County and City Data Book* (Washington, DC: U.S. Government Printing Office, 1949), 1952. In 1947 the ten largest cities were, in order, New York, Chicago, Detroit, Philadelphia, Cleveland, St. Louis, Los Angeles, Baltimore, San Francisco, and Washington, DC.

middle class. As late as 1959 median income among central city families was $20,400, only $2,200 less than median family income in the suburbs and $1,000 above the national average for all families.[15]

The Labor Force and Occupations and Earnings

In 1947 white men accounted for about two thirds of the labor force. This proportion is large but the group's importance was even larger because the other major labor force groups—white women, black men, and black women—were concentrated by custom and legal segregation into a limited number of occupations.

Compared with today's labor force these white men were experienced workers. There had been no 1920s baby boom to yield large numbers of young workers twenty years later. And Social Security and private pensions were not sufficiently developed to permit large-scale retirement among older workers.[16] Sixty percent of white male workers were over age 35 (compared with 47 percent today), and even among white men over age 65 one half still worked.[17] While the men were experienced, they did not have much formal education. Two thirds had not finished high school, while only one eighth had some college. Beneath these averages were clear differences by age: white men in their late 20s averaged 12.5 years of education while white men in their late 40s averaged 9 years. The better education of young men compressed the usual pattern in which income increases with age (and experience). In 1947 the average income gap between 30-year-old and 40-year-old white men was 7 percent. By the late 1960s, when 40-year-old men were relatively better educated, the gap had opened to 13 percent.

To describe white men's occupational structure it is useful to think of five occupational classes:

- *Professional and managerial workers:* managers, administrators, scientists, teachers, lawyers, doctors, ministers, and so on

[15] See Larry H. Long and Donald C. Dahmann, "The City-Suburb Income Gap: Is It Being Narrowed by a Back-to-the-City Movement?" U.S. Bureau of the Census, *Special Demographic Analyses*, CDS-80-1 (Washington, DC: U.S. Government Printing Office, 1980). Incomes are expressed in 1984 dollars.

[16] We discuss the evolution of the Social Security program in Chapter 8. On the evolution of private pensions, see Alan S. Blinder, "Private Pensions and Public Pensions: Theory and Fact," Working Paper no. 902 (Cambridge, MA: National Bureau of Economic Research, 1982).

[17] The proportion today is about one fifth.

- *Other white collar workers:* sales clerks, clerical workers, technicians

- *Blue collar workers:* craftsmen, precision workers, machine and equipment operators, laborers, handlers

- *Service workers:* cooks, custodians, barbers, beauticians, protective service workers including police and firemen, and so on

- *Farmers and farm-related occupations*

Note that most *service workers* are employed in the service *sector,* but the service sector also contains certain blue collar workers (auto mechanics, telephone repairmen), professional and managerial workers (doctors, lawyers, managers), and so on.

By this typology, white men's work was a blue collar affair. In a random sample of 100 white men, 47 would have been craftsmen, machine operators, laborers, and other blue collar workers. Thirty two would have been white collar workers (with half in management and the professions). Thirteen would have been farmers, six would have been service workers, and two would have been in the military (Table 3.2).

The men would have averaged $11,500 in annual earnings, an average that obscures several variations. One was age. As workers grew older, their earnings increased until their mid-to-late 40s, after which they began to decline. Far larger were variations by occupation.[18] While all white men averaged $11,500, white male farmers averaged $8,000 and white male doctors averaged $27,000.

Compared with white men, black men in the late 1940s were in a very weak position from which they were slowly emerging. Ten years earlier, on the eve of World War II, half of all black men had worked in the rural South—both the Southeast and the Southwest— while another quarter lived in southern cities.[19] Only one third had gone beyond the seventh grade (compared with three quarters of white men). Their incomes, nationwide, averaged $3,300, less than

[18] Some of the variation in both age and occupation corresponds to differences in education. For example, the average 30-year-old was better educated than the average 40-year-old. The gap between their earnings was therefore smaller than it would have been if they had had the same education.

[19] See, for example, James P. Smith and Finis Welch, "Race Differences in Earnings: A Survey and New Evidence," in Peter Mieszkowski and Mahlon Straszheim, eds., *Current Issues in Urban Economics* (Baltimore: John Hopkins University Press, 1979), pp. 40–73.

TABLE 3.2

Occupational Distribution, 1949

In the 1950 census, white men were the dominant labor force group, and they were heavily concentrated in blue collar occupations. Black men were concentrated in the lower rung of blue collar occupations (for example, laborers) and in agriculture. White women worked in clerical and sales jobs and as teachers, but significant numbers also worked as machine operators (largely as garment and textile workers). About three black women in five worked either as domestics or as other service workers (cooks, custodians).

	White Men	Black Men	White Women	Black Women
NUMBER OF WORKERS (in millions)	39.9	4.3	13.3	2.0
OCCUPATIONAL DISTRIBUTION				
Professional and Managerial Workers	17%	4%	14%	6%
Other White Collar Workers	15	6	48	7
Blue Collar Workers	47	49	23	18
Service Workers	6	13	14	59
Farmers and Farm-Related	13	26	1	10
Total	98%	98%	100%	100%

NOTES: Many persons who work in the Service Sector are not service workers, but rather professional, managerial, other white collar workers, and blue collar workers. Totals do not always add up to 100 percent because persons in the armed forces are excluded.

SOURCE: Author's tabulations of the 1950 Census Public Use Microdata Sample files.

half of white men's average income. This weak position was reinforced by both legal and informal discrimination.

The demands of war production had opened up manufacturing jobs for blacks and had encouraged migration out of the South, largely to northern and midwestern cities. Migration was also forced by the mechanization of southern agriculture and the elimination of farm employment. By the end of the 1950s, fully one third of the southern black population would move to other regions. But in 1947 the migration was still in progress, and a quarter of all black men were still concentrated in southern agriculture. Those not in agriculture were in low level blue collar occupations and in personal service work, while only 10 percent held white collar jobs (Table 3.2). Nonetheless, the migration through the late 1940s had been sufficient to raise black men's average earnings to $5,800, or 51 percent of white men's.[20]

For white women it is easy to imagine the late 1940s as a period of regression, with the war's labor shortage easing and "Rosie the Riveters" going back to the kitchen. There is some truth here, but only some. During the war women's labor force participation—the proportion of all women over age 14 who were working or looking for work—peaked at 35 percent in 1944. That participation rate was high for its time, but it was far lower than today's 54 percent rate. At the war's end, it declined only modestly to about 31 percent in the early postwar years.

This 31 percent figure was an average of participation rates that declined by age and reflected a straightforward pattern. White women worked until they married; then they stopped. Labor force participation rates of single white women in their 20s, 30s, and 40s were about 80 percent. For married women in their 20s, 30s, and 40s rates were 20–25 percent, and few women returned to work even after their children had grown. Statistics suggest that working women had about 1.5 more years of schooling than working men, but this reflected the fact that most working women were young women who had been educated more recently when people stayed in school longer.[21]

When white women did participate in the labor force, they worked in a relatively small number of occupations. A third worked in administrative support jobs including secretaries, clerks, and receptionists. Another fifth worked as machine operators, largely in garment manufacturing and textiles. These two occupations—together with sales, teaching, nursing, and various personal services (cooks, waitresses, beauticians)—accounted for three quarters of all white women's jobs (Table 3.2).

Comparing women's and men's earnings must be done with some care. Most women worked less than full time, and so meaningful comparisons are restricted to men and women who are year-round, full-time workers. Statistics for the mid-1950s, the earliest

[20] See U.S. Bureau of the Census, "Money Income of Households, Families and Persons in the United States: 1983," *Current Population Reports*, series P-60, no. 146 (1985), table 40. Note that these figures refer to income (from all sources) rather than earnings per se. Comparable historical series restricted to earnings—wages, salaries, and self-employment income—are not available.

[21] See June O'Neill, "The Trend in the Male-Female Wage Gap in the United States," mimeographed (Washington DC: Urban Institute, revised March 1984).

available, suggest that full-time white women workers averaged about $11,000 in income, 65 percent of the average income of white men who worked full time.[22]

Unlike white women, black women had always worked in large numbers, reflecting economic necessity. In 1947 their labor force participation rate averaged 50 percent across all age groups (compared with 31 percent for white women), and they were less likely than white women to leave the labor force when they married and had children.[23] In the labor market they shared many of the disadvantages of black men: geographic concentration in the South, an average of 7 years of schooling, and official and informal discrimination.

These disadvantages were reflected in black women's jobs. In 1950 two fifths of black women worked as household domestics and another fifth worked in cafeterias, as custodians, and in other personal service jobs. Low-rung occupations translated into low earnings. In the mid-1950s black women who worked full time averaged $5,700 in income, half as much as white women.

Family Structure and the Government

We could describe family structures in 1947 as traditional, but it would be an understatement. Few unmarried people could afford to live alone and 94 percent of the population lived in families. Of these families, 80 percent had both a husband and wife under age 65 and in most of these husband-wife families the wife didn't work.

The number of independent elderly families was relatively small (Table 3.3). This reflected, in part, a life expectancy that was three years less than it is today,[24] but it also reflected the large number of older parents who lived in their children's homes.

---

[22] See *Current Population Reports*, series P-60, no. 146, table 40 (1985).

[23] See Suzanne M. Bianchi and Daphne Spain, *American Women in Transition*, The Population of the United States in the 1980s: A Census Monograph Series (New York: Russell Sage Foundation, 1986).

[24] This figure is shorthand for a more complicated set of statistics. In terms of total life expectancy, the greatest postwar gains have come from declines in infant mortality and the diminishing chance that young children will die before their first birthday. Nevertheless, the more relevant statistics—for example, the additional life expectancy of a man who was 40 years old in 1922 (and so would be 65 years old in 1947) versus the additional life expectancy of a man who was 40 years old in 1960—show a similar increase.

TABLE 3.3

Family Structures, 1949

In the late 1940s, family structures were highly traditional. Relatively few persons lived outside families. Relatively few families had working wives. And among nonelderly white families, only one in fifteen were headed by single women. But among black families, families headed by single women were becoming important, already accounting for one nonelderly family in six.

Age	White	Black*	All*
FAMILIES (38.5 MILLION; 139 MILLION PERSONS)			
Head Aged 65 or Over	13%	10%	12%
Husband-Wife Family Under 65			
Wife Works	16	23	18
Wife Does Not Work	65	52	60
Female-Headed Family Under Age 65	6	15	10%
Total	100%	100%	100%
UNRELATED INDIVIDUALS (9.0 MILLION PERSONS)			
Persons Aged 65 or Over			23%
Males			
Aged 35–64			21
Aged 34 or Under			21
Females			
Aged 35–64			22
Aged 34 or Under			13
Total			100%

*Includes other nonwhite races.

SOURCE: U.S. Bureau of the Census, 1950 Census of Population.

The number of families headed by a woman under age 65 was also small, though there were important differences by race. Among all white families under age 65, one in fifteen was headed by a woman. The corresponding proportion among black families was one in six.

Not all of these black female-headed families lived in central cities, but the problem of urban black families headed by women had existed for some time. In 1899 the sociologist W. E. B. DuBois described the large numbers of such black families in Philadelphia's poor seventh ward. Many of these women described themselves as widows, but DuBois' description is more ambiguous:

The economic difficulties arise continually among young waiters and servant girls; away from home and oppressed by the peculiar lonesomeness of a great city, they form chance acquaintances here and there, thoughtlessly marry and soon find they cannot alone support a family; then comes a struggle which generally results in the wife's turning laundress, but often results in desertion or voluntary separation.

The great number of widows is noticeable. The conditions of life for men are much harder than for women and they consequently have a much higher death rate. Unacknowledged desertion and separation also increases this total. Then, too, a large number of these widows are simply unmarried mothers and represent the unchastity of a large number of women. [pp. 67–68]

Fifty years later, St. Clair Drake and Horace Cayton (1945) elaborated on this description for the black lower class of Chicago:

Its people are the large mass of poorly schooled and the economically insecure who cluster in the "worst" areas or nestle in the interstices of middle-class communities. The lower-class world is complex. Basic to it is a large group of disorganized and broken families, whose style of life differs from that of other social classes, but who are by no means "criminal" except so far as the children swell the ranks of the delinquents, or the elders occasionally run afoul of the law. Existing side by side with these people is a smaller, more stable group made up of "church folks" and those families (church and non-church) who are trying to "advance themselves." In close contact with both these groups are the denizens of the underworld—the pimps and prostitutes, the thieves and pickpockets, the dope addicts and reefer smokers, the professional gamblers, cutthroats, and murderers. The lines separating these three basic groups are fluid and shifting, and a given household may incorporate individuals of all three types, since, restricted by low incomes and inadequate housing, the so-called "respectable" lowers find it impossible to seal themselves off from "shady" neighbors among whom they find themselves. The "church folks," despite their verbal protests, must live in close contact with the world of "sin." [p. 600]

Over time, lower-class patterns and families headed by women (overlapping but separate concepts) would become an increasing source of income inequality among blacks but also among whites. We trace their development in the chapters that follow.[25]

If female-headed families were significant among blacks, they were still rare in the population as a whole. This fact, together with the high labor force participation of older workers, meant that almost all U.S. families (95 percent) had at least one member who worked all or part of the year. And among all families, earnings—including wages, salaries, and income from self-employment—constituted about 90 percent of all income reported by the census.

The situation today is quite different. Earnings now make up about 80 percent of all census income (rather than 90), while almost 10 percent of income comes from government payments. In 1947 government payments were limited, but, then as now, payments came through two kinds of programs. One was a set of social insurance programs, including Social Security and unemployment insurance, to which wage earners directly contributed. The other was a set of means-tested programs, including Aid to Families with Dependent Children (AFDC) and county relief, which were aimed specifically at the poor and funded from general tax revenues.

In 1947 many social insurance programs were still in their infancy. Relatively few persons had paid into Social Security long enough to have qualified for benefits, so that in 1950 the program paid benefits to 2 million persons over age 65, only 16 percent of the over-65 population.[26] Other social insurance programs like Medicare simply didn't exist.

Antipoverty programs were similarly quite small. Food stamps and Medicaid would not exist for another twenty years while AFDC paid benefits to 600,000 families, about one family with children in every forty.[27]

A small welfare state meant small domestic government expenditures, and in the lull between World War II and the Korean war defense expenditures were small as well. Low government expenditures meant low taxes. A family with the median income ($14,100) paid federal income taxes and Social Security payroll taxes totaling

[25] See, for example, Glen C. Loury, "The Family as Context for Delinquency Prevention: Demographic Trends and Political Realities," paper prepared for the Executive Session on Delinquency and the Family, John F. Kennedy School of Government, Cambridge, Massachusetts, November 10–12, 1985.

[26] On the number of Social Security recipients, see *Historical Statistics* (1975), series H125-171.

[27] *Historical Statistics* (1975), series H346-367.

about 7 percent of income, while state and local taxes (sales taxes, property taxes) added about 3.5 percent more. The resulting tax burden was 10.5 percent, less than one half of what it is today.[28]

The Income Distribution

We conclude our discussion of the late 1940s by describing the 1949 family income distribution. What was its shape? And what was its content? In Table 2.1 we saw census statistics describing the shape of the family income distribution, but these statistics contain several limitations. The census defines income as pretax money payments. If taxes go up or down, families' purchasing power will change but the census statistics will not show it since they count income before taxes. If families get income in "nonmoney" forms—prepaid health insurance from their employer, food stamps, or Medicare insurance coverage—census statistics will not show that either. (Government benefits paid in cash such as AFDC are counted like other money income.)

The virtue of the census definition is simplicity. The census depends heavily on citizen cooperation, and people will not answer detailed questions about their state income tax or the kind of hospitalization insurance they have. But we need a better sense of the distribution's true shape.

Much of the data required for this true distribution do not exist. It is hard to reconstruct the amount of state and local taxes paid by different income groups in 1949. It is even harder to get data on the distribution of employee fringe benefits. Despite these problems, we can construct an "upper bound" estimate of 1949 income equality.[29] We begin with the work of economist Joseph Minarik (1985), which allows us to adjust census income statistics for the payment of federal income taxes and payroll taxes (Table 3.4). Ideally, we would make additional adjustments for three more factors:

[28] Tax estimates by the author are based on Joseph J. Minarik, *Making Tax Choices* (Washington, DC: Urban Institute, 1985).

[29] One can argue that this definition of income is itself too restrictive. For example, we might further include the estimated benefits received by families from public schools, subsidized student loans, street lamps, and a large variety of government expenditures. But valuing such income is well beyond the scope of this book. For some examples, see Benjamin I. Page, *Who Gets What from Government*, (Berkeley: University of California Press, 1983); and Patricia Ruggles and Michael O'Higgins, "The Distribution of Public Expenditure Among Households in the United States," *Review of Income and Wealth* 27, no. 2 (June 1981); 137–63.

TABLE 3.4

Approximating the "True" Family Income Distribution, 1949

With available data, it is possible to correct census income distribution statistics only for federal and payroll taxes paid and for differences across quintiles in family size. It is not possible to make corrections for state and local taxes paid and for nonmoney income received from employers (for example, prepaid health insurance). Since these unmade corrections all favor middle- and upper-income groups, the figures below can serve as an upper limit to family income equality in 1949.

	1st Quintile (poorest)	2nd Quintile	3rd Quintile	4th Quintile	5th Quintile (richest)
1 Census Definition (Pretax, Money Income only)	4.5%	11.9%	17.3%	23.5%	42.7%
2 Census Definition less Federal Income Taxes and Payroll (Social Security Taxes)	5.4	12.6	17.8	23.1	41.1
3 Line 2 Adjusted for Differences Across Quintiles in Average Family size	5.8	13.1	18.6	23.2	39.3

NOTE: Family size adjustments are made on a per capita basis without adjustments for economies of scale, and other factors.

SOURCE: See Appendix D.

- *State and local taxes:* In the late 1940s these taxes were generally regressive, falling most heavily on low-income persons.
- *Employer-provided fringe benefits:* In the late 1940s these benefits were relatively small, and such benefits that existed went to middle- and upper-income families.
- *Government-provided "nonmoney benefits":* Major programs in this group—food stamps, Medicaid, and Medicare—did not yet exist. Existing programs like the occasional distribution of surplus commodities were relatively small.

Correcting for these problems would result in an income distribution *less* equal than appears in Table 3.4, line 2. It follows that the true family income distribution was certainly no more, and probably a little less equal than line 2 indicates.

To understand the content of the distribution—that is, what kinds of families were in each quintile—it is useful to review points made in this chapter:

- *Age:* Men's earnings rose modestly with age and experience through their mid-40s. (They would have risen more steeply

TABLE 3.5

*Composition of the Family Income Distribution by Type of Family
and by Occupation of Family Head, 1949*

In the family income distribution of the late 1940s about one half of the first quintile represented families headed by a man or woman aged 65 or over or by a woman under age 65. As we move up the distribution, the proportion of these kinds of families diminishes and the proportion of husband-wife families increases. The top quintile contains predominantly middle-aged, husband-wife families—that is, families in their peak earning years.

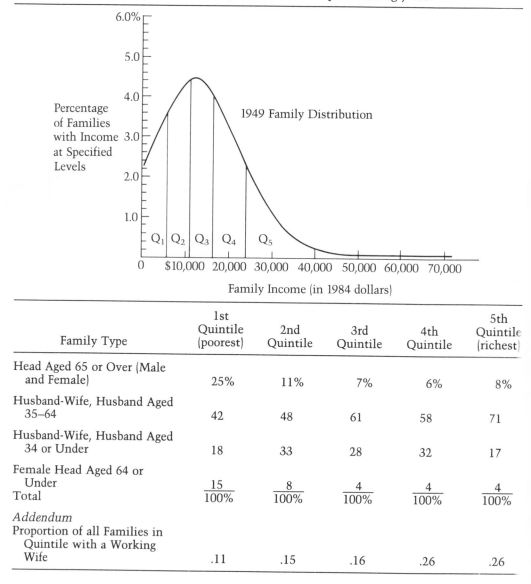

Family Type	1st Quintile (poorest)	2nd Quintile	3rd Quintile	4th Quintile	5th Quintile (richest)
Head Aged 65 or Over (Male and Female)	25%	11%	7%	6%	8%
Husband-Wife, Husband Aged 35–64	42	48	61	58	71
Husband-Wife, Husband Aged 34 or Under	18	33	28	32	17
Female Head Aged 64 or Under	15	8	4	4	4
Total	100%	100%	100%	100%	100%
Addendum Proportion of all Families in Quintile with a Working Wife	.11	.15	.16	.26	.26

TABLE 3.5 *(continued)*

In the early postwar years 80 percent of all families were headed by men who worked, while 93 percent had at least one working member. Among family heads who worked, those in service and agricultural occupations were concentrated in the bottom quintile, those in professional and managerial occupations were concentrated in the top two quintiles, and those in blue collar occupations—the largest classification of the time—were represented in significant numbers throughout the top four quintiles.

Occupation of Family Head	1st Quintile (poorest)	2nd Quintile	3rd Quintile	4th Quintile	5th Quintile (richest)
Professional and Managerial	7%	11%	12%	20%	36%
Other White Collar	3	9	10	13	12
Blue Collar	15	39	41	46	34
Service and Agricultural	37	16	17	12	10
Head Does Not Work	38	25	20	9	8
Total	100%	100%	100%	100%	100%
Addendum Proportion of All Families in Quintile with No Member Working	.25	.08	.02	.01	.01

SOURCES: U.S. Bureau of the Census, *Historical Statistics of the United States;* and author's tabulations of the 1950 Public Use Microdata Sample tables.

but younger men had significantly higher education.) After a worker reached his mid-40s, earnings declined. This means that higher quintiles contained increasing proportions of middle-aged families.

- *Occupation:* Regardless of age certain occupations, including farming and much service work, paid particularly low wages and were concentrated in low quintiles. Professional occupations paid above-average wages and were concentrated in higher quintiles.

- *Geography:* Incomes in the southeastern states were far lower than elsewhere. City-suburban income distinctions were relatively small.

- *Family structure:* Elderly families and families headed by single women had incomes well below average. Families with two earners were relatively rare.

Together, these relationships help explain the distribution described in Table 3.5 and Figure 3.2. In 1949 the lowest quintile

FIGURE 3.2

Distribution of Families Across Quintiles
by Residence, Age, and Race, 1949

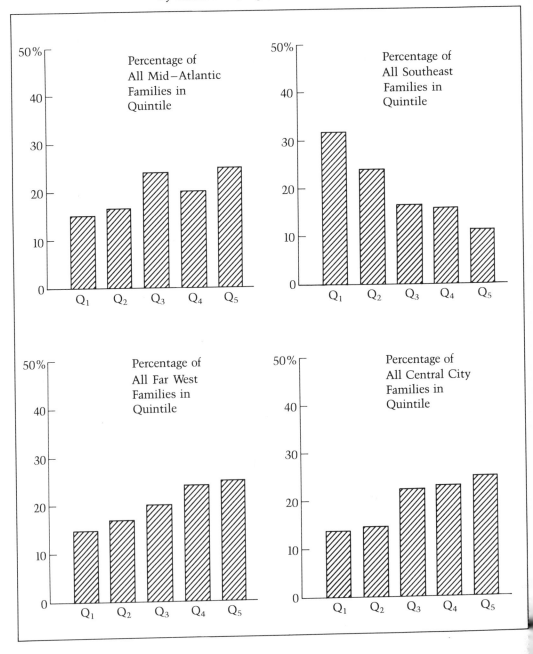

FIGURE 3.2 *(continued)*

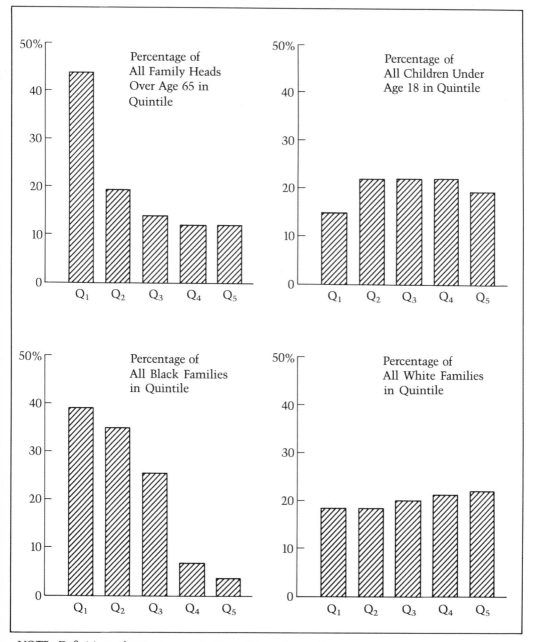

NOTE: Definitions of regions appear in Figure 3.1. Each set of bars sums to 100%.

SOURCE: Author's tabulations of the 1950 Census Public Use Microdata Sample.

stopped at an income of $6,725 (in 1984 dollars), and by construction one fifth of all families in the United States had incomes below this level. But in most dimensions these families differed sharply from U.S. averages.

The quintile was heavily skewed toward the elderly and the small number of families headed by women. These groups together comprised 19 percent of all families (of any income level), but they comprised 40 percent of families in the lowest quintile. Nevertheless, retirement was rare, welfare was limited, and three quarters of all families in the quintile had at least one worker, usually in agriculture or personal service work. The concentration of elderly and female-headed families also gave the bottom quintile a relatively small family size, and when our "upper bound" on income equality is adjusted for family size it becomes slightly more equal (Table 3.4, line 3).

The bottom quintile was also heavily skewed toward the low-wage Southeast and contained a quarter of all white families and half of all black families who lived in that region. Conversely, it contained relatively few central city families (from any region), reflecting central cities' still strong economies.

As we move up the distribution, all of these characteristics reverse. Families were less likely to be elderly or headed by a single woman and more likely to be headed by a middle-aged man. In the top quintile (where family incomes were $21,900 or more), 99 percent of the families had at least one worker while 40 percent of the workers were in professional jobs. The top quintile contained only 4 percent of black families and only 13 percent of white families from the Southeast, but it contained 30 percent of the families who lived in central cities.

How well did children do in the distribution? On the whole, fairly well. Only 15 percent of all children were in the lowest quintile, reflecting the way the elderly dominated the bottom of the distribution. Again, there were differences by race: The 15 percent figure included nearly half of all black children. But taken as a group, children were higher in the distribution than the typical family.

This was the income distribution in the late 1940s. In the chapters that follow, we trace its development through the postwar years.

4

INCOME, CONSUMPTION,
AND GOVERNMENT ECONOMIC POLICY

Making Up for Lost Time: 1947–1959[1]

B Y THE end of World War II the nation had lived through seven-
teen years in which material aspirations had been put on the
shelf. During the Great Depression there was no income. During the war there was income but no consumer goods. The experience left us ambivalent.

We had high hopes for the postwar economy, but we also had a
sense of foreboding. If a Great Depression could happen once, it
could happen again, especially since war production was ending. And
depression was not the only danger. When the government relaxed
wartime wage and price controls, producers quickly pushed up prices
and labor staged a wave of strikes to recoup foregone wartime pay
increases. In a 1946 Gallup Poll economic worries topped the list of

---

[1] In this chapter I have benefited greatly from two superb essays on the early postwar
period. One is Alan S. Blinder's "The Level and Distribution of Economic Well-Being."
The other is Robert J. Gordon's "Postwar Macroeconomics: The Evolution of Events and
Ideas." These essays are in Martin Feldstein, ed., *The American Economy in Transition*
(Chicago: University of Chicago Press, 1980).

the most important problems facing the country, a position they would not hold again until the mid-1970s.[2]

Yet the fears were not borne out and the economy did very well. Life was not perfect. Between 1947 and 1959 there would be another war, three bouts of inflation, and three recessions, the last of which would be quite serious. But over the period median family income would grow from $14,100 to $19,300 (all incomes are in 1984 dollars). Had poverty statistics been kept, they would have shown the proportion of the population in poverty declining from 32 to 22 percent.[3] (See Table 4.1.)

Why did incomes grow so fast? The answer is instructive because it illustrates something of what government macroeconomic policy can and cannot accomplish. The growth of 1947–1959 was a case where policy was quite passive.

We commonly talk about gross national product (GNP), the dollar value of the economy's total annual output. But economists also talk about *potential* GNP, the value of output that would be produced if the economy were operating at full employment.[4] Federal government macroeconomic policies—monetary, tax, and expenditure policies—regulate demand for the economy's output. By regulating demand, they attempt to make actual GNP coincide with potential GNP, avoiding unemployment and foregone production (when demand falls below potential GNP) and inflation (when demand exceeds potential GNP).

While macroeconomic policies are important, they can only raise living standards in the short run. If the economy is in recession (and actual GNP lies below potential), increased demand can stimulate GNP to reach its potential and raise average incomes in the process. But additional income increases depend on the growth of potential GNP and, in particular, the growth of output per worker. In the long run, the amount of output per worker sets limits on a worker's

[2] See Tom W. Smith, "America's Most Important Problem—a Trend Analysis, 1946–76," *Public Opinion Quarterly* 44, no. 2 (1980):164–80.

[3] See Charles Murray, *Losing Ground* (New York: Basic Books, 1984), figure 4.5.

[4] This definition evades the problem of assigning a number for the "full employment" unemployment rate. In theory, full employment is the lowest unemployment rate the economy can achieve without causing inflation to accelerate. In practice, government economists used a 4 percent full employment rate in the 1950s and 1960s and about a 6.5 percent rate in the 1970s and early 1980s. The difference in rates was partly due to the growing proportion of teenagers and older women in the labor force, two groups that have historically done more "job shopping" and so have traditionally exhibited higher unemployment rates.

TABLE 4.1

Living Standards in the 1950s

Between the end of World War II and 1959 median family income grew by more than one third. Tax rates remained relatively low, while growing real wages substantially reduced the proportion of the population in poverty. Government expenditures increased substantially, with the lion's share going to national defense and Social Security.

	1949	1959	Growth per Decade
Median Family Income (1984 dollars)	$13,540	$19,300	+42.5%
Tax Burden at the Median Family Income	12.2%	13.1%	
Ratio of Black-to-White Median Family Income	.50	.51	
Income Share of Lowest Quintile of Families	4.5%	4.9%	
Percentage of all Persons in Poverty	32.0% (est.)	22.4%	
Government Expenditures per Person (1984 dollars)			
All Government Expenditures	$ 1,599	$ 2,409	+50.7%
National Defense	377	849	
Payments to Individuals	334	469	
All Other Expenditures	888	1,091	

NOTE: The 1949 recession depressed 1949 income below 1947 income by 5 percent, which made the ten-year growth rate appear larger than it otherwise would have been.

SOURCES: Median family income, the ratio of black-to-white median income, and income shares, come from U.S. Bureau of the Census, *Current Population Reports,* series P-60, no. 146. Tax burdens are estimated by the author using the work of Joseph Minarik, *Making Tax Choices* (Washington, DC: Urban Institute Press, 1985). The 1949 estimate of the poverty rate comes from Charles Murray, *Losing Ground* (New York: Basic Books, 1984), figure 4.5. The 1959 estimates of poverty come from U.S. Bureau of the Census, *Current Population Reports,* series P-60, no. 147. Statistics on government expenditures come from U.S. Department of Commerce, Bureau of Economic Analysis, *National Income and Product Accounts of the United States, 1929–76* (1981).

income. Economists refer to output per worker as productivity and so the growth of incomes over time depends on the growth of productivity.

In the first part of this century output per worker hour grew by 2.0–2.5 percent per year, a result of a more educated work force, increased efficiency, and technological change.[5] This growth in productivity continued through the Great Depression, but from 1947 to 1965 GNP per worker grew by 3.3 percent a year, a remarkably high figure. A difference of one-and-a-fraction percentage points may not seem very large. But as the economist Herbert Stein (1980) noted in a different context:

> . . . the difference between a growth rate of 3 percent and a rate of 4 percent was not one percent as commonly thought at the time but 33.3 percent. This means that in some sense we would have to increase the total of resources devoted to producing growth—the investment, the research, the education and so on— by one-third [to obtain the higher growth]. [p. 173]

Stein was speaking metaphorically, for there is no precise relationship between various "inputs" and increased productivity. Nonetheless, the unusually high productivity growth of 1947–65 did have some concrete explanations. One was a set of stockpiled innovations in electronics, transportation, and petrochemicals that had been developed during the Great Depression and World War II. Another was favorable demographics in the form of a labor force which was very experienced and was growing very slowly. A third was a public that wanted to put the Great Depression behind it and would sacrifice personal convenience to make money.

Equally important were the rapidly expanding markets which producers faced. The country was starved for basic durable goods. Our trading partners had been devastated by the war and their needs further increased U.S. demand. These markets created a climate for improved productivity in both obvious and subtle ways. Donald F. Barnett and Louis Schorsch (1983) describe the direct links:

> Booming markets foster the construction of new plants, which are generally larger and more advanced technologically; both of these characteristics reduce labor requirements [and so increase output per worker]. . . . rapid market growth also tends to boost profits and cash flow. The availability of funds for investment then accelerates the modernization of existing facilities. Finally, rapid market growth makes it easier to maintain high operating

---

[5] See John W. Kendrick, *Postwar Productivity Trends in the United States, 1948–69* (New York: National Bureau of Economic Research, 1974), pp. 51–59.

rates, lowering unit costs and thus improving profitability. All of these characteristics contribute to productivity growth. [p. 143]

In a less obvious way, expanding markets improved productivity by reconciling divergent corporate goals. In 1932 Adolf Berle and Gardner Means addressed the tensions that arise in a modern corporation because the owners (shareholders) and managers are not the same people. A shareholder wants improved profits (and therefore improved productivity). A manager wants improved profits, but he also wants the corporation to grow in ways that enhance his position and prestige. In a stagnant market, improved profits may require a manager to shrink operations, something he will not want to do. When markets are booming, a corporation can simultaneously become larger and more efficient and these tensions do not arise.[6] But after taking account of innovations, demographics, and expanding markets, productivity growth seemed to benefit from a dose of good luck.[7]

In the glow of remembrance, rising living standards suggests a tranquil Ozzie and Harriet economy. A more accurate picture comes from Joseph Schumpeter's term "creative destruction," in which old products, firms, and areas are being displaced even in a healthy economy. Over the 1950s the number of persons employed on farms dropped from 7 million to 4 million, a decline equal to 5 percent of the nation's labor force. Total manufacturing employment was growing but within the total, steel employment fell by 25,000 (−4 percent) while aircraft employment increased by 363,000 (139 percent). Changing industrial patterns meant changing plant locations and over the decade manufacturing production jobs in the ten largest central cities declined by one fifth.[8] Dislocations abounded, but because real wages were growing more people (including many of the dislocated) won than lost.

How was the new money spent? Largely to make up for the time lost since 1929. The automobile market had been brought to a halt

---

[6] A thoughtful elaboration of this argument with new evidence is contained in Dennis C. Mueller, *The Corporation: Growth, Diversification, and Mergers* (London: Gordon & Breach, 1987).

[7] For example, in the work of Edward Denison, quantifiable factors can account for about two thirds of productivity growth during this period, while he refers to the unexplained remainder as the "residual." See Edward F. Denison, *Trends in American Economic Growth, 1929–82* (Washington, DC: Brookings Institution, 1985).

[8] See Chapter 6 for a discussion of both agricultural migrations and the declining number of production jobs in central cities.

by the depression and the war, but at the war's end it exploded. The number of private automobiles on the road had grown by only 3 million in all of the 1930s, but it grew by 12 million between 1946 and 1950 and 21 million more between 1950 and 1960. By 1960 there were 62 million cars on the road, one for every 1.8 adults.

Over the same period the number of owner-occupied homes doubled from 17 million to 33 million. As with cars, the demographics for home ownership had been present throughout the depression: The problem was insufficient income, but after the war incomes were growing. At the same time housing was more affordable. The availability of automobiles meant that building sites were no longer tied to public transportation and whole new areas were opened up. The new land combined with improved mass construction techniques to keep housing prices low. In the mid-1950s the average home in Levittown, New Jersey, had monthly carrying charges of $475 while the average family had monthly income of $2,100 (in 1984 dollars). On a national basis, the average 30-year-old man could carry the mortgage on an average home for 14 percent of his gross pay.[9] The affordability of cars and housing meant that the middle-class dream was becoming available on an increasingly wide basis.

More important than the consumption of housing and cars was our consumption of children. Children, like consumer goods, cost money and hard times, *ceteris paribus*, mean falling birth rates.[10] From 1929 to 1944 the number of children under age 14 *declined* by 1.5 million. But between the end of the war and 1960 the number of children under 14 increased by 20.3 million in what we call the baby boom. Some of these children represented births that had been postponed during the depression and the war. But most were the children of younger men and women who had been raised in the depression. They had lived first on low incomes and then on rationed consumption. When they formed their own families in the 1950s, they found

---

[9] On Levittown, see Herbert Gans, *The Levittowners* (New York: Pantheon, 1967), pp. 22 and 34. The figures have been converted to 1984 dollars. The nationwide figure comes from Frank Levy and Richard C. Michel, "An Economic Bust for the Baby Boom," *Challenge*, March–April 1986, pp. 33–39.

[10] The qualifying *ceteris paribus* is important. In the mid-1960s the birthrate began to fall from its baby boom high levels even though times were very good. At least part of the reason was an expanded set of opportunities for women together with a growing interest among women in working. Chapter 8 discusses this change in greater detail.

that they truly could have it all—they could live better than they had seen their parents live and they could have large families, too.[11]

The fast growing number of children led to a statistical paradox. *Family* incomes were growing rapidly, but consumption expenditure per capita—that is, per man, woman, and child—was growing far more slowly (Figure 4.1). Usually slow growth is a sign of trouble, but here it reflected an optimism that workers could support large families.

Living standards improved in other ways. The proportion of households with radios grew from 85 to 95 percent. The proportion of households with televisions grew from essentially nothing to 85 percent. Families acquired vacuum cleaners, washing machines, and other time-saving devices which would ultimately help women into the labor force.[12]

Diets improved: Per capita consumption of beef and veal increased by one quarter; per capita consumption of potatoes declined by one fifth; lard consumption declined; butter and margarine consumption increased; the introduction of frozen foods increased the availability of vegetables and juices throughout the year.[13] In today's world of sushi and the Cajun revolution, these improvements seem tame, but they brought about significant improvements in nutrition.[14] And because agricultural productivity grew so fast (the opposite side of farm worker dislocation), improved diets did not require increased food expenditures (Figure 4.1).

We have focused on the increased consumption of goods. Expenditures on services rose just as rapidly as expenditures on goods. Using National Income Accounts definitions,[15] we see that expenditures on medical care, recreation, telephones, personal care, and other consumer services all increased such that services accounted for one fifth of all consumer expenditures in both 1947 and 1959. Twenty years later increasing service consumption (and growing ser-

---

[11] This argument has been developed most elegantly by Richard Easterlin in *Birth and Fortune* (New York: Basic Books, 1980).

[12] I am thankful to Maureen Steinbruner for this point.

[13] See Blinder, "The Level and Distribution of Economic Well-Being," for a similar discussion.

[14] On increases in nutrient intake, see U.S. Bureau of the Census, *Historical Statistics of the United States: Colonial Times to 1970* (1975), series G849-856. On the Cajun revolution, see Paul Prudhomme, *Paul Prudhomme's Louisiana Kitchen* (New York: Morrow, 1984).

[15] See the discussion on National Income Accounts data in Figure 4.1.

FIGURE 4.1

Changes in Consumption Expenditure per Person, 1949–1959
(in 1984 dollars)

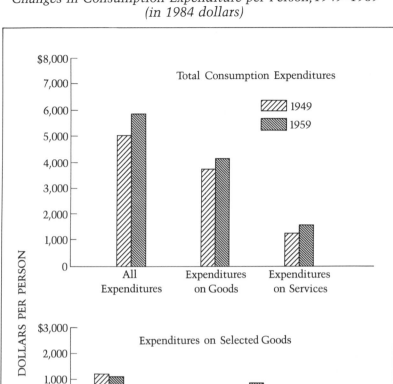

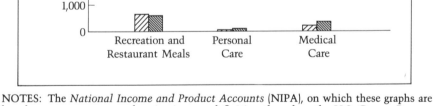

NOTES: The *National Income and Product Accounts* (NIPA), on which these graphs are based, uses a more comprehensive income definition than does the U.S. Census Bureau. For example, the NIPA definition of medical expenditures includes the cost of employer-provided health insurance, but most families would not think about such insurance when reporting their incomes to the census. For this reason, the income level implied by NIPA is higher than the income level in official census statistics. (NIPA estimates are generally not available on a family-by-family basis and so they can be used only occasionally in this volume.)

Under NIPA conventions, housing expenditures are considered a service while restaurant meals are considered a good. Those classifications have been reversed here to conform with popular definitions.

SOURCES: U.S. Department of Commerce, Bureau of Economic Analysis, *National Income and Product Accounts of the United States*, various years.

vice employment) would be used as evidence of a second-rate economy, but during the 1950s it was just another part of the larger theme of making up for lost time.

The Drive for Full Employment: 1960–1969

If we have only dim memories of the 1950s, many of us have a clearer memory of the 1960s. It was a decade when government assumed a much larger role in taxing, spending, and managing the economy.

The new economic intervention was a natural development of the 1950s growth. From 1947 through 1959, the economy had experienced very rapid long-term growth, but it had also seen three recessions. In each case a Keynesian-activist President might have tried to reduce unemployment through tax cuts and/or increased government spending, but neither President Truman nor President Eisenhower was predisposed to such activism. Both men were concerned with the corrosive effects of inflation. Eisenhower, in particular, felt that periodic economic slumps kept inflation in check and attempts to shorten recessions would ratchet inflation upward. His view was politically acceptable because both the 1948 recession (under Truman) and the 1954 recession had been mild. But the 1958 recession was both deep and long, with unemployment averaging a then high 5.4 percent from 1958 to 1960. Nonetheless, Eisenhower held firm against activist policies.[16]

Compared with the Great Depression, the 1958 recession was not serious, but a decade of postwar recovery had made the depression a fading memory. People were less ready to accept any economic downturn and were more willing to see the government experiment with antirecession policies. John Kennedy's 1960 campaign

---

[16] The description as it applies to Truman is a little unfair. In 1948 the Republicans had forced Truman to accept a cut in taxes from their wartime high levels. When the economy entered the recession of 1949, Truman felt that since a tax cut had recently been passed and presumably was just starting to work, a second tax cut designed specifically to fight the recession was unnecessarily risky.

Eisenhower's reluctance to stimulate the economy has been detailed by Richard Nixon in *Six Crises* (New York: Doubleday, 1962). Nixon and his adviser Arthur Burns feared that a continued recession would cost Nixon the 1960 presidential election. He appealed to Eisenhower to take some action to stimulate the economy, but Eisenhower held fast.

promise to "get the country moving again"[17] was an attempt to tap this feeling.

In contrast to the Truman-Eisenhower years, the Kennedy-Johnson years were a high point of Keynesian activism and the initial success was enormous. A number of authors have described the role of good decisions in this success.[18] Less obvious were the roles of luck and circumstance which made the 1960s an ideal Keynesian test case.

Consider the context. Productivity growth remained at a high 3.3 percent per year, which permitted average wages to increase by 3 percent per year without creating inflationary pressures. In addition, Kennedy (and then Johnson) inherited low inflationary expectations. Getting the country moving (through Keynesian stimulation) could lower unemployment, but it ran the risk of increasing inflation. Had we entered the 1960s with high inflation, Keynesian policies would have been ruled out. But Eisenhower's policies had kept the economy slack and inflation averaged only 1 percent per year from 1958 to 1960. In this way, Eisenhower had removed a potential obstacle to the Keynesian experiment.

A second Eisenhower legacy was a federal budget with, in economists' terms, a large "full employment surplus." Keynesian policies required deficits only during a recession. If taxes are already low vis-à-vis expenditures, a further stimulating tax cut can leave a permanent (or "structural") budget deficit that continues even when the economy reaches full employment and stimulation is no longer needed. During the late 1950s Eisenhower ran a stringent fiscal policy so that had the economy been at full employment, the budget would have shown a large surplus. This full employment budget surplus provided Kennedy and Johnson with the margin for Keynesian tax cuts: They could cut taxes knowing that the budget would come into balance as the economy reached full employment.[19]

To list these happy circumstances is to belittle neither economic policy nor the role of policy-makers. Many presidents have squandered opportunities, whereas the Kennedy-Johnson application

---

[17] See Theodore H. White, *The Making of the President, 1960* (New York: Atheneum, 1961).

[18] See, for example, Walter Heller, *New Dimensions in Political Economy* (Cambridge, MA: Harvard University Press, 1960).

[19] This, in fact, happened. In 1965 the federal budget ran a small surplus, and in 1966 it ran a small deficit.

of Keynes began brilliantly. But the opportunity was there. If we miss this point and think rising incomes in the 1960s reflected smart policies alone, we will conclude that the 1970s stagnation came only from government ineptitude and that is simply wrong.

The early results of the Kennedy-Johnson policies were all that could be hoped for. After 1963, unemployment declined steadily. In 1965, it stood at 4.4 percent and median family income stood at $22,900 (in 1984 dollars), a $3,600 increase in five years. The increased income reflected both sustained productivity growth and the Keynesian stimulation that was getting more people into jobs. Despite the brisk recovery, inflation was running at under 2 percent per year.

In 1965 events began to sour. The country became increasingly involved in the Vietnam war. Increased involvement meant increased expenditures. Since the war was too unpopular to permit new taxes, President Johnson financed Vietnam's opening phase by new deficit spending.[20] In the process he turned economic folk wisdom on its head. A war was supposed to be good for the economy. It was, after all, the only time when government could increase spending and run deficits—that is, practice Keynesian economics—with a straight face. But attitudes had changed in the early 1960s and by 1965 the government, without the benefit of war, had stimulated the economy to nearly full employment.

This made the Vietnam deficits a very mixed blessing. In the short run, they further stimulated the economy and produced much faster growth and lower unemployment than any president would have dared chosen—a boom of enormous proportions. But this boom sowed the seeds for stubborn inflation that would prove very difficult to break.

The boom accelerated income growth for the rest of the decade. As the economy approached full employment, worker productivity began to grow more slowly, averaging 2.2 percent per year (versus 3.3 percent per year from 1947 through 1965). But slower productivity was offset by falling unemployment, and over the decade median family income grew from $19,300 to $26,700 (Table 4.2), a growth rate comparable to the 1950s. Moreover, low unemployment meant that income gains were distributed more equally than would otherwise have been the case.

---

[20] For an excellent discussion of this period, see Arthur Okun, *The Political Economy of Prosperity* (Washington, DC: Brookings Institution, 1969).

TABLE 4.2

Living Standards in the 1960s

During the 1960s median family incomes again increased by over one third. By the end of the decade tax burdens had also increased to finance the Vietnam war. As incomes rose, the proportion of the population in poverty continued to drop sharply. Government spending rose as sharply as it had in the 1950s, but far less went into defense and far more went into such new programs as aid to education and health insurance for the poor and elderly.

	1959	1969	Growth per Decade
Median Family Income (1984 dollars)	$19,300	$26,700	+38.3%
Tax Burden at the Median Family Income	13.1%	20.9%	
Ratio of Black-to-White Median Family Income	.51	.61	
Income Share of Lowest Quintile of Families	4.9%	5.6%	
Percentage of all Persons in Poverty	22.4%	12.1%	
Government Expenditures per Person (1984 dollars)	$ 2,409	$ 3,774	+56.6%
National Defense	849	968	
Payments to Individuals	469	798	
All Other Expenditures	1,091	2,008	

SOURCES: Median family income, the ratio of black-to-white median income, and income shares, come from U.S. Bureau of the Census, *Current Population Reports,* series P-60, no. 146. Tax burdens are estimated by the author using the work of Joseph Minarik, *Making Tax Choices* (Washington, DC: Urban Institute Press, 1985). Estimates of poverty come from U.S. Bureau of the Census, *Current Population Reports,* series P-60, no. 147. Statistics on government expenditures come from U.S. Department of Commerce, Bureau of Economic Analysis, *National Income and Product Accounts of the United States, 1929–76* (1981).

For example, throughout the postwar period, black men had unemployment rates about twice those of white men, but the 1960s expansion made this two-for-one relationship something positive: For every 1 point drop in the white unemployment rate, the black rate dropped 2 points. In 1968–69 the black male adult unemployment rate stood at 3.8 percent, 6 percentage points below its 1955–65 average (and about 10 points below its 1984 level).

Low black unemployment was strong medicine for black incomes. Over the postwar years the proportion of black families headed by women had risen from 15 percent to 22 percent in 1960 and 31 percent in 1969. (See Chapter 8.) By itself this should have caused the black-white income gap to grow, but the improved economy was so powerful that the ratio of black-to-white median family incomes increased from .49 to .61. More generally, the income share of the lowest quintile increased, and the combination of rising and more equal incomes caused the proportion of the population in poverty to fall from 22 to 12 percent (Table 4.2).

By the end of the decade, Congress had raised taxes to pay for Vietnam, but after-tax income had still risen sharply over the decade. Expenditures on cars and houses grew but at slower rates than they had grown in the 1950s, as the most urgent postwar needs were filled. At the margin, consumption was shifting toward services. Per capita expenditures on recreation and meals had grown slowly in the 1950s, but over the 1960s they grew by 40 percent. Per capita expenditure on medical care grew even faster in the 1960s than it had in the 1950s (Figure 4.2).

The shift toward services was also evident in the apparently rapid growth of government spending. We say "apparently" because government spending in the 1960s was characterized not so much by a growth of dollars as by a growth of new initiatives. In the "conservative" 1950s, government expenditures (federal, state, and local) had actually grown faster than private consumption spending. (Table 4.1). This expenditure did not make news because the lion's share went into two traditional programs: national defense and Social Security. Only a few initiatives—such as the new network of federal highways—stood out.

Over the 1960s government expenditure per person grew only slightly faster than it had grown in the 1950s (Table 4.2). But now traditional programs took a smaller portion of the increment and new money went into new programs: health insurance for the elderly and poor families, community action antipoverty programs, aid to elementary and secondary education, and so on.

Behind the new programs was a coincidence of economics and politics. Between World War II and the mid-1960s, family incomes had increased by 40 percent. The government apparently could avoid recessions as well as depressions, and economic growth was beginning to look automatic. Cars and single family homes were widely available, and an increasing proportion of the population saw itself

FIGURE 4.2

Changes in Consumption Expenditure per Person, 1959–1969
(in 1984 dollars)

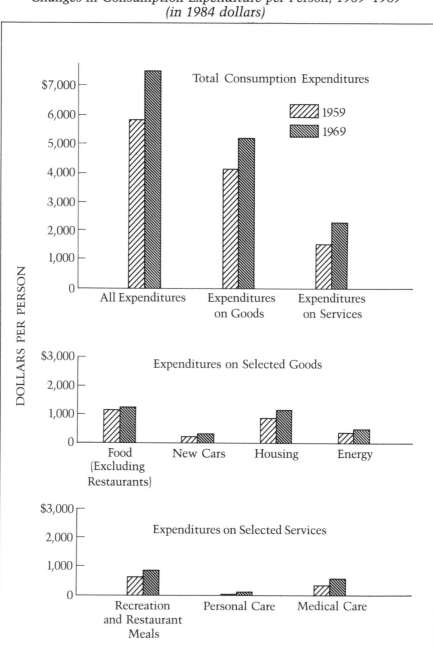

SOURCES: U.S. Department of Commerce, Bureau of Economic Analysis, *National Income and Product Accounts of the United States,* various years. Also see NOTES, Figure 4.1.

as middle class. We were ready to consider increased public spending to "make the society a better place."[21]

During the 1950s the congressional Democrats had built an agenda of domestic programs, but Eisenhower generally was not interested.[22] In a curious sense, his attitude may have further stimulated public receptivity to Democratic ideas: Had Eisenhower tried, say, a war on illiteracy which then failed, the public might have become skeptical about what government could accomplish. But his lack of initiatives meant no failures, so that the public was willing to listen.

By the mid-1960s Eisenhower's caution had been swept away. The civil rights movement was gaining strength. Kennedy had been assassinated and Lyndon Johnson assumed office. Johnson skillfully presented the Democratic agenda as a way to heal the nation.[23] Congressional Republicans might have blocked the agenda on fiscal grounds, but many of them were dragged from office by Senator Barry Goldwater's disastrous presidential candidacy in the 1964 election. Their Democratic replacements found a delightful prospect: The economic expansion was raising tax revenues so fast that the government had to initiate new spending, cut taxes, or do both. To do nothing would create large budget surpluses which would slow down the economy. The 1965–66 Congress passed medical insurance for the elderly and indigent (Medicare and Medicaid), federal aid to public schools, the original War on Poverty legislation, a substantial increase in grants to state and local governments, and much more.

Even more ambitious than the actual programs were the promises they embodied. Some were performance promises, like the promise that government dollars could teach all poor children how to read. But others were promises of entitlement in which the gov-

---

[21] In 1964, 44 percent of respondents saw themselves middle class or higher, up from 37 percent in 1952. On the complementary relationship between private consumption and public expenditure, see Albert O. Hirschman, *Shifting Involvements* (Princeton, NJ: Princeton University Press, 1982); and Frank Levy, "Affluence, Altruism and Happiness in the Postwar Period," in Martin David and Timothy Smeeding, eds., *Horizontal Equity, Uncertainty and Economic Well-Being* (Chicago: National Bureau of Economic Research, University of Chicago Press, 1985), chap. 1.

[22] The best description of how Democrats built their agenda during the Eisenhower years and then passed much of it when Lyndon Johnson became President is contained in James L. Sundquist, *Politics and Policies: The Eisenhower, Kennedy, and Johnson Years* (Washington, DC: Brookings Institution, 1968).

[23] See Levy, "Affluence, Altruism," for an examination of public opinion polls which showed people in the mid-1960s as both quite optimistic about their economic future and generally agreeable to increased spending for the poor.

ernment, for example, would provide certain levels of medical care for the elderly no matter how expensive it became. These entitlements assumed that long-run economic growth would continue. If it didn't, things would get very expensive.

The Troubles Begin: 1970–1972

When the economy goes badly, politicians get the blame and so it is not surprising that they should want the credit when things go well. Johnson took full credit for the sustained boom of the 1960s, and Keynesian economists confidently talked of "fine tuning" the economy to achieve maximum performance. This view obscured the underlying factors that lay beyond any politician's immediate control. Two of these factors we have already seen: continued productivity growth and the absence of inflationary expectations. The third was stability in raw materials prices. By the mid-1970s all of these factors had reversed. Incomes (and politicians) suffered correspondingly.

Inflationary expectations began to form in the late 1960s. The economic boom had left the country with very low unemployment but a high (for that time) inflation rate of 5.5 percent. When Richard Nixon took office in 1969, he planned to induce a short recession, break the inflation, and stimulate a new expansion in time for the 1972 election.[24] History was on his side. In each of the earlier postwar recessions (1948, 1954, and 1958–60), one year of recession was sufficient to bring inflation below 1 percent, but in 1970 the plan did not work. By August, 1971, after eighteen months of recession, inflation was still running at 4.7 percent while unemployment was at almost 6 percent.

This was the first evidence of inflationary expectations, or "stagflation," a situation in which employers and workers anticipate inflation and push for higher wages and prices even though the economy is slack.[25] The result is a self-fulfilling prophecy. In retrospect,

[24] For a good, partisan discussion of this period, see Alan S. Blinder, *Economic Policy and the Great Stagflation* (New York: Academic Press, 1979).

[25] Here, as in many other things, an excellent source is the work of the late Arthur Okun. See *Prices and Quantities* (Washington, DC: Brookings Institution, 1981), his work on stagnation and the "invisible handshake" in which employers and employees come to expect cost-of-living salary adjustments even in slack markets.

this early stagflation was a by-product of the late 1960s boom. The late Arthur Okun (1980), a key architect of 1960s economic success, summarized the relationship well:

> In subtle ways, I believe the depression mentality [and the drive to combat recession] fostered inflation vulnerability. There was an imbalance in policy: it is inconceivable that a four-year recession would have been tolerated in the way that a four-year boom was tolerated in the late 1960's. And when the economy is made depression-proof and deflation-proof, private expectations and conventions become asymmetrical, introducing inflationary bias into the system. [pp. 168–69]

Nixon, feeling the pressure of the upcoming election, responded with a mixed policy. He used wage and price controls to break inflation and accepted a monetary expansion by the Federal Reserve to lower unemployment.

The combination of policies represented a distinct gamble. Wage and price controls can reduce inflation when the economy is slack—when there is no underlying scarcity. But because monetary policy was stimulating the economy, controls could only suppress inflation until they were removed or until they simply broke down. Nixon, by pursuing both policies, was gambling that the controls would at least hold through the 1972 election.

The gamble worked. Inflation cooled, unemployment fell, and 1972 median family income reached $27,600, $900 more than it had been in 1969. But as the controls were lifted, inflation began to reappear. At this point the country experienced another piece of bad luck—shortages in the supply of two key raw materials.

The first was the 1972–73 food shortage, which led to a rapid inflation in food prices. The shortage was driven by a worldwide failure of harvests and a bad Peruvian anchovy catch which disrupted the production of animal feeds.[26] In the United States, the situation was made worse by a large (and disadvantageous) wheat sale to Russia. Between 1972 and 1974 food prices in the United States rose by 34 percent.

---

[26] See Dale E. Hathaway, "Food Prices and Inflation," *Brookings Papers on Economic Activity*, no. 1 (1974), pp. 63–116.

The Quiet Depression: 1973–1984

The rise in food prices was quickly followed by the 1973–74 oil shortage. Unlike the food shortage, the oil shortage was contrived, a conscious policy imposed by the Organization of Petroleum Exporting Countries (OPEC) in the wake of the 1973 Arab-Israeli War. It resulted in a tripling of oil prices and while it was buried in the rhetoric of the exhaustion of resources, it is best understood as OPEC's attempt to run oil production as a monopoly industry.[27] (In this sense, the Arab-Israeli war served as the catalyst for cartel co-operation.)

These "supply shock" inflations were quite different from inflation in the late 1960s. That earlier inflation came from an overstimulation of demand for output and was at least accompanied by low unemployment. Shortages in food and oil could cause rapid inflation (and strengthen inflationary expectations) even when the economy was stagnant and unemployment was high.

The OPEC increase, in particular, could not have come at a worse time. The country remained divided over the Vietnam war. Vice President Spiro Agnew had been forced to resign, under threat of trial for corruption, and Nixon himself was besieged by the Watergate hearings.[28] The government was left with little authority to face a very difficult problem because the OPEC price increase did more than exacerbate inflation; it also caused large amounts of income to be sent overseas to foreign oil producers. These oil payments were equivalent to a giant tax and so helped to increase unemployment even as inflation was rising. By the time President Nixon resigned and Gerald Ford took office, inflation had reached 12 percent while unemployment was 5.6 percent and rising fast. Not until 1976 would the economy begin to recover.

The food and oil inflations caused a substantial erosion in average family incomes. Median family income continued to rise in 1973 to a postwar high of $28,200, but between 1973 and 1975 it fell by

[27] An alternative explanation is that demand in the 1960s had expanded rapidly while petroleum producers had allowed their prices to remain low. In this view the 1973–74 price increase was merely a "catch-up" to free market levels.

[28] I am indebted to Robert Reisner, Washington, DC, Director of Market Opinion Research, for reminding me of these connections. On one particular evening the newscaster Walter Cronkite had to expand the *CBS Evening News* from its normal half hour to one hour to cover the events of the day, which included the Agnew resignation and the continuing Arab-Israeli "Yom Kippur" war.

$1,700 to slightly below its 1969 level. Under normal circumstances, th.s income loss would have been erased by little more than two years of economic growth. But in the final piece of 1970s bad luck, productivity growth collapsed.

Recall that in the 1950s and early 1960s rapid productivity growth (3.3 percent per year) led to rapid income gains. After 1966 productivity growth had slowed to something like historical trends (2.5 percent per year), but beginning in 1974 productivity growth averaged .8 percent per year for the next eight years.

The productivity stagnation is one of the central events of this book, and it is particularly maddening that it cannot be completely explained. The most careful studies point to factors like these:[29]

- The rapid increase in energy prices suddenly changed the techniques required for efficient production, making certain kinds of capital equipment obsolete and so lowering the amount of capital per worker.

- When baby boomers and older women entered the labor force in great numbers, they lowered average labor force experience. They also caused the labor force to grow rapidly enough to further dilute capital equipment per worker.

- Increased government regulation of business diverted research efforts away from more efficient production (as measured in productivity statistics) and toward the reduction of pollution and increased worker safety.[30]

In this list, energy prices and the fast-growing labor force are the most important. Both worked to reduce the amount of (nonobsolete)

---

[29] For conflicting appraisals of the importance of different factors in the productivity slowdown, see the work of Lester Thurow and Edward Denison. Thurow gives the greatest weight to insufficient savings and capital formation while Denison gives the least. In practice, however, some of the differences are less than they appear. For example, the rapid oil price increases clearly made some capital obsolete, while the rapid growth of the labor force diluted capital per worker below what it otherwise would have been. These were both "explanations" in themselves, but both implied the need for higher levels of investment. See Denison, *Trends in American Economic Growth;* and Lester C. Thurow, *The Zero-Sum Solution* (New York: Simon & Schuster, 1985).

[30] For a case study of how antipollution regulations may have diverted research efforts from ways to increase output, see Martin N. Baily and Alok K. Chabrabarti, "Innovation and Productivity in U.S. Industry," *Brookings Papers on Economic Activity,* no. 2 (1985), pp. 609–32. Because we measure a firm's output by its sales, we have no way of correcting the fact that the output is accompanied by clean, rather than dirty, air. To the extent that the 1970s were characterized by less output but cleaner air, standard productivity statistics will understate the gains in well-being.

capital per worker, an important productivity determinant. Even when all the factors are considered, however, they predict a slow-down in productivity growth from 2.3 percent per year to about 1.5 percent per year. The remaining slowdown of .7 percent per year is still unexplained, but it surely reflects the changing economic climate. Earlier, we saw that the 1950s' high productivity growth was fostered by rapidly growing markets for U.S. goods. Under normal circumstances, this growth would have slowed by the mid-1960s. Consumers at home were relatively well off. Overseas our trading partners had rebuilt their economies and wanted to export to us (to expand their own markets) rather than buy our imports. But growth did not slow because the Vietnam boom was sufficient to keep markets expanding.

It was after 1973 that the slow growth of markets emerged. The war demands were over. To cool inflation, policy-makers were willing to tolerate fairly high unemployment, which further constrained demand. On top of this, slow-growing markets were surrounded with enormous year-to-year uncertainty—about next year's prices and next year's unemployment rates. In this situation, many corporate managers kept expanding on the assumption that markets would come around again. Economist Dennis C. Mueller reviews a wide range of evidence suggesting that diversified corporations, in particular, continued to pursue existing product lines (with resulting low productivity and profits) rather than make the wrenching changes which slack markets and high energy costs required.[31]

This problem was not unique to the United States. Productivity growth also fell sharply in most European countries after 1973, and it subsequently revived there only because the countries were willing to tolerate historically high rates of unemployment. The fact that so many countries faced productivity problems immediately after 1973 suggests the destructive force of the inflation and uncertainty of the post-OPEC economy.[32]

Because productivity grew slowly the country could not quickly recoup the income losses of 1974–75, and the economy soon became an inversion of the Eisenhower years. In those years average incomes grew rapidly even though the government made few interventions to

[31] See Mueller, *The Corporation*, sect. H.

[32] See Denison, *Trends*, p. 7, and the references cited therein. Note that we do *not* list the shift of employment to the service sector as a cause of the productivity slowdown. We explain why in Chapter 5.

achieve full employment. Beginning in 1975 Presidents Gerald Ford and Jimmy Carter actively moved to reduce unemployment, but stagnant productivity meant that income gains were small. By 1979 the adult male unemployment rate had fallen to 4.2 percent (down from 6.8 percent in 1975), but median family income was $28,030, still slightly below its 1973 level.

The situation, moreover, was getting worse, not better. Because productivity was growing so slowly, workers' push for higher wages and firms' push for higher profits led directly to more inflation. Economic problems once again reached the top of the Gallup Poll's problem list.[33] In the first half of 1979 inflation reached an annual rate of 12 percent, a dangerously high figure. In the best of circumstances government policy would have had to abandon further stimulation to help cool inflation.

The best of circumstances, however, was not what we received. In late 1979 a coalition of Iranians overthrew the Shah of Iran. With Iranian oil production disrupted, OPEC announced a four-fold increase in the price of oil. The cycle began again. By the fall of 1980 inflation still exceeded 11 percent even though unemployment was 7.5 percent. These conditions helped set the stage for Jimmy Carter's election defeat by Ronald Reagan.

When President Reagan took office, his economic program promised a painless end to inflation and an immediate return to rapid economic growth.[34] It was an impossible boast. The 1970s inflation had been strongly reinforced by the second OPEC price increase, and so Reagan was left with a painful choice: Reduce inflation or reduce unemployment, but not both at once.

When confronted with the choice, Reagan opted to reduce inflation. In 1981–82 the Federal Reserve continued a very tight monetary policy (begun in 1979) and the President stood aloof. He gave clear signals that he would not intervene in the economy even when the adult male unemployment rate exceeded 9 percent.[35] Because of

[33] See Smith, "America's Most Important Problem."

[34] For example, the Reagan Administration predicted that if its program were adopted, 1984 inflation would stand at 5.5 percent, unemployment would stand at 6.4 percent, and real Gross National Product would stand at $1,718 billion (in 1972 dollars, the standard benchmark for real GNP). In 1984 inflation more than met the target, standing at 4.3 percent, but unemployment was 7.1 percent and GNP was $1,639 billion, about the level the administration had forecast for 1983. See U.S. Office of Management and Budget, *America's New Beginning: A Program for Economic Recovery* (Washington, DC: U.S. Government Printing Office, February 18, 1981).

[35] One such signal was Reagan's willingness to fire air traffic controllers, a group whose union had supported him, when they went on strike early in his administration.

his posture, inflation fell more quickly than most observers had expected and this was a major achievement. But the price was paid in short-term growth. Despite the recovery of 1983–84, 1984 median family income stood at $26,433. This was about its level when President Reagan was campaigning in 1980, $1,600 less than in 1979 be-

TABLE 4.3

Living Standards, 1973–1984

From 1973 through 1984 median family income declined by 6 percent. Families were pushed into higher tax brackets by the late 1970s inflation, but federal income taxes were then reduced by the Reagan Administration. A slack economy and declining government means-tested benefits meant a less equal income distribution. Less equality and declining incomes meant that the proportion of the population in poverty increased. Government spending grew more slowly than it had in the 1960s, and through most of the decade defense spending declined in part to accommodate the growth of social insurance programs including Social Security and Medicare.

	1973	1984	Growth over 11 Years
Median Family Income (1984 dollars)	$28,200	$26,433	−6.2%
Tax Burden at Median Family Income	20.9%	22.4%	
Ratio of Black-to-White Median Family Income	.58	.56	
Income Share of Lowest Quintile of Families	5.5%	4.7%	
Percentage of all Persons in Poverty	11.1%	14.4%	
Government Expenditures per Person (1984 dollars)	$ 4,124	$ 4,792	+16.2%
National Defense	728	910	
Payments to Individuals	1,138	1,721	
All Other	2,258	2,161	

NOTE: In 1979, prior to President Reagan's defense buildup, defense spending per capita had declined to $687.

SOURCES: Median family income, the ratio of black-to-white median income, and income shares come from U.S. Bureau of Census, *Current Population Reports*, series P-60, no. 151. Tax burdens are estimated by the author using the work of Joseph Minarik, *Making Tax Choices* (Washington, DC: Urban Institute Press, 1985). Estimates of poverty come from U.S. Bureau of the Census, *Current Population Reports*, series P-60, nos. 147 and 149. Statistics on government expenditures come from U.S. Department of Commerce, Bureau of Economic Analysis, *National Income and Product Accounts of the United States, 1929–76* (1981), and updates of the national accounts through 1985 in *Survey of Current Business*, no. 3 (March 1986), pp. 76–83.

fore the second OPEC price increase, and $1,700 less than in 1973. (See Table 4.3.)

By 1984 we had been through eleven years in which average family incomes had not increased (and early 1985 figures showed little additional progress). But events did not stand still and beneath the stagnant average, inequality was slowly growing and changing. Some of the changes resulted from government policy, others were inadvertant, and not all of the changes could be seen in census statistics.

The clearest statistical change was the decline in the lowest quintile's share of income, a share that fell from 5.6 percent of all family income in 1969 to 5.2 percent in 1979 and 4.7 percent in 1984. A part of the decline flowed from macroeconomic policy.

After 1973 threats of inflation caused the government to tolerate two severe recessions. From 1965 through 1973, adult men (ages 20 and over) averaged 3 percent unemployment. From 1974 through 1984 they averaged 6 percent unemployment. Higher unemployment reduced the income of low skilled workers in particular and was one factor in the increase of families headed by women. Both mechanisms reduced incomes in the poorest quintile of families. After 1980 the severe recession and an overvalued U.S. dollar were particularly hard on manufacturing and blue collar workers, which increased income inequality further (see Chapter 5).

Policy played a second role through government programs. By 1973 the major social insurance programs—Social Security, Medicare—had benefits that were automatically adjusted for the cost of living. But benefits for the major low-income program—Aid to Families with Dependent Children (AFDC)—were set separately by each state on an annual basis. Through the 1970s states were hard pressed for revenues and they chose to increase AFDC benefits more slowly than inflation. When President Reagan came to office, AFDC benefits were further reduced through eligibility restrictions that were part of his administration's economic program. In the depths of the 1980–82 recession, real AFDC expenditures were about 20 percent lower than they had been in 1976. This also reduced income in the bottom quintile.[36]

The combined impact of this inequality and stagnant incomes is captured in calculations by economist Katherine Bradbury (1986).

---

[36] These developments are discussed more fully in Chapters 7 and 8.

Bradbury shows that between 1973 and 1984, the percentage of all families with incomes over $50,000 (in 1984 dollars) had risen slightly from 14.9 to 15.6 percent, but the percentage of all families with incomes between $20,000 and $50,000 had declined from 53.0 to 47.9 percent while the percentage of all families with incomes less than $20,000 had risen from 32.1 to 36.4 percent. (See Figure 2.2.)

A more subtle change in inequality involved housing and the role of mortgages. Over the 1970s home prices rose much faster than most other prices. This was, in part, a reflection of baby boom cohorts who were now looking for places to live, but it also reflected a stagnant economy in which real estate was a better investment than most stocks and bonds.[37] If a family had bought its home before the early 1970s, these housing prices were of little concern since their mortgage payments were fixed in dollar terms.[38] But for families who had not yet bought homes, it was a different story. Recall that in the 1950s a typical 30-year-old man could make the monthly payments on a typical home using 14 percent of his gross monthly pay. By the early 1970s this ratio had climbed a little, so that in 1973 a young man would have had to spend 21 percent of his gross earnings for payments on a typical home. But in 1984 a 30-year-old man—now a member of the baby boom cohorts—would have had to spend *44 percent* of his gross earnings to carry a median-priced home.[39] The middle-class dream was becoming more expensive.

This kind of inequality was largely missed in official statistics. Young families postponed marriage until they were established and, when they did marry, they increasingly relied on two earners. Thus, *family* income inequality was not as affected as wage trends would suggest. Similarly, the census measures dollar incomes—not incomes after mortgage payments—so that the rising price of housing had no impact on the income distribution. But it was a far cry from the 1950s when a second income could go for the extras.

---

[37] For a good discussion of housing prices during this period see John A. Tucillo, *Housing and Investment in an Inflationary World* (Washington, DC: Urban Institute, 1980). As an example of the weakness of corporate investment, the New York Stock Exchange common stock index stood at 57.4 in 1973, 45.7 in 1975, 53.7 in 1977, and 58.3 in 1979. It was not until the end of 1980 and the election of Ronald Reagan that the index began to rise.

[38] Even if a family's dollar wages did not keep up with inflation, the fact that their mortgage payments were fixed might allow their purchasing power to remain relatively intact.

[39] See Levy and Michel, "An Economic Bust for the Baby Boom."

An Alternate View

Statistics exist to prove any point, and so it is not surprising that we can find one statistic that contradicts this gloomy picture. Between 1973 and 1984 real consumer expenditure per capita increased by 15 percent. Much of the new money went to such necessities as housing, utilities, and medical care (Figure 4.3). Still the growth in spending per capita was equivalent to its growth in the 1950s and suggests that the 1973–84 period was actually quite dynamic.

The contradiction is easily reconciled. The post-1973 growth in consumption per capita did not reflect a booming economy, but rather two national trends: the growing proportion of the population who worked and our increased willingness to take on debt.

The major success of the 1970s economy was its ability to absorb new workers. (In this it was quite unlike Europe which tolerated high rates of unemployment.) During the 1970s and early 1980s the biggest baby boom cohorts began their careers while women of all ages entered the labor force in large numbers.[40] In addition, these late baby boomers delayed marriage and had relatively few children (see Chapter 8). More workers and fewer children meant that the proportion of the entire population in the labor force rose from 41 percent in 1970 to 49 percent today (this despite the fact that older men were retiring at earlier ages).

Not even an economist would argue that these trends were all induced by the stagnant economy,[41] but they helped offset the effects of stagnation. Because an increasing proportion of the population was at work, income per *capita* (that is, per man, woman, and child) kept growing even though income per *worker* did not. In this way the decade was a reversal of the 1950s. Then, income per worker was growing by 30 percent per decade but income per capita was growing at half that rate because we were sufficiently optimistic to have large numbers of children.

The effect of demographic changes on consumption was reinforced by taking on new debt. Debt comes in many varieties: consumer debt, the government's debt, the debt in our international

[40] This is discussed more fully in Chapter 7.

[41] In particular, the birthrate began falling sharply, and women's labor force participation began growing sharply in the 1960s when the economy was strong. These trends are discussed in Chapters 7 and 8.

FIGURE 4.3

Changes in Consumption Expenditure per Person, 1973–1984
(in 1984 dollars)

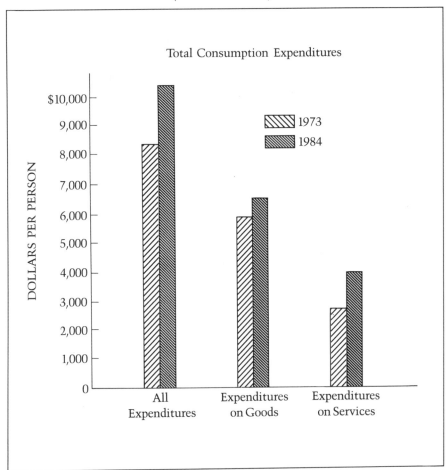

trade balance. In GNP accounts, these different pieces can be combined into a single equation:[42]

| Personal Savings | + | Savings by Business | + | Government Savings | + | Foreign Capital Inflow | = | Domestic Investment |

The equation describes the way in which each dollar of investment must be financed by a dollar from one of four sources: individ-

---

[42] See, for example, Richard N. Cooper, "Dealing with the Trade Deficit in a Floating Rate System," *Brookings Papers on Economic Activity*, no. 1 (1986), pp. 195–207.

FIGURE 4.3 *(continued)*

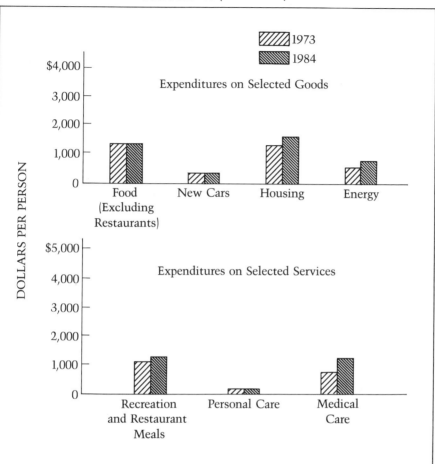

SOURCES: U.S. Department of Commerce, Bureau of Economic Analysis, *National Income and Product Accounts of the United States*, various years.

uals, businesses (through their retained earnings), the government sector (through budget surpluses), or capital borrowed from foreign countries.

A comparison of this equation in the early 1970s and the mid-1980s shows the following:

- The individual savings rate has declined from 5.4 percent to 3.8 percent of GNP. But the business savings rate has increased correspondingly from 11 percent to 14 percent of GNP.

- The government sector (federal, state, and local) has moved from running a small surplus in the early 1970s to running a deficit equal to 3.4 percent of GNP per year, a reflection of the $220 billion annual deficits in the federal budget. Thus, government has changed from being a small generator of savings to becoming a significant user of savings. The total domestic savings rate (individual plus business plus government) fell from 16.8 percent to 14.7 percent of GNP.

- The rate of investment has remained constant at 16.5 percent of GNP, despite reduced domestic savings, because we are borrowing heavily from abroad. In the early 1970s we were a net supplier of capital for other countries. By 1985, our net borrowing from other countries equaled 3.5 percent of GNP per year.

The emergence of the federal budget deficit follows naturally from our story. It reflects our willingness to cut taxes, coupled with our reluctance to cut expenditures. The combined effect of these policies is to put more money in our pockets to keep consumption growing, but the choice is possible only because foreign countries are lending us money.

Foreign investment in the United States is not automatically bad. If foreign funds increase the level of U.S. investment, both the United States and foreigners will benefit. But the U.S. rate of investment is no higher today than it was in 1973, despite the foreign capital.[43] Foreign funds have been used to offset government deficits and thus to finance extra U.S. consumption.[44] This is a strategy for postponing stagnation's effects, but it involves borrowing from the future. Eventually, the foreign funds must be paid back with interest. And because they were used to finance consumption, rather than additional investment, the repayment will require reducing our consumption below what it otherwise would have been. The need for foreign capital also led to high U.S. interest rates and an overvalued U.S. dollar overseas, the foundations of an enormous trade deficit. We examine these issues beginning in Chapter 5.

---

[43] One could reasonably argue that the rate of investment should be greater now than it was in 1973 to keep up with rapid labor force growth, and so 'ur relatively constant rate of investment is insufficient.

[44] That is, the deficit reflected the fact that government wanted to cut taxes without making corresponding cuts in government expenditure. Tax cuts without expenditure cuts was a way to increase purchasing power.

The decline in the birthrate was, in its way, a different kind of borrowing from the future. That decline is heavily concentrated among middle-income families. Later we shall see that about one fifth of all U.S. children now live in poverty. This proportion reflects not only what poor families are doing, but what middle-income families are not doing. The result is that one fifth of our next generation is being raised in abysmal circumstances. We return to this issue in Chapters 8 and 9.

A Sense of Perspective

Economic trends are notoriously sensitive to their starting dates. Are we living better today (1986) than we lived in the 1920s? The answer is yes. And are we living better today than we did in the 1980–82 recession? The answer again is yes. But are we living as well today as we did in 1973? The answer is no. We appear to be doing better, but this is only because we have borrowed against the future in ways that must eventually be repaid.

The economy, of course, is much more than consumption standards. It is industry and the labor force and geography and families. It is to those other elements that we now turn.

5

THE INDUSTRIAL STRUCTURE

Are Services to be Feared?

FOR THE first twenty-six years of the postwar period, real wage growth was so steady that it came to be taken for granted. Wage growth affected us in obvious ways, like the number of cars we could afford, but it also affected our outlook on economic life. It shaped our perceptions of the normal path of a man's career; of the difficulty in abolishing poverty; of the relationship between one generation and the next, and, in particular, of the economy's transition to a service society.

Recall that as early as 1947 more than half of all hours of employment were in the service sector industries: transportation and communication, wholesale and retail trade, finance, the service industry per se, and government. Most observers found the trend benign. The distinguished economist Colin Clark (1940) described: ". . . the most important concomitant of economic progress, namely, the movement of the working population from agriculture to manufacture and from manufacture to commerce and services." [p. 176]

Four decades later the perception was quite different. The continuing shift of employment to services was seen as the force behind an increasingly immobile, unequal society. Bruce Steinberg (1982), a writer for *Fortune* magazine, gave a representative summary:

> . . . the decline of the middle [of the income distribution] really began during the long expansion of the late Seventies, when families began to find the economic ground under them shifting.
>
> The key to what's going on lies in the explosive growth of the service economy, which has brought on massive upheaval in employment patterns. [p. 77]

Steinberg argued that the earnings distribution in the service sector was inherently less equal than the earnings distribution in the goods-producing industries: mining, construction and manufacturing.[1] These industries, he said, paid middle-class wages, while services ranged from fast food to investment banking. As service sector employment grew, earnings inequality would have to grow as well.

Steinberg was representative of a number of authors who argued that the trend toward services was creating a two-tier job market: the very high paid and the very low paid, with a shrinking number of jobs in the middle.[2] And, in fact, while the family income distribution has remained relatively constant, the distribution of men's earnings has become less equal.

In Chapter 2 we summarized inequality in family incomes by use of the Gini coefficient (Table 2.1). In 1947 the Gini coefficient of the family income distribution stood at .38. It fell slowly, reflecting the slightly more equal income distribution, until it reached .35 in the late 1960s. During the 1970s it rose again, reaching .37 in 1979 and .39 in 1984.

---

[1] Technically, agriculture is also in the goods-producing sector. But agricultural earnings are relatively low and highly unequal, and no one argues that the declining share of the labor force in agriculture has hurt earnings inequality. For this reason, we will describe the economy in terms of agriculture, the service sector, and the goods-producing sector.

[2] A list of authors who see a two-tier economy is contained in Chapter 1, footnote 2. Among the authors who disagree are Neal H. Rosenthal, "The Shrinking Middle Class: Myth or Reality?," *Monthly Labor Review*, March 1985, pp. 3–10; Robert J. Samuelson, "Middle-Class Media Myth," *National Journal*, December 31, 1983, pp. 2673–78; and Robert Z. Lawrence, *Can America Compete?* (Washington, DC: Brookings Institution, 1984), pp. 80–81. Some of the differences arise because different authors look at different statistics: annual earnings, hourly wages, hourly wages of full-time workers, and so on.

By comparison, the Gini coefficient of men's annual earnings was larger to begin with and was increasing for most of this period. The economists Peter Henle and Paul Ryscavage show that in 1958 it stood at .40 and it rose steadily in subsequent years, reaching .44 in 1977.[3] In 1984 it stood at about .46.[4]

Henle and Ryscavage calculate that the distribution of women's annual earnings was even more unequal, but showed no postwar trend. In 1958 the Gini coefficient for women's earnings stood at .47 (versus .40 for men), which reflected the wide variation in women's annual hours of work, but in subsequent years it showed almost no change.[5]

For this reason most analyses of the two-tier labor market have focused on inequality in men's earnings, and we will follow that convention here. An example makes the issue concrete. In 1969, at the peak of the Vietnam boom, the man who stood at the 75th percentile of the male earnings distribution made $28,659 (in 1984 dollars) while the man who stood at the 25th percentile made $8,981, a ratio of 3.2 to 1 (Figure 5.1). In 1984 the two comparable men made $28,710 and $7,200, respectively, a ratio of 3.99 to 1. This growth in earnings inequality leads to a series of questions:

- How important is the service sector in the growing inequality of men's earnings?

- In terms of employment, we have been a service economy for the entire postwar period. If the service sector played an important role in increasing earnings inequality, why wasn't its role noticed earlier?

- If the service sector has not increased earnings inequality, why does its growth raise such concern?

As we answer these questions, we shall see that the issues between Clark and Steinberg have more to do with demography and the general state of the economy than with the service sector per se. From 1947 to 1973 the transition to a service economy proceeded in a generally benign fashion. It was in the stagnant economy of the last twelve years that the transition became increasingly dangerous.

---

[3] See Peter Henle and Paul Ryscavage, "The Distribution of Earned Income Among Men and Women, 1958–77," *Monthly Labor Review*, April 1980, pp. 3–10.

[4] This is the author's estimate based on grouped data.

[5] Inequality between women's and men's earnings is examined in Chapter 7.

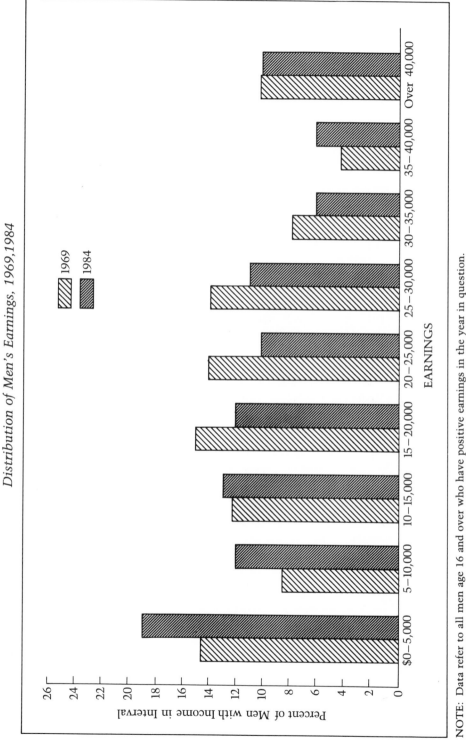

FIGURE 5.1

Distribution of Men's Earnings, 1969,1984

NOTE: Data refer to all men age 16 and over who have positive earnings in the year in question.

SOURCES: 1970 Census of Population and March 1985 Current Population Survey.

When Wages Were Growing

The shift to services calls to mind yesterday's $25,000-a-year steel worker who now clerks in a K-Mart at $4.25 per hour. Since 1980, 6 percent of the labor force have been displaced from their jobs and many have taken big pay cuts. The pay cuts are a new problem; displacement is not. Even when the economy was healthy, workers were displaced all the time. Beginning in the 1890s New England steadily lost textile mills, first to the Southeast and then to overseas. During the 1950s the number of workers on farms dropped by 2.9 million, about 5 percent of the U.S. labor force. From the end of World War II through 1963 Chicago lost one third of its blue collar manufacturing jobs.

This was part of what Joseph Schumpeter (1942) meant by "creative destruction":

> The opening up of new markets, foreign or domestic, and the organizational development from the craft shop and factory to such concerns as U.S. Steel illustrate the same process of industrial mutation—if I may use that biological term—that incessantly revolutionizes the economic structure *from within*, incessantly destroying the old one, incessantly creating a new one. This process of Creative Destruction is the essential fact about capitalism. It is what capitalism consists in and what every capitalist concern has got to live in. [p. 83]

As the name implies, the process involves substantial dislocation and pain. But when average real earnings are growing throughout the economy, this pain is substantially reduced.

For the first two thirds of the postwar period real wages were growing with this effect. From 1947 to 1973 real earnings grew at 2.5–3.0 percent per year. A good index of this growth was the path of a man's earnings as he moved from age 40 to age 50. By the time most men are 40, their big promotions are behind them and *in any one year* 40-year-old and 50-year-old men have similar incomes. But as men actually pass from age 40 to 50 their earnings can increase if earnings are increasing throughout the economy.

Table 5.1 shows that prior to 1973 this is exactly what happened. In the table we can follow the arrows to trace men's real in-

TABLE 5.1

Men's Income Growth Before and After 1973 (in 1984 dollars)

Arrows trace the path of an average man's income as he passes from age 30 in 1949 to age 40 in 1959, and so on. After 1973, incomes stagnated.

Age	1949	1959	1969	1973	1984
25–34 years	$12,000	16,916	22,593	23,579	17,538
35–44 years	$12,858	18,958	25,628	28,118	23,418
45–54 years	$11,987	17,290	24,421	27,279	24,132

NOTE: Figures represent men's median income for the cohort and year in question. To maintain decade intervals between observations, the table's last year should have been 1983: 1984 was chosen instead because the economy was still recovering from recession in 1983 and the reader might assume that 1983 incomes were particularly depressed for that reason. In 1983 the corresponding income figures were ages 25–34, $17,519; 35–44, $23,394; 45–54, $24,097

SOURCES: All statistics from U.S. Bureau of the Census, *Current Population Reports,* series P-60, various numbers.

comes as they grew older.[6] In 1949 an average 40-year-old man (35–44 in the table) was earning $12,858. Ten years later (and despite displacements) this average man, now 50, had an income of $17,290, an increase of 34 percent. During the 1960s a similar passage from age 40 to 50 increased earnings by 29 percent. This growth extended the years of a man's career in which his earning power increased.

The growth of earnings also helped young men get off to a quick start. Suppose that an 18- or 19-year-old man was preparing to leave home. As he left, he took a look at his father's salary and what it would buy and he kept the memory as a personal yardstick. Before 1973 he would have measured up quickly. By the time the young man was 30 years old, he would have been earning about 15 percent more than his father had earned when the young man was leaving

---

[6] Our real interest is not in annual incomes but in hourly or weekly earnings. The census typically does not publish average weekly earnings by age, so that we have been forced to use annual incomes of prime-age men as a proxy. (Because these are prime-age men, most of their income comes from earnings.) The census publishes similar income statistics for women by age, but these statistics confound trends in weekly earnings with rapid increases in the number of women who worked. For this reason, we have not constructed a comparable table for women, but one comparison is suggestive. Among women who worked full time, annual real income rose by 9.2 percent between 1955 (the earliest data available) and 1959, 54 percent between 1960 and 1969, and − 1 percent between 1973 and 1984.

home. The young man knew early in his career that he could live as well as he had seen his parents live.[7]

Real wage growth also made the poverty problem appear manageable. In Chapter 4 we saw how economic growth was the major force behind poverty reduction in the 1950s and 1960s. The force was, more precisely, the growth of real wages, which allowed low-income workers to make progress vis-à-vis the poverty line.

Finally, the growth of earnings blurred distinctions between goods-producing jobs and service sector jobs. Throughout the postwar period, goods-producing workers earned 10–15 percent more than service-producing workers of the same age and education. The difference reflected the larger plant sizes and greater unionization of goods-producing firms.[8] But real wages in both sectors were rising so fast that sectoral differences were blurred. In 1959 a 30-year-old man in durable manufacturing was earning about $18,950 while a 30-year-old man in retail trade was earning $2,600 less, but over the next ten years each man's earnings would increase by $8,000. When your own situation is improving so fast, your neighbor's better situation is less of an irritant.

These were the virtues of wage growth and they continued from the end of World War II until 1973. Then wages turned stagnant, and each of the virtues was turned on its head:

- A man who became 40 years old in 1973 now earns about 14 percent less (rather than 25 percent more) than he did then (Figure 5.2).

- A young man who left his parents' home in 1973 is now earning 25 percent less (rather than 15 percent more) than his father had earned in the early 1970s.

- The proportion of the population in poverty in 1984 was 14 percent, 3 percentage points higher than it had been in 1973.

- Wages in both goods production and service production have stopped growing. Because all wages are stagnating, moving to a higher-paying sector seems like the only way to get ahead,

---

[7] Richard Easterlin develops similar comparisons for points in time, rather than over time. See his *Birth and Fortune* (New York: Basic Books, 1980).

[8] See Victor R. Fuchs, *The Service Economy* (New York: National Bureau of Economic Research and Columbia University Press, 1968).

FIGURE 5.2

*Average Income Gain for Men Passing from Age 40 to Age 50
(in 1984 dollars)*

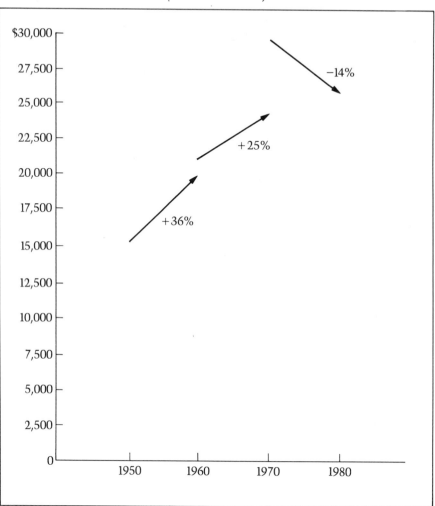

SOURCES: U.S. Bureau of the Census, *Current Population Reports*, series P-60, various numbers.

and the service-manufacturing wage gap has become an increasingly raw issue.[9]

A Service-Stagnation Connection?

In Chapter 4 we saw that the slowdown in productivity and wage growth came from a combination of factors—the rapid increase in energy prices, a fast growing labor force, a strong inflation, and slow-growing markets which threw corporations off stride. But taken together these factors could explain only a part of the slowdown, and it is reasonable to ask whether the growth of the service sector played a role.

Obviously, productivity in some services grows very slowly. Musicians today require the same time to play the Brandenburg Concertos as when Bach wrote them. A men's barber takes the same time to cut a head of hair as he did in 1947.[10] Couldn't the shift toward services have contributed to the productivity slowdown?

If the shift did contribute, its contribution was small. Begin with the fact that barbers and classical musicians are in highly labor-intensive services. There is little place for capital and technology to enter to raise output per worker. In this they are exceptional. Recent estimates suggest that for the service sector as a whole, the level of capital per worker is now on a par with capital per worker in goods production.[11] And the effect of the capital is obvious. Imagine airlines without jets or travel agents without computerized bookings or a telephone system in which operators made all connections by hand

---

[9] There are two ways in which the decline in earnings may be overstated. The first is that during the 1970s certain fringe benefits—for example, employer-provided health insurance—grew rapidly more expensive, and so the value of a worker's *total* compensation grew faster than would be implied by money earnings alone. The second is that throughout this book we are adjusting for inflation using the Consumer Price Index, which during this period was heavily influenced by the rising cost of home purchase. While this is appropriate for younger workers (most of whom have not yet bought homes), it may overstate inflation for older workers. For them, a more appropriate inflation adjustment may be the Personal Consumption Expenditure Index, but this does not change the results very much. In the case of men passing from age 40 to 50, the Consumer Price Index adjustment has them moving from a 29 percent increase (in 1959–69) to a 14 percent decline (in 1973–84) while the Personal Consumption Expenditure Index has them moving from a 29 percent increase to a 6 percent decline.

[10] But beauticians' productivity has improved. See Fuchs, *The Service Economy*, chap. 6.

[11] See the work of financial economist Stephen Roach, as quoted in Richard I. Kirkland, Jr., "Are Service Jobs Good Jobs?" *Fortune*, June 10, 1985, pp. 38–43.

and you can see how much output per worker has increased in most service industries. Official statistics show this. From 1947 to 1973 output per hour of labor in service sector industries rose at 1.9 percent per year.[12] This growth rate was slower than the productivity growth in agriculture (4.0 percent per year) or in goods production (2.9 percent per year), but it was sufficient to help justify growing wages.

Because output per worker grows more slowly in the service sector than in other sectors,[13] a gradual shift of labor toward services might cause a gradual decline in overall productivity growth. But after 1973 productivity growth declined abruptly—not gradually. Since 1947 (and, in fact, since 1910) output per worker had grown at rates averaging 2.5–3.3 percent per year.[14] From 1973 to 1982 it grew at only .8 percent per year. Consider the contrast: Between 1947 and 1973 *service sector* productivity grew at 1.9 percent per year (see above), but between 1973 and 1982 *combined* productivity for services, goods production, and agriculture only grew at .8 percent per year (see Figure 5.3). It is this break in trend that points to macroeconomic shocks—energy price increases, the rapidly growing labor force, suddenly stagnant markets—as the chief causes of productivity slowdown.

Even if barbers and classical musicians are exceptions, they still make an important point. How can one justify paying them higher wages if their productivity hasn't improved? To answer this question, imagine what would happen if barbers' wages did not increase. In 1949 the typical barber was earning $9,900 per year (in 1984 dollars). Barbering is an occupation that requires both skill and training. If that same salary held today, skilled people would have better opportunities and barbering would become like the old Groucho Marx joke: We wouldn't want our hair cut by anyone who wanted to cut it. In reality, the typical full-time barber now earns about $17,500. Imbedded in this salary is the fact that the real cost of haircuts has risen relative to the cost of oranges or radios or computers, all of which come from more productive industries. But during this time our real incomes have also grown, and we can afford the higher hair-

---

[12] This calculation was made by the author based on National Income Account data.
[13] There is, in addition, the question of how good a job we do in measuring the output of services, particularly in the government where we do not have output prices.
[14] The figures refer to growth rates averaged over decades.

FIGURE 5.3

The Year-to-Year Growth Rate of Worker Productivity, 1947–1985

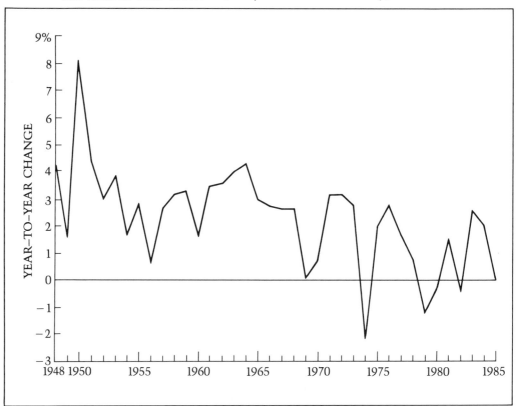

NOTE: Each point refers to the percentage change from the previous year.

SOURCE: U.S. Council of Economic Advisors, *Economic Report of the President; 1986, table B-43.*

cut costs. In this way the benefits of high productivity industries are spread throughout the economy.[15]

In sum, the growing service sector has made only a small contribution to stagnation. (Conversely, stagnation has made a big contribution to anxiety over the service sector.) But if services are not an important cause of stagnation, there remains the potential relationship between the growing service sector and increased earnings

[15] The reader may recognize this as the argument of economist William Baumol explaining why certain labor-intensive services—the arts, domestic help—seemed to cost so much more over time. See his "Macroeconomics of Unbalanced Growth: The Anatomy of the Urban Crisis," *American Economic Review* 57 (June 1967): 415–26.

inequality. To understand this relationship, we first need to see why the service sector grew.

How the Service Sector Grew

When Colin Clark equated the growth of service sector employment to progress, he had two things in mind. One is the tendency for the economy (business and consumers) to demand more services as it becomes richer. The other is the way in which service industries use relatively large amounts of labor.

In Chapter 4 we saw how services became an increasingly important part of personal consumption spending. The source of these statistics, the National Income Accounts, treats housing expenditures as a service and restaurant meals as a good. But even when these items are reclassified to conform with public perception (as they were in Figures 4.1–4.3), services over the postwar period grew from 26 to 34 percent of all personal consumption. It is easy to see why. When a family's income doubles, it will not double the amount of food it eats at home. But it may more than double its expenditures on services like vacation travel, medical care, insurance protection, or college education for the children. Added to this is their increasing demand for government products—better schools, better libraries, and more parks—which are also services.

Business demand for services grew in a similar way. At the end of World War II, 29 percent of all services were actually purchased by business to produce other goods and services.[16] A manufacturer of kitchen stoves needed telephones, transportation, utilities, a sales network, and other service sector products as a normal part of production. As the economy matured, business expanded its service demand to include more lawyering, accounting, data processing, management consulting, and other products, so that today 36 percent of all services are purchased by business.[17]

---

[16] Technically, this fraction is:

$$1 - \frac{\text{All Final Sales of Service Sector Output}}{\text{Total Service Sector Output}}$$

[17] See Kirkland, "Are Service Jobs Good Jobs?" To the extent that this growing demand is accompanied by increased contracting out, the shift to services looks more dramatic than it is. For example, if the aforementioned stove company had kept an accountant on its payroll, she would have been tabulated as a manufacturing employee. But if she leaves to join an accounting firm and takes the stove company's business with her, she will be tabulated as a service sector employee even though she is doing the same work.

It follows that if GNP doubles over time, demand for services (from consumers and business) will more than double. This is part of what Clark meant, but there is more.

If the service sector had very rapid productivity growth, it could produce this increased output with a constant or declining share of the labor force. But because service sector productivity is relatively low, an increase in service demand means a relatively large increase in service sector employment. Service *output* as a proportion of GNP has risen relatively slowly: 40 percent in 1947 and 46 percent in 1984. But service *employment* as a proportion of the labor force has grown more rapidly.[18]

As Clark implied, the employment trend toward services is nothing new. Service industries accounted for 53 percent of all hours of employment in 1947 and 72 percent today (Table 5.2). In this shift the "old line" service industries—transportation and communication, wholesale trade, retail trade—grew no faster than employment as a whole. The finance, insurance, and real estate industry grew more rapidly, but began from a very small base and so was not numerically important. The bulk of new service sector employment came from two other industries: the government and the census-defined "service industry" (an industry within the service sector).

The growth of government employment followed the growth of government expenditures described in Chapter 4. Between 1947 and 1969 total employment in the economy increased by 21 million persons (on a full-time equivalent basis), and almost 8 million of these jobs were in government. During the 1970s the growth of government slowed, but governments at all levels still employ one worker in six nationwide.

The census-defined service industry is a collection of small industries that are too small to warrant individual classification: hotels, barbers, moviemakers, private hospitals, law firms, private colleges, accounting firms, and so on. Within this group, the greatest employment gains have been in health care and business services (for example, accounting, data processing).

If the trend toward service employment was so obvious in the 1950s and 1960s, why didn't it create more alarm? In part, because

---

[18] See Victor R. Fuchs, "Economic Growth and the Rise of Service Employment," in Herbert Giersch, ed., *Towards an Explanation of Economic Growth* (Tubingen: Mohr, 1981).

TABLE 5.2

Distribution of Full-Time Equivalent Employment
by Sector and Industry, 1947–1983

Throughout the early postwar period the service sector had an increasing *share* of employment, but *absolute* employment in goods production was increasing as well. It was only in the 1970s and, in particular, after 1979 that the number of persons in goods production—particularly in manufacturing—began to decline.

	1947	1959	1969	1979	1984
PERSONS ENGAGED IN PRODUCTION (IN THOUSANDS)	57,320	63,770	78,478	94,332	100,502
SHARE BY SECTOR AND INDUSTRY					
Agriculture	11.3%	7.4%	4.0%	3.3%	3.0%
Goods-Producing Sector					
Mining	1.7	1.2	.8	.9	1.0
Construction	5.6	5.5	5.4	5.8	5.5
Manufacturing	26.5	25.6	25.5	22.1	19.2
Durable Goods	(14.4)	(14.6)	(15.2)	(13.5)	(11.5)
Nondurable Goods	(12.1)	(11.0)	(10.3)	(8.5)	(7.7)
Service-Producing Sector					
Transportation, Communication, and Public Utilities	7.4	6.4	5.7	5.5	5.2
Wholesale Trade	4.6	5.2	5.1	5.6	5.7
Retail Trade	14.6	13.9	13.3	14.6	15.3
Finance, Insurance, and Real Estate	3.3	4.2	4.6	5.5	6.1
Services	13.0	14.6	16.8	19.5	22.7
Government and Government Enterprises	11.8	16.2	18.7	17.1	16.4
Total	99.8%	100.2%	99.9%	99.9%	100.1%

NOTE: Persons engaged in production equals the number of full-time equivalent employees plus the number of self-employed persons working in an industry. Numbers may not add to 100 percent due to rounding.

SOURCES: U.S. Department of Commerce, Bureau of Economic Analysis, *National Income and Product Accounts of the United States, 1929–76* (1981), table 6.11B; *Survey of Current Business*, vol. 63, no. 7 (July 1983), table 6.11B; vol. 66, no. 7 (March 1986), table 6.10B.

during these decades service sector growth did *not* mean goods production decline. The proportion of all men working in mining, construction, and manufacturing stood at 39 percent in 1949, 41 percent in 1959, and 41 percent in 1969. Nonetheless, service sector employment could grow very fast because agricultural employment was declining and, more important, because large numbers of women were entering the labor force.

Among traditional women's occupations, clerical work is distributed across all industries, but the others—teachers, nurses, sales personnel, and so on—are in the service sector. From 1950 to 1969 service sector employment increased by 22 million persons (full-time plus part-time), and women constituted 70 percent of this increase. The economist Victor Fuchs notes that this growth contained an element of feedback: More working induced a need for more restaurant workers, more day care teachers, and other service jobs.[19]

But during the 1950s and 1960s goods production employment was also growing. The growth was not fast—6 million new jobs versus 22 million new jobs in the service sector. Still, it was sufficient to keep about 40 percent of all male workers in goods-producing jobs. (Figure 5.4).

To this point, we have implicitly assumed that goods-producing jobs are good and should be preserved. Is this really true? It is, and for two reasons.

There is, first, the question of individual mobility. Goods-producing industries provide blue collar jobs where men without high levels of education can do physical work and often receive good pay. In the 1979 census construction trades workers averaged $21,660 per year, and 80 percent had a high school diploma or less. Metal and plastic processing machine operators averaged $19,500, and 90 percent had a high school diploma or less.[20] Unions have achieved their greatest success in blue collar occupations, which explains a portion of these earnings, but the earnings also reflect the nature of the work. In the service sector, many good jobs require high levels of training or an ability to deal smoothly with the public. These are attributes which many less educated men do not have, and their opportunities and wages in the service sector are correspondingly lower.[21]

The second reason is the interdependency of goods production and services. If manufacturing output declines, many high-paying service jobs will evaporate. We have seen how many service jobs actually "service" the production of physical goods. When a factory

[19] See Fuchs, "Economic Growth and the Rise of Service Employment."

[20] See U.S. Bureau of the Census, *Earnings by Occupation and Education*, Report PC80-2-8B (May 1984), table 2. (Figures are converted to 1984 dollars.)

[21] For a discussion of the nature of service work, see Thomas M. Stanback, Jr., et al., *Services: The New Economy* (Totowa, NJ: Allanheld, Osmun, 1981).

FIGURE 5.4

Number of Men and Women Workers by Sector of Employment

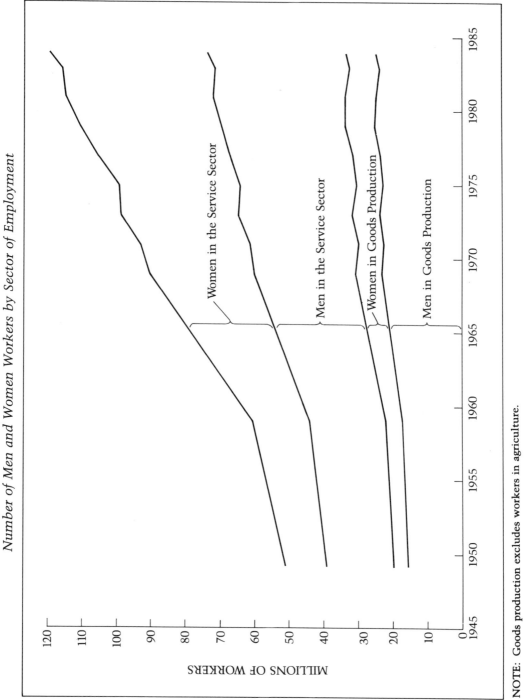

NOTE: Goods production excludes workers in agriculture.

SOURCES: U.S. Bureau of the Census, *Current Population Reports*, series P-60, various numbers.

shuts down, it no longer needs telephones or rail service or insurance or a lawyer. Economist Lester Thurow (1985) summarizes the argument well:

> One has only to look at Great Britain to see what happens to service industries when manufacturing collapses. The decline of the City of London as a financial hub is directly traceable to the decline of British industry. As American industry declines, the financial institutions that serve it will also decline. American banks, for example, will get some business from foreign manufacturing firms, but most of the foreign business will go to foreign banks. If anyone thinks otherwise, just remember the large equity positions that Japanese, German, French, and other banks hold in their national industrial firms. Controlling large equity positions, foreign banks can and do tell industrial managers what to do [including whom to bank with]. [p. 56]

From the perspective of the mid-1980s, we can add a third reason: A mix of manufacturing and services that requires the United States to run a $150 billion annual trade deficit is simply the wrong mix.

The Problems of the 1970s

Employment in goods production—particularly manufacturing—is sensitive to economic downturns. When unemployment rises, demand for cars, houses, and investment equipment all slow even as the demand for services continues. In Chapter 4 we saw how the 1970s became a succession of recessions: Richard Nixon's planned recession (to break inflation) of 1970–71; the deep recession that followed the 1973–74 OPEC price increase; the deeper recession that followed the 1979–80 OPEC price increase. All these extracted a cost in goods production employment. Over the 1950s and 1960s, mining, construction, and manufacturing had created 6 million new jobs. From 1969 through 1979 these industries created only 2.1 million additional jobs. This was the decade in which the baby boomers entered the work force, and the number of new jobs was not sufficient to keep up with labor force growth. The proportion of male workers in goods production fell from 41 to 39 percent, while the proportion of men in manufacturing per se fell from 30 to 26 percent. As economist Robert Lawrence (1984) writes: "there is no puzzle in explaining [the slow growth of] aggregate manufacturing production: it is almost exactly what one should have expected given the performance of the total economy" (p. 21).

Lawrence is correct in part but he understates the problem. Even in a good economy, the 1970s would have been a time when U.S. corporations had to learn new ways of doing business. Recall that in the 1950s and 1960s corporations relied on the rapid growth of markets to reconcile improved productivity (and profits) and the desire for expansion (see Chapter 4). By the early 1970s the environment had changed. Markets for manufactured goods were growing more slowly and in some markets—automobiles, machine tools, and consumer electronics—producers like West Germany and Japan had equaled or surpassed U.S. efficiency. In addition, advanced technology was shortening the average time between a new product's introduction and its successful "cloning" by other (often foreign) firms.[22]

This was creative destruction with a vengeance, and it required enormous changes in management style. The slack economy and rising energy prices only made the situation worse. Beneath the slow growth of manufacturing employment, worker displacement grew more frequent. This displacement would have been hard in any circumstances, but in the post-1973 period incomes were rising slowly for workers who *held* their jobs. Workers who lost their jobs faced a long-term cut in their standard of living. Moving to a better job seemed the only way to get ahead, and the slow growth of "good" jobs in goods production was a source of real worry.

A symbol of this worry was the loss of blue collar jobs in the steel industry. Steel is an important case because it faced shrinking markets even before the 1970s. In 1959 the United States imported more steel than it exported for the first time in the twentieth century. Imports reflected the effects of a long steelworker strike, but they also pointed to the industry's underlying weakness. At the close of World War II, the U.S. steel industry had enjoyed worldwide leadership in both capacity and productivity, and as economists Donald Barnett and Louis Schorsch show, the industry assumed that the postwar dominance would last indefinitely.[23]

Domestic steel firms invested heavily in expanded capacity us-

---

[22] On the nature of the product cycle and the movement of production to other countries, see Raymond Vernon, "International Investment and International Trade in the Product Cycle," *Quarterly Journal of Economics* 80 (May 1966): 190–207.
[23] See Donald F. Barnett and Louis Schorsch, *Steel: Upheaval in a Basic Industry* (Cambridge, MA: Ballinger, 1983) chap. 2.

ing proven, open hearth technology. While the expansion promoted corporate growth, it was hard on efficiency because Europe and Japan began to rebuild their steel industries around the new, more efficient, oxygen furnace technology. As foreign steel producers supplied a growing share of the world market, recently expanded U.S. firms were forced to operate below capacity. This further decreased U.S. firms' competitiveness and reduced the profits available for further modernization. In 1953 the U.S. steel industry employed 620,000 production workers. By 1970 it employed 513,000 production workers. The further decline to 451,000 in 1979 was only a continuation of a long-term trend.

There was, however, a second part to the story. While big U.S. steel corporations were shrinking, U.S. "mini-mills" were growing. Mini-mills are small firms built around arc furnaces and continuous casting, and each firm specializes in a limited number of products. By the early 1980s they supplied about one fifth of the total U.S. steel market. Because of their small size and specialization, they are better able to absorb rapidly improving technology and they are typically fully competitive with foreign producers. Mini-mills do not solve all problems: They pay wages lower than those paid by larger firms.[24] But on balance, the mini-mills show the steel industry's lack of competitiveness came as much from organizational problems as from an inevitable national decline.

Problems of the Early 1980s

Adjusting to slow-growing markets was difficult, but the worst was yet to come. The deep recession of 1980–82 struck a tremendous

---

[24] The issue of wages in big steel is itself a source of controversy. By the early 1970s the industry felt it had been seriously hurt by strikes. In exchange for no-strike pledges, workers were given a substantial wage increase and an automatic cost-of-living adjustment in case of future inflation. Recall that in the early 1970s an inflation rate of 5.5 percent was considered politically unacceptable. But in 1974 oil price increases pushed inflation to 12 percent, and only once in the next eight years did inflation fall below 6 percent. During these years most wages in the economy lagged behind inflation while wages in big steel kept pace. By 1979 production workers in nondurable manufacturing (for example, food, textiles, and chemicals) had gross pay averaging $338 per week. Production workers in durable manufacturing had gross pay averaging $415 per week. But among these durable goods workers, steel production workers' pay averaged $612 per week. Thus, high steel workers' wages were, in a sense, unintended and made the big steel producers that much more vulnerable to import competition. Autoworkers also received automatic cost-of-living provisions in the early 1970s and faced similar problems.

blow to manufacturing. During the subsequent recovery, government policy ensured that the problem would get worse. In Chapter 4 we saw how the federal government postponed the effects of stagnation by significantly reducing taxes without reducing expenditures. To finance the resulting government deficit, it was necessary to maintain very high interest rates to attract foreign capital into the country. The capital inflow created a strong dollar overseas, which made it difficult for even efficient manufacturers to export products while it made foreign imports cheap. This meant that the recovery of 1982–84 was very lopsided. Service jobs were growing while manufacturing jobs were on hold. Between 1979 and 1984 the proportion of men employed in goods production fell further from 39 to 36 percent, a decline concentrated in manufacturing per se. It was now common to see television news stories of workers who had lost $10-per-hour manufacturing jobs and who were now clerking fast foods. Bureau of Labor Statistics Surveys confirm that these stories were more than lurid journalism: The Bureau defined displaced workers as those who were over 20 years old, had lost their job due to plant closings or employment cutbacks between January 1979 and January 1984, and had worked for the firm at least three years prior to losing their job.

By this definition, the Bureau counted 5.1 million displaced workers—about 5 percent of the entire U.S. work force. Manufacturing, which accounts for one quarter of *all* employment (men and women), accounted for one half of the displaced workers.

As of January 1986, a year into economic recovery:

- 30 percent of the displaced workers were reemployed at wages equal to or better than those in the job they lost
- 30 percent were reemployed at wages lower than those in the job they lost
- 40 percent were unemployed or had dropped out of the labor force[25]

The stagnation and chaotic conditions of the last decade had made the employment shift to services into an extremely painful process. This was not, however, the end of the story. Economic recovery continued through 1986. By the autumn of 1986 interest rates

---

[25] Paul O. Flaim and Ellen Sehgal, "Displaced Workers of 1979–83: How Well Have They Fared?" *Monthly Labor Review*, July 1985, pp. 3–16.

were falling and the dollar was beginning to weaken against foreign currencies. Employment in goods production—particularly, manufacturing—had stopped its decline and it appeared that some of the worst aspects of the 1973–85 period could be reversed. We explore these prospects in more detail in Chapter 9.

A Two-Tier Economy?

Even if manufacturing employment recovers, a majority of all men will be employed in services, and so it is still important to examine the argument raised by Steinberg and others: that the shift to services has helped increase the inequality in men's earnings and will ultimately propel us to a "two-tier" economy with high- and low-paying jobs and nothing in the middle. Richard Cyert (1984), the president of Carnegie-Mellon University, summarizes the argument well:

> The effect of this movement over time [of employment to the service sector] will be to change the income distribution in the country. The shift from manufacturing to service jobs will be one in which the income distribution will become more skewed than it is currently. . . . Putting it another way, we will have a reduction in the number of middle-income people. The economy will tend to be polarized into two classes, the low- and high-income groups.

This argument is bolstered by two kinds of evidence. The first is that men's earnings *have* become less equal over the last fifteen years. The second is that Bureau of Labor Statistics occupational projections apparently show a polarized occupational structure. As Steinberg (1983) notes:

> Projections by the Bureau of Labor Statistics indicate that the jobs likely to increase more will continue to be those at opposite ends of the earnings spectrum. Strong growth is expected in the number of professional and technical workers—more are high paid, with some notable exceptions like nurses. Even stronger growth should occur at the low end, among such service workers as janitors, fast-food workers, and hospital orderlies. [p. 78]

The argument is plausible, but the balance of evidence suggests that it is wrong. We are developing a two- or even three-tier economy, but the long run trend toward services is not the cause.[26]

To see this, we return to 1969, a year of very low unemployment in which the family income distribution was as equal as it has been in this century. As the argument suggests, census statistics show that men's earnings in the service sector were less equally distributed than in the goods sector. We can summarize this inequality both by Gini coefficients and by the "75/25 ratio": the ratio of earnings at the 75th percentile of the distribution to earnings at the 25th percentile of the distribution. Among men in the service sector, this ratio was $29,115/$8,837, or 3.29. Among men in the goods-producing sector, the ratio was $30,175/$13,401, or 2.25. The respective Gini coefficients were .38 and .31 (Figure 5.5).

These 1969 data are consistent with the two-tier hypotheses, but a second calculation is not. If we recompute the 75/25 ratios for only those men who worked full time, the distributions look much closer: ratios of 2.00 in services and 1.95 in goods production, while the two Gini coefficients are .26 and .24. It follows that differences in earnings inequality between the two sectors were caused by the frequency and/or role of part-time workers.[27]

The relative frequency of part-time workers is not a factor: In both the goods-producing and service sectors, one third of all men worked part time, but the *role* of these workers differed between the sectors.

In the goods-producing sector, part-time workers often "looked like" full-time workers: They included construction workers who worked less than full time because of the weather and manufacturing workers who worked less than full time because of layoffs.

In the service sector part-time workers are heavily concentrated in retail sales. Many of these men were young and worked part time by choice. (The statistics include all men aged 16 and over.) In this they are like construction workers who expect to be working less

---

[26] This argument builds on the work of Henle and Ryscavage, "The Distribution of Earned Income," and the unpublished doctoral dissertation of Joung Young Lee, Department of Economics, University of Maryland, April 1985.

[27] In their article, Henle and Ryscavage show a similar result: that even as the Gini coefficient of all men's earnings was increasing between 1955 and 1978, the Gini coefficient for men who worked full-time remained stable.

FIGURE 5.5

Distribution of Men's Earnings in Goods and Services Production, 1969

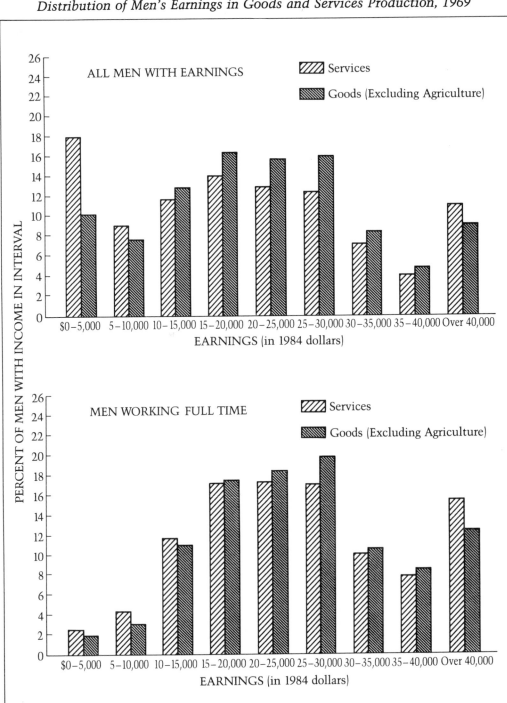

NOTE: Graph includes all men, 16 years and over.

SOURCE: March 1970 Current Population Survey.

than full time. But where construction wages are representative of the goods-producing sector, retail sales jobs pay less than the average service sector job. The large group of part-time workers in retail sales is the most important factor in explaining why 1969 service sector earnings were relatively unequal.

That was the story for 1969. Between 1969 and 1979 the story remained largely unchanged. There were, as we have seen, substantial shifts within goods production. Steel employment declined by 73,000 (11 percent); electronic equipment employment increased by 137,000; aircraft employment fell by 190,000 (a reflection of the end of the Vietnam war); employment in industrial instruments and computers increased by 144,000. On a national basis these changes were largely offsetting. The proportion of all men in goods production declined slightly from 41 to 39 percent, and earnings inequality among men who worked full time remained unchanged. Earnings inequality among *all* men grew over the decade, but this result was driven by the influx of young people into part-time jobs.

In the more recent period, 1979–84, the story changed. In this time earnings inequality increased for all workers *and* for full-time workers (Figure 5.6). But the problem was not that male workers shifted to services: rather, earnings inequality among full-time workers grew in *both* the goods- and the service-producing sectors, with Gini coefficients of .29 and .27, respectively.

A part of the inequality reflected the deep 1980–82 recession and the income cuts taken by displaced workers. But a second part of the growing inequality occurred between age groups. In the 1970s the baby boomers of the 1950s began their careers. By the law of supply and demand, their large numbers meant a growing gap between the incomes of younger and older workers. For most of the 1970s the gap was kept within bounds, but in the 1979–84 period the gap widened rapidly. The median income of 40-year-old men exceeded the median income of 30-year-old men by 21 percent in 1975 and 25 percent in 1979, but increased sharply to 34 percent by 1984.[28] As Robert Lawrence (1984) writes:

> The U.S. economy has displayed remarkable flexibility in providing employment for the massive numbers of young people and

[28] A small part of this gap may also be due to the fact that as the larger baby boom cohorts entered the labor force, the age gap between "25-to-34-year-olds" and "35-to-44-year-olds" was actually widening because the average age within both groups was declining but was declining faster in the younger group.

FIGURE 5.6

*Distribution of Men's Full-Time Earnings
in Goods and Services, 1979 and 1984*

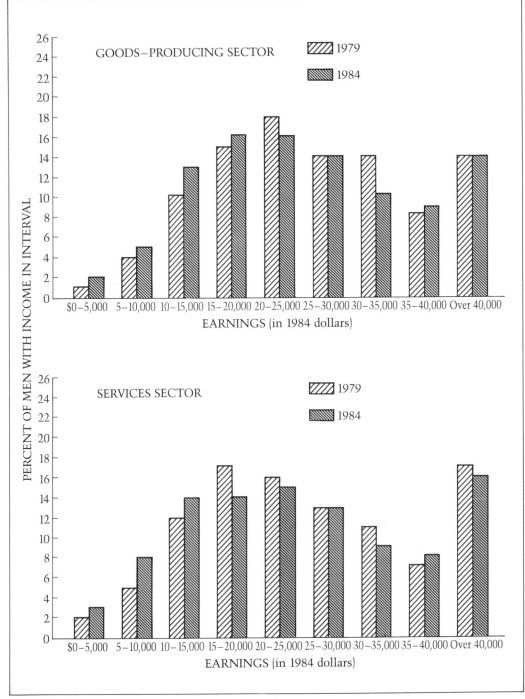

SOURCES: March 1980 and March 1985 Current Population Survey.

females who entered the job market over the past decade and a half. While these enhanced opportunities appear to have offset the impact of a large cohort for all but the youngest females, increasing competition from both male and female job seekers has depressed the earnings of young males.

The period's high inflation undoubtedly helped this process. Since the early 1980s we have seen a growing number of union wage "give-backs" and "two-tier" contracts in which new workers enter the firm at reduced pay.[29] These visible paycuts are highly controversial, but the rapid inflation of 1979–82 gave employers the option for similar savings in a much less visible way. If inflation rises at 10 percent, a 6 percent money wage increase is a 4 percent real wage cut. But the cut is far less controversial than a money pay cut, particularly if it is focused on entry-level jobs—the jobs that young workers will soon take. We shall return to the baby boomers' troubles in Chapter 7.

We need to confront one other issue: the previously mentioned Bureau of Labor Statistics (BLS) projections, which show large numbers of job openings concentrated at the top and bottom of the job ladder. These data have been examined by BLS economist Neal Rosenthal, who finds that the numbers have been misinterpreted.

Rosenthal points out that projections refer to job *openings* rather than *jobs*. The distinction is important. An investment banker "job slot" generates few job openings because the person who holds the job wants to keep it for some time. But a job slot in a fast food store can generate numerous openings because the persons who hold it keep quitting, often for better work. As Rosenthal (1985) says: ". . . despite large numbers of openings in these [low-paying] occupations, there is no indication that the number of workers having low earnings is increasing because the rate of increase of employment in these jobs is generally not faster than that for the total economy." [p. 8]

A Summing Up

If the shift to services is as benign as Colin Clark described it, why has it received such attention? There are two reasons. The first

---

[29] On wage developments in the early 1980s, see Daniel J. B. Mitchell, "Recent Union Contract Concessions," *Brookings Papers on Economic Activity*, no. 1, 1982, pp. 165–201.

is that for the last fifteen years we have seen something more than the normal shift of employment to services. Since the early 1970s manufacturing has wrestled with the problems of competing in a slow-growing, highly competitive market. Since 1980 manufacturing has carried the burden of a highly overvalued U.S. dollar, a burden of our own making. The effect has been to compress 20 or 30 years of long-run change into less than a decade.

The second reason is the stagnation of living standards that has occurred since 1973. Recall that arguments surrounding the service sector were developed to explain the decline in middle-class jobs. To the economic analyst, middle-class jobs refer to jobs in the middle of the earnings distribution. This naturally leads to examinations of whether the middle of the earnings distribution has shrunk and whether the service sector was responsible.[30]

But the decline of middle-class jobs can mean something much simpler: A declining proportion of jobs pay enough to afford the middle-class standard of living. On this point the numbers are clear. In 1973 men who worked full time had a median income of $26,000.[31] In light of postwar experience, this median income should have grown to about $31,000 in 1984, even allowing for the baby boom. But, in fact, men who worked full time in 1984 had a median income of $23,218. The typical worker could afford less of the good things of American life and so was a ready audience for arguments that the middle class was vanishing.

Does this mean that the "two-tier" job market is meaningless? Not quite. Younger workers are clearly falling behind older workers in wages. And there is a "third tier" to the economy, a growing number of prime-age men who have dropped out of the labor force altogether. We begin to explore these issues in Chapter 6, but as we do we should remember that they have less to do with the changing industrial structure than with a bad period in our economic life.

---

[30] The authors cited earlier—those who both see and deny the two-tier labor market—all approach it in terms of earnings inequality rather than earnings growth.
[31] Again, all incomes in 1984 dollars.

6

THE GEOGRAPHY OF INCOME

The Role of Migration

IN THE spring of 1986 the Massachusetts unemployment rate averaged 3.8 percent. New York City regained fiscal autonomy from the state-created Municipal Assistance Corporation. But in Texas the governor required state agencies to cut budgets as an austerity measure while in Lafayette, Louisiana, families walked away from recently purchased homes.

Little of this would have been predicted a decade earlier. Then Texas and Louisiana were riding the crest of an energy boom. Massachusetts was a "snowbelt" state most noted for the industry it had lost. New York City threatened to become the first major city to declare bankruptcy since the Great Depression.

We have seen how the economy is constantly changing and change has a geographic dimension. The rise and fall of firms and industries means the rise and fall of cities and states and regions. The easiest way to see these movements is to look at the migration of people. In the 1940 census 5.4 percent of the population reported that they had been living in a different state in 1935. This statistic included the large Dustbowl migration from Oklahoma and Texas to

California. But postwar migration would become much larger still. In the 1960 census 9.3 percent of the population reported that they had been living in a different state five years earlier, and a 9–10 percent rate would continue to the present.[1]

Most people, of course, were following jobs and jobs showed similar movements. Between 1960 and 1970 U.S. manufacturing employment increased by 2.6 million, but in Texas it increased by 247,000 while it declined by 50,000 in Massachusetts, 120,000 in New York state, and 60,000 in Philadelphia.[2]

These moves had consequences for both the people involved and the content of the income distribution. Recall from Chapter 3 that the 1947 map of U.S. incomes had one principal distinction: Family incomes in the Southeast were 40 percent less than incomes in other regions. Some of this difference reflected the extremely low incomes of rural black families, but the Southeast was really a region apart and wages were low for everyone: Black Alabama families averaged $3,800, white Alabama families averaged $8,960, and all families in New York averaged $15,500. (All incomes are in 1984 dollars.) Absent from the map was an income gap between central cities and their still small suburbs. Central cities still held much of the urban middle class, and so city–suburban income differences were modest.

The migration of people and jobs over almost four decades eventually reversed this picture. By the early 1980s regional differences in family incomes had become less important as southern incomes gained parity with the rest of the country. Now the big income distinctions were within regions as central cities fell increasingly behind suburbs.[3] These new distinctions did not reflect city-suburban wage differences (many central city workers were commuters) but rather the increasing number of central city families headed by women.

The major migration routes were already in existence by the end

[1] See Larry H. Long, *Migration and Residential Mobility in the United States*, The Population of the United States in the 1980s: A Census Monograph Series (New York: Russell Sage Foundation, 1987 [forthcoming]) chap. 3.

[2] For trends in jobs by state, see U.S. Department of Labor, *Handbook of Labor Statistics* (Washington, DC: U.S. Government Printing Office, December 1983). On jobs by industry for big cities, see U.S. Bureau of the Census, *County and City Data Book* (Washington, DC: U.S. Government Printing Office), published at five year intervals.

[3] For a discussion of this theme from a regional development perspective, see Peter Mieszkowski, "Recent Trends in Urban and Regional Development," in Peter Mieszkowski and Mahlon Straszheim, eds., *Current Issues in Urban Economics* (Baltimore, Johns Hopkins, 1979), pp. 3–34.

of World War II. And like the growth of the service sector, migration was not at first viewed as a threat. From the perspective of a governor or mayor, it was only one among several factors influencing an area's economy and the other factors were all positive. Population was increasing rapidly (the baby boom), and real wages were increasing rapidly as well. Whatever the migration patterns, most states and cities had growing economies even though other areas might be growing faster.

By the mid-1970s the context had changed. After 1964 the birthrate fell sharply for fourteen years. After 1973 wages stopped growing. At this point, local economic growth became more dependent on attracting people and jobs from elsewhere and one area gained only at the expense of another.[4]

The net effect of these migrations was to rearrange the income distribution's content. Overall, family income inequality did not change much, but within the distribution southern families moved up while central city families declined.

The Convergence of Incomes Across Regions

In Chapter 3 we saw that the 1947 economic map was dominated by two groups of states: the Mid Atlantic states (New York through the District of Columbia) and the Great Lakes states (Ohio through Wisconsin). Together, these nine states accounted for 42 percent of the nation's population and 60 percent of all manufacturing jobs.

Like most maps, this point-in-time picture obscured people on the move. Retired whites from the North were moving south, primarily to Florida. Whites from the North and South (i.e., the Southeast and Southwest) were moving to California. Blacks from the South were moving to eastern and midwestern cities.

With the exception of the retirees, most of these moves involved looking for better jobs, and in the early postwar years better jobs meant manufacturing jobs. Manufacturing could provide good wages for men with limited education (Chapter 5). Men leaving agriculture

---

[4] For a discussion of how migration became more important as the birthrates declined, see Peter A. Morrison, "Current Demographic Change in Regions of the United States," in Victor L. Arnold, ed., *Alternatives to Confrontation* (Lexington, MA: Heath, 1980) chap. 2.

typically had little education, and so the availability of manufacturing work was particularly important for them. By this measure, some places were ripe for sending migrants and others were ripe for receiving them.

The Great Plains states—Minnesota, the Dakotas, Missouri, and Kansas—were ripe for sending. Their economies were heavily dependent on agriculture, which was becoming increasingly mechanized. Higher productivity (and slow-growing demand for food) meant fewer opportunities at home. People—particularly young people[5]—began to look elsewhere.

The Far West (California through Washington and Nevada) was an obvious place to look. During World War II the West Coast had taken the lead in the fast-growing aircraft industry and was becoming a manufacturing power. Between 1929 and 1947 California's manufacturing employment had grown from 350,000 to 660,000.[6] This *rate* of growth was twice the national average, and in absolute terms, the number of new jobs equaled the number added by such traditional manufacturing states as Ohio and Illinois.

The Southeast (West Virginia through Arkansas and everywhere south) was really two regions: Florida and the other states. As postwar incomes rose and more families could afford retirement, they found Florida's climate and living costs attractive, and the state's economy did well. The other southeastern states were far more depressed, and in these states manufacturing was regarded with ambivalence. It created jobs that paid well (vis-à-vis agriculture), but it also threatened to bring in unions and other pressures on segregated race relations. There had been some growth of manufacturing, predominantly in textiles, a part of which had been attracted from New England. But other employers were put off by the poorly educated labor force and too much hot weather. In 1947 these states accounted for 24 percent of the U.S. population but only 11 percent of all manufacturing jobs. The lack of manufacturing jobs was compounded by the continued mechanization of southern agriculture which eliminated jobs in farming. The region was a place of surplus labor and a ready source of out-migration.

[5] As Long points out, interstate migration is usually concentrated in two age ranges: younger persons aged 25 to 35 who are just starting out and older persons aged 65 to 70 who are moving for retirement reasons. See Long, *Migration and Residential Mobility*.

[6] For an analysis of regional patterns of manufacturing growth in the post-1929 period, see Victor R. Fuchs, *Changes in the Location of Manufacturing in the United States Since 1929* (New Haven: Yale University Press, 1962).

Even New England, while not as weak as the Southeast, was not strong. Its agriculture had long since ceased to be competitive, and it was steadily losing textile manufacturing jobs to the Southeast. Between 1929 and 1947 its manufacturing employment grew by 18 percent, about one half as fast as the rest of the nation. Except for lower Connecticut, a suburb for New York City, New England was also a source of out-migration.

In the early postwar years, then, significant numbers of people had reason to move, and the resulting flows were large. Over the 1950s the Great Plains states had *net* out-migration (persons moving out minus persons moving in) equal to 5 percent of their 1950 population. New England (excluding Connecticut) experienced a similar loss. The southeastern states (excluding Florida) lost a net of 1.2 million whites and 1.6 million blacks, almost 10 percent of their 1950 population.

The migrants' destinations varied by race. Among whites, the largest movements were to California (net in-migration of 2.8 million) and Florida (1.6 million). Black migration had three main destinations, including the industrial belt from Ohio to Michigan (504,000), New York and New Jersey (362,000), and California (255,000). (See Figure 6.1.) Blacks, far more than whites, migrated to central cities. Over the 1950s the proportion of *all* blacks living in central cities rose from 41 percent to 51 percent.[7]

People were moving for better opportunities, and in the process they were reducing regional income differences. When poor families (black and white) left the Southeast, they were raising the average income of the region. And when they moved to northern states, they were typically lowering, *ceteris paribus,* average incomes in that region.

In a static economy this migration would have led to charges of exporting the poor. There was some of this, but in most areas migrants led to a *relative* increase or decrease around a rising trend. New York state is an example. Over the 1950s it had net out-migration of 72,000 whites and net in-migration of 255,000 blacks, a net increase of 180,000 persons. But this in-migration was dwarfed by the state's own birthrate. The 1950s was the baby boom decade and

[7] On interstate migration flows, see U.S. Bureau of the Census, *Historical Statistics of the United States: Colonial Times to 1970* (Washington, DC: U.S. Government Printing Office, 1975), series C25-75. On the proportion of blacks living in central cities, see series A276-287.

FIGURE 6.1
Major U.S. Migration Flows in the late 1940s and 1950s
(persons per year)

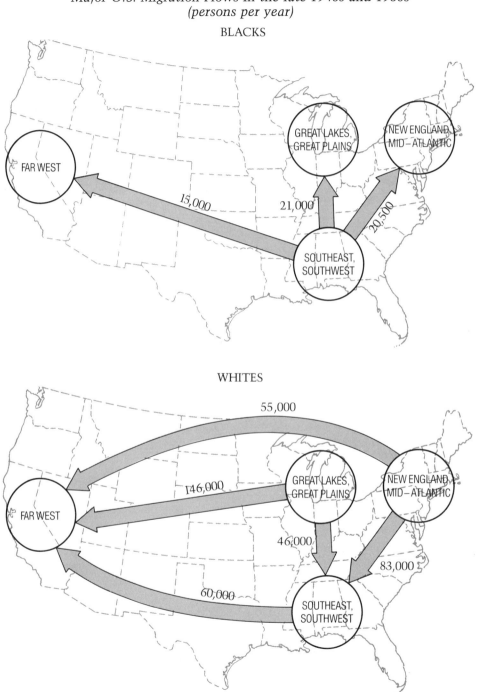

BLACKS

WHITES

New York's population, exclusive of migration, increased by 1.8 million persons. It was also a decade of growing wages, and the median family income of New Yorkers grew from \$15,200 to \$22,700. Migration had its effect. The *rate* of growth of New York's incomes—49 percent—was slower than the rate of growth in, say, Alabama (78 percent), but incomes were growing fast enough to keep in-migration from becoming an issue.

In a similar way growing wages and growing population cushioned shifts in the country's industrial base. During the 1950s employment in durable goods manufacturing increased by 1.2 million (14 percent), but three quarters of this increase came from new industries: electronic equipment, aircraft and parts, and industrial instruments.[8] Steel industry employment actually declined (see Chapter 5). The implications for regions were obvious. From 1949 through 1959 the Far West added 400,000 new manufacturing jobs while the Mid Atlantic region added none. But rapid productivity growth and the baby boom were sufficient to keep population and income growing everywhere.

The 1960s Boom

During the 1960s boom, even more than in the 1950s, regional weaknesses were obscured. Over the decade average family incomes rose sharply in all states: from \$24,000 to \$29,000 in New York, from \$14,000 to \$20,600 in Alabama, from \$24,000 to \$30,400 in California, and from \$23,400 to \$31,000 in Illinois. These increases, as we have seen, reflected both strong real wage growth and significant declines in unemployment.

Beneath these growing incomes, the industrial base continued to move south and west. In Chapter 5 we saw that aggregate manufacturing demand is particularly sensitive to the overall economy and during the 1960s boom *national* manufacturing employment increased by 20 percent. But within this national total, manufacturing employment in the Mid Atlantic states again failed to increase while manufacturing employment in the Great Lakes states increased by only 12 percent. Gains in manufacturing were concentrated in the Far West, and in 1963 California passed New York to become the most populous state in the nation.

[8] See Fuchs, *Changes in the Location of Manufacturing.*

It was also in the 1960s that the Southeast made a breakthrough. By the end of the decade some of the hardest civil rights battles had been won, and this reduced the hostility to new industry. The interstate highway system (begun under Eisenhower) and network television were linking the region to the rest of the nation while the spread of air conditioning was increasing the region's amenities. Over the decade total nonagricultural employment (even excluding booming Florida) grew by 3.5 million persons, a 45 percent increase that was significantly faster than in the rest of the economy. Through these new industries, southern income levels continued to move closer to the national averages.

Shifting opportunities were reflected in migration statistics. Over the 1960s the Great Lakes and Mid Atlantic regions each had net out-migration of 550,000 whites and an approximately equal in-migration of blacks. In each region high birthrates and the economic boom meant that population and income were still growing. But through migration flows, incomes across regions were becoming more equal.

The End of Growth

The baby boom ended in 1964 and the growth of wages ended in 1973. By the mid-1970s the more vulnerable regions were clearly exposed. The bad economy was hard on most regions, but stagnant markets and then the overvalued dollar were particularly hard on heavy industry which was concentrated in the Mid Atlantic and Great Lakes states.

Between 1970 and 1984 Pennsylvania lost one manufacturing job in four—400,000 jobs in all. New York also lost 400,000 (−23 percent); Ohio lost 300,000 (−21 percent); Michigan lost 228,000 (−18 percent); Illinois lost 228,000 (−17 percent). Manufacturing employment in the Southeast and Far West, by contrast, continued to grow moderately. And with the post-OPEC rise in energy prices, the southwestern states—particularly Texas, Louisiana, and Oklahoma—experienced substantial income gains.

Again, migration followed the new opportunities. Over the 1970s and early 1980s the Mid Atlantic and Great Lakes states each had a net out-migration (including all races) of 1.8 million persons. The Southeast, excluding Florida, had net *in*-migration of 2.9 million persons. The shift in opportunities was such that the traditional routes of black migration were now reversed: Blacks, on net, were leaving the North to go to the South.[9]

Unlike the 1950s and 1960s there were no high birthrates or rising wages to give all regions a cushion. By the middle 1970s it was common to see low-level regional warfare, with "snowbelts," "sunbelts," and "rustbowls" competing for government contracts and limited economic growth.[10]

Words like snowbelt and sunbelt suggest that all postwar migration might be explained by something as simple as Horace Greeley's invocation to "go West." But as we have seen, the true driving force was industrial change and Schumpeter's creative destruction. In the early postwar period California's good climate was important in making the state a focus for the aircraft industry. (The climate was reinforced by an aggressive state government and a high-quality university system.) Through the industry, the state received enormous demand from both commercial airlines and government defense and aerospace contracts. As the aircraft industry grew, other industries grew around it both to support aircraft production and to serve the growing number of aircraft workers. In a similar fashion, the OPEC price increases of 1973–74 and 1979–80 meant that *domestic* oil and gas could also command high prices. The economies of energy states including Oklahoma, Louisiana, Texas, and Alaska benefited correspondingly.

The changing industrial structure explains some movements that Greeley would not have predicted. During the late 1970s Massachusetts and New Hampshire showed themselves to be highly competitive in electronics. Like California, Massachusetts industry benefited from high-quality universities and significant defense contracts which helped boost the economy.[11] By the spring of 1986, the OPEC cartel had collapsed. Oil prices were falling rapidly and Texas

[9] On the reversal of black migration to the North, see Larry H. Long, "Interregional Migration of the Poor: Some Recent Changes," U.S. Bureau of the Census, *Current Population Reports*, Special Studies series P-23, no. 73 (Washington, DC: U.S. Government Printing Office, 1973).

[10] See, for example, "The Second War Between the States," *Business Week*, May 17, 1976, pp. 92–114; and Peggy L. Cuciti, "Troubled Local Economies and the Distribution of Federal Dollars," a Congressional Budget Office Background Paper (Washington, DC: U.S. Government Printing Office, August 1977).

[11] On the role of government spending in influencing regional growth, see George E. Peterson and Thomas Muller, "Regional Impact of Federal Tax and Spending Policies" in Arnold, *Alternatives to Confrontation*, chap. 6.

FIGURE 6.2

Average Family Incomes for Selected Regions, 1949–1979 (in 1984 dollars)

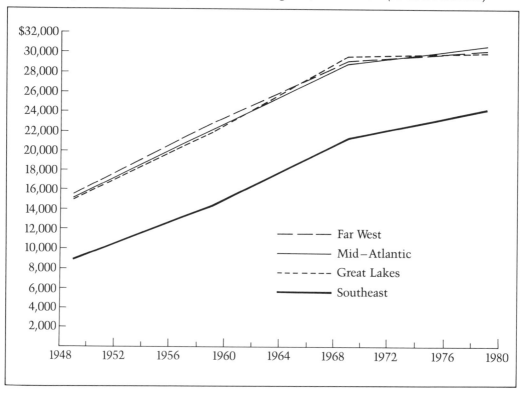

NOTE: Average refers to mean across states in region.

SOURCES: State income figures from U.S. Census of Population, 1950–1980.

and Louisiana were attempting to deal with huge budget deficits, but Massachusetts had the lowest unemployment rate in the country.[12]

Beneath all these movements, income differences among regions continued to decline. In 1949 family incomes in the Southeast had been 40 percent lower than in the rest of the country. By the early 1980s the gap had closed to 18 percent (Figure 6.2).

---

[12] On the dependence of Texas on oil, see David Maraniss, "For West Texans, It's Merely Boom and Bust, as Usual," *Washington Post* February 11, 1986, p. 1. As Maraniss notes, every $1 fall in the price of a barrel of oil costs the state government $100 million in tax revenues and costs the state $3 billion in total economic activity and 25,000 jobs.

The Decline of Central Cities

While regional incomes became more equal, *intra*-regional inequality was growing. The source of the inequality was the widening income gap between central cities and suburbs. In one sense the cities' decline was an unintended by-product of economic growth.

Historically, cities had been places where producers could be close to cheap transportation and close to each other while workers could live close to their jobs. Economic growth undermined all of these functions. After World War II the mass availability of automobiles and the improved highway system made it possible for plants and workers, pursuing their best interests, to locate further from the city center.[13] Their dispersal was reinforced by the changing nature of the country's output. Where transportation had been an important cost element in food or steel, it was far less important in computer chips or in most services. A few Southwest cities like Houston could capture the dispersal by continually annexing new territory. But most city boundaries had been frozen by the 1930s, and so these older cities faced the problem of continually replenishing their economies.

At the close of World War II these problems had not yet surfaced. Central cities still dominated their metropolitan areas (Chapter 3). They housed the middle class as well as the poor, and they contained enough manufacturing to provide rural in-migrants with jobs. In reality this domination had been heavily subsidized by the Great Depression and the war.

The depression and the war had slowed the production of new cars and houses and so slowed suburban growth. The needs of war production had kept central city manufacturing plants in use beyond their normal lives.[14] All of this made central cities stronger than they otherwise would have been, but even during the depression the underlying trends were apparent. Demographer Larry Long shows that between 1935 and 1940 the largest net migration between two states was the move from New York to New Jersey. It was largely a

---

[13] This process of dispersal is almost as old as cities themselves. See, for example, Raymond Vernon, *The Changing Economic Function of the Central City* (New York: Area Development Committee of the Committee for Economic Development, January 1959).

[14] See John E. Kain, "The Distribution and Movement of Jobs and Industry," in James Q. Wilson, ed., *The Metropolitan Enigma* (Cambridge, MA: Harvard University Press, 1968), chap. 1.

move to the suburbs, and it involved more people than the move from the Oklahoma Dustbowl to California.[15]

When the war ended, the rapid availability of automobiles and the low price of housing made it possible for many more families to buy their own homes in the suburbs (Chapter 4). Almost all these families were white, and they were joined by other white families moving from rural areas. The rate of suburbanization was remarkable. Over the 1950s the population of the suburbs grew by 20 million, while the population of the entire United States grew by only 30 million. By 1960 the proportion of the population living in the suburbs had climbed from 23 to 31 percent.[16]

During the 1950s the suburbs' gain was not the cities' loss. The same factors that had lifted older industrial regions—high birthrates, rapid wage growth—also helped central cities. New York City is a case in point. Between 1950 and 1960 New York's suburban ring grew from 1.7 million to 2.9 million persons, but the city's own population held steady at 7.8 million persons. The city had sustained its population through high birthrates and significant in-migration from rural areas. Many of the in-migrants were black, and over the decade the proportion of blacks in the city's population rose from 10 to 15 percent. Chicago, Philadelphia, and other older cities had similar experiences.

The in-migrants were coming in search of higher incomes, and in these early postwar years the cities could accommodate them. Cities had both cheap housing and, most important, manufacturing jobs. In part because of war production, manufacturing was still a central city activity. In 1947 the ten largest central cities contained 2.5 million manufacturing production jobs, one fifth of all such jobs in the nation.[17]

Because of these jobs, cities could still serve as a place for rural migrants to get a start. By 1959 cities had seen large out-migration of middle-class families to the suburbs and large in-migration from rural areas. Despite this, median income among central city families was $20,400, only $2,100 lower (11 percent) than median income in

---

[15] See Long, *Migration and Residential Mobility*.

[16] See U.S. Bureau of the Census, *Historical Statistics* (1975), series A82-90.

[17] U.S. Bureau of the Census, *County and City Data Book, 1949* (Washington, DC: U.S. Government Printing Office, 1952).

the suburbs, and well above the family income outside metropolitan areas.[18]

The situation, however, was fragile. Central city manufacturing jobs largely involved old plants. When firms considered new investment, improved transportation often led them to build new plants outside the city rather than retool. Similarly, city plants produced "old" products like garments and tires. The growth of the aircraft industry did a great deal for a few far western cities—Seattle, Los Angeles, Long Beach—but it helped Pittsburgh and other older cities very little. The resulting loss of manufacturing jobs was striking. Between 1947 and 1963 manufacturing production jobs in the United States grew slightly from 11.9 million to 12.2 million. But among the ten largest central cities in 1947, only one, Los Angeles, gained production jobs over the period (55,000). The other nine cities lost production jobs totaling 680,000 (Figure 6.3).

During this period, *total* city employment declined less dramatically as losses in production jobs were offset by growing employment in services, including an expansion of local governments (Figure 6.3). But many of these new jobs were in teaching, medicine, financial operations, and other white collar occupations that required substantial education. Other service jobs had lower skill requirements, but were often "women's" work: sales clerks, clerical workers, waitresses, nurses' assistants. For poorly educated black men from rural areas, things were getting worse.

From a mayor's perspective, this situation could easily feed on itself. In the early 1960s the cities continued to lose middle-class families and manufacturing jobs. But city economies were still stronger than many places in the rural Southeast, and so cities continued to attract in-migrants, many of them black. If a city did not have the jobs to raise an in-migrant's income, it would be left with a growing low-income population and an increasingly stagnant tax base. A weak tax base logically requires reduced expenses, but, as economist George Peterson argues, this is not easy to do. More than in most businesses, city budgets represent on-going capital commitments: the maintenance of roads, sewers, bridges, hospitals, and

[18] See Larry H. Long and Donald C. Dahmann, *The City-Suburb Income Gap: Is It Being Narrowed by a Back-to-the-City Movement?* U.S. Bureau of the Census, Special Demographic Analyses, CDS-80-1 (Washington, DC: U.S. Government Printing Office, 1980).

FIGURE 6.3

*Total Employment and Manufacturing Production Employment
for Selected Central Cities, 1947–1963*

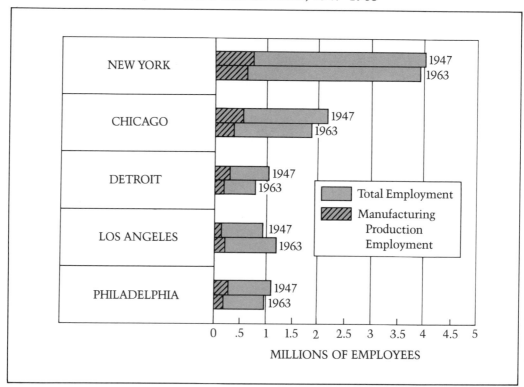

SOURCES: U.S. Bureau of the Census, *County and City Data Book*, 1947 and 1963.

schools. As this capital stock ages, it becomes increasingly expensive to maintain. A city's largest element of variable cost is its labor force, and as Peterson (1976) says:

> . . . in terms of budget expense, a city's labor force tends to act as another fixed overhead item whose cost must be spread over fewer taxpayers once net out-migration commences. It is difficult to reduce public employment under the best of circumstances, but the pressure to retain public sector jobs is doubly great when a city is suffering private sector job loss. [p. 45]

Few public employees would vote for a candidate who proposed job cuts, and few low-income families, already dependent on public services, would vote for a candidate who wanted service cuts. The result of these pressures was often higher expenditures, higher taxes, and an even greater incentive for the out-migration of jobs and middle-income families.

Earlier we saw how the late 1960s economic boom helped to hide the weaknesses of older industrial regions. The effect of the boom on central cities was more ambiguous. Cities shared in low unemployment rates, but in one important dimension the boom did little good: Between 1960 and 1970 the proportion of all black families headed by women rose from 22 to 31 percent, and these female-headed families were heavily concentrated in central cities.[19]

Why did the black family break down when times were good? Like the case of the productivity slowdown (Chapter 4), we have no single answer. The outlines of an answer begin with the W. E. B. DuBois quote in Chapter 3: If a man can't bring income to a marriage—if he will be another mouth to feed rather than a breadwinner—many women would rather raise their children alone than keep the man as a husband. In DuBois' time, black men's incomes were kept low by discrimination which excluded them from good jobs. In the postwar period, central cities' loss of manufacturing jobs had a similar effect.[20]

Official statistics show that the late 1960s were a time of major black progress (Chapter 4). Nonetheless, a significant minority of black men may have been in economic trouble. The Census Bureau has long acknowledged difficulty in properly counting black men. In 1969 census statistics show 1.39 million black women but only 1.18 million black men aged 25 to 34, a difference of 15 percent.[21] As economist Robert Lerman notes, the census has developed independent estimates from birth and death certificates suggesting that only one third of this gap is real, the result of high arrest and homicide rates among black men.[22] But this means that 10 percent of 25–34-

[19] See, for example, U.S. Bureau of the Census, "24 Million Americans: Poverty in the United States: 1969," *Current Population Reports* Washington, DC: US Government series P-60, no. 76 (1970).

[20] The major elaborator of DuBois' ideas is William Julius Wilson. See his *The Declining Significance of Race* (Chicago: University of Chicago Press, 1978).

[21] See U.S. Bureau of the Census, "Income in 1969 of Families and Persons in the United States," *Current Population Reports*, series P-60, no. 75 (Washington, DC: U.S. Government Printing Office, 1970).

[22] Personal communication, 1986.

year-old black men were not counted by the census and so are not included in any unemployment statistics.

By the late 1960s the scarcity of working black men was compounded by what William Julius Wilson calls the isolation of the ghetto.[23] The problem began as the economic boom and the civil rights revolution focused increasing attention on the urban poor. This attention led to increased federal aid to cities, but it also led to an enormous rise in expectations among the poor themselves and, ultimately, a series of major riots in black neighborhoods including New York City's Harlem and Bedford Stuyvesant (1964), Cleveland's Hough (1964), Los Angeles' Watts (1965), and Detroit's 12th Street (1967) in which 43 persons were killed.

One response to the riots was a decision among local governments to make welfare benefits more accessible to pacify the population.[24] A second response was a decision by many black middle- and working-class families that the time had come to leave the ghettos.

As Wilson and journalist Nicholas Lemann argue, racial discrimination had historically kept black neighborhoods economically integrated. Through churches, schools, newspapers, and other institutions, the black middle and working class kept constant pressure on the black lower class—the families described by DuBois—to improve themselves and to economically assimilate. By the late 1960s residential discrimination was declining. In the aftermath of the riots, many middle-class and working-class families moved, often to other parts of the city.[25]

For some of those who stayed behind, the results were disastrous: neighborhoods with weak middle-class institutions where welfare was increasingly available and lower-class culture (including

---

[23] See William Julius Wilson and Robert Aponte, "Urban Poverty," *Annual Review of Sociology*, no. 11 (1985), pp. 231–58.

[24] See Frances Fox Piven and Richard A. Cloward, *Regulating the Poor* (New York: Pantheon, 1971), chaps. 8–10.

[25] See Wilson and Aponte, "Urban Poverty"; and Nicholas Lemann, "The Origins of the Underclass," *Atlantic*, June 1986, pp. 31–55 (part 1) and July 1986, pp. 54–68 (part 2). Because much of the movement of blacks took place within cities, it is not easy to trace with published data. But beginning in the 1970s the census began to publish separate data for "poverty areas," also called "low-income areas," census tracts in which 20 percent or more of the population was poor in the 1970 decennial census. Between 1973 and 1983 the number of blacks living in central city poverty areas declined from 7.7 million to 7.1 million persons, or from 33 to 25 percent of the black population. Among the blacks who remained in these areas, the poverty rate rose from 39 percent in 1973 to 50 percent in 1983.

female-headed families) could expand. We will return to this problem of the underclass in Chapters 7–9.

A more general response to the riots was accelerated black and white migration, not just out of poor neighborhoods but out of cities per se. This migration was particularly important because the baby boom had ended and migration, for cities as for regions, became the principal determinant of population. Of the sixty cities that had 1960 populations of 200,000 or more, nearly half had absolute population declines from 1960 to 1970.[26]

After 1973 the national economy stagnated and the situation in cities grew worse. New York City was an extreme case. Between 1969 and 1977 the city's employment declined by 700,000 (18 percent), and in 1975 its government almost declared bankruptcy.[27] Employment in many cities was more stable, but most cities lost population. During the 1960s central cities as a group had net out-migration of 345,000 persons per year. During the 1970s central cities' net out-migration averaged 1.3 million persons per year. Between 1970 and 1980 cities had lost 13 million persons through migration, an amount equivalent to one fifth of their total 1970 population.[28] By the early 1980s almost one half of the U.S. population lived in suburbs.

As had always been true, families who left the cities had higher incomes than families who stayed, and this was reflected in a growing city-suburb family income gap. Recall that as late as 1959 the size of that gap was $2,100, or 11 percent. By 1983 it had widened to 24 percent—$23,300 in central cities versus $30,600 in suburbs.[29] (See Figure 6.4.) Unlike regional income differences, the city-suburban income gap did not reflect different wages, but different family structures. By 1983 one quarter of all central city families were

[26] See George E. Peterson, "Finance," in William Gorham and Nathan Glazer, eds., *The Urban Predicament* (Washington, DC: Urban Institute, 1976), chap. 2.

[27] On New York City employment declines, see Samuel M. Ehrenhalt, "Growth in the New York City Economy, Problems and Promise," paper presented at the eighteenth annual Institute on the Challenges of the Changing Economy of New York City, New York, May 8, 1985. Ehrenhalt shows that over the 1970s employment grew by 24 percent in Los Angeles–Long Beach and by 6 percent in Chicago, but it declined by 15 percent in Philadelphia.

[28] See U.S. Bureau of the Census, "Geographical Mobility, March 1975 to March 1980," *Current Population Reports*, series P-20, no. 368 (Washington, DC: U.S. Government Printing Office, 1982).

[29] See Long and Dahmann, "The City-Suburb Income Gap." (Incomes in 1984 dollars.)

FIGURE 6.4

Median Family Income in Central Cities and Suburbs (in 1984 dollars)

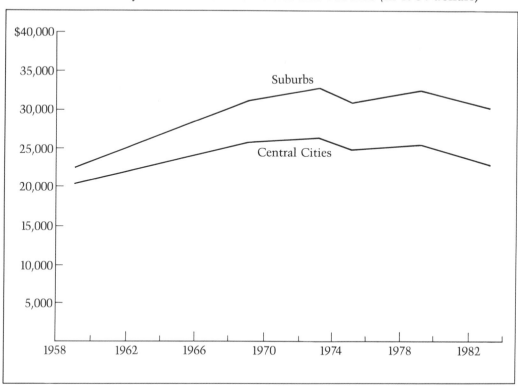

SOURCES: Long and Dahmann (1980); and U.S. Bureau of the Census, *Current Population Reports*, series P-60, various numbers.

headed by a woman.[30] If we look only at families with two parents, the city-suburban income gap closes by one third.

There was one saving grace. The same bad economy which had hurt cities played a part is raising the age at which young persons married, which led to an increasing number of "young singles." Many of these young men and women chose to live in cities for the excitement of city life and to be near people like themselves. Because they had only themselves to support, they were relatively well off; and if we look at data on average income per person (whether or

[30] See U.S. Bureau of the Census, "Money Income of Households, Families and Persons in the United States, 1983," *Current Population Reports*, series P-60, no. 146 (Washington, DC: U.S. Government Printing Office, 1985), table 21.

not that person lives in a family), city and suburban income levels look much closer.[31] We return to young singles in Chapter 8.

By the mid 1980s some cities were participating in the nation's economic recovery. New York City, for example, had gained back most of the employment it had lost in 1969–77, but the new jobs increasingly required skills that the poorest of city residents do not have. Samuel Ehrenhalt (1985), Commissioner of Labor Statistics for the New York Region, summarizes the problem well:

> A very basic difference [in today's job market] is that the lower level job entrant of yesterday did not have to possess the basic literacy, numeracy, interaction and communication skills needed today.
>
> Increasingly, workers need to be able to successfully function in a word-oriented, information-intensive work environment such as the modern office. They need to be able to learn on a continuing basis, to have a foundation of fundamental knowledge, to reason, draw conclusions, and express ideas. The demands of the New York City job market of today simply do not match up well with a 38 percent high school dropout rate and 40 percent of the resident population age 25 and over without a high school diploma. These groups will face a difficult and increasingly uphill battle in gaining a foothold in today's economy. [p. 57]

Geography and Family

By the early 1980s the early postwar geography of income had been reversed. The income gap between the Southeast and the rest of the nation, while still observable, was less than it had been. Now the important income distinctions were within regions—in particular between central cities and their suburbs. Where the old distinctions had come from regional wage differences, the new distinctions came from the large number of families headed by a woman who lived in cities. Where the old distinctions were ground down by migration and industrial change, the new distinctions looked much more durable.

---

[31] See Long and Dahmann, "The City-Suburb Income Gap."

THE LABOR FORCE:
OCCUPATIONS AND EARNINGS

Upward Mobility[1]

IN JUNE 1986 the American Medical Association issued a report announcing that physicians were in oversupply. The solution, they suggested, was to restrict the number of new medical school graduates. Dr. Arnold Relman, editor of the *New England Journal of Medicine*, gave the rationale: "All over the country, doctors are more concerned about their economic future than I can ever remember. There is more pressure on the doctor to maintain his income than is good for the public or the profession."[2]

Limiting new doctors to boost doctors' salaries is not a new idea. In 1934 the president of the American Medical Association made the same suggestion: "A fine piece of educational work could well be done if we were to use only half of the 70-odd medical schools in the U.S."[3] In 1934 doctors could argue for this policy based on real hardship. In 1986 the issue seemed to be failed expectations.

---

[1] In writing this chapter, I have benefited substantially from the labor market writings of economist Richard Freeman. See, in particular, *The Over-Educated American* (New York: Academic Press, 1976).

[2] Quoted in Milt Freudenheim, "AMA Report Sees Too Many Doctors," *New York Times*, June 14, 1986, p. 1.

[3] Freeman, *The Over-Educated American*, p. 118.

In the 1950s and 1960s expectations did not fail so frequently. Upward mobility—becoming a doctor or a lawyer or just a college graduate—was one way to pursue the middle-class dream. But while upward mobility is a central part of American life, it has two limits. One limit is the economy's health. When real wages are stagnant, as they were after 1973, all occupations will suffer and people will do less well than they had anticipated.

A second limit, suggested by the doctors, comes from supply and demand. Today four workers in every 1,000 are doctors, with average year-round earnings of about $100,000. (Income figures are in 1984 dollars.) It does not follow that if we were all doctors, we would all earn $100,000. To the contrary, as more people enter a high-income occupation competition will increase. Earnings in the occupation will grow more slowly and perhaps even decline. This process can take some time. High-paying occupations typically take several years of training and so the supply of new workers is often slow to catch up with demand.[4] But the market works eventually and while it may narrow an individual's options, it has a silver lining for it also helps to narrow the extent of earnings inequality.

These limits are most useful in discussing the earnings and occupations of white men. At the end of World War II, white men constituted almost two thirds of the labor force and they were still more than half of the labor force as late as the early 1980s.[5] Beyond their numerical importance, they had the greatest freedom to pursue educational and job opportunities during the postwar period.

One might argue that the term "white men" is too heterogeneous: The white coal miner's son in West Virginia had far less opportunity than the white physicist's son *or* daughter in California. This criticism is surely correct. But compared with white women and black men and women, the average white man faced far fewer constraints of custom and of legal segregation in his choice of a career. It follows that once we have described the absolute progress of white men, the progress of the other groups is best told in two ways: in absolute terms, and in relative terms vis-à-vis white men.

---

[4] Economists will recognize this slow convergence as part of the "cobweb" model, in which a long production process—for example, the four years it takes to raise a beef cow—leads to a situation in which this year's supply is a response to the prices (and demand) that existed some time ago. For the best application of this model to the market for trained manpower, see Freeman, *The Over-Educated American.*

[5] See, for example, U.S. Department of Labor, *Employment and Training Report of the President: 1982* (Washington, DC: U.S. Government Printing Office, 1982), table A-4.

Occupations and Earnings: White Men

In Chapter 3 we defined an occupational structure using five classifications:

- Professional and managerial workers
- Other white collar workers
- Blue collar workers
- Service workers
- Farmers and farm-related occupations

Most occupations require at least some training, and most people do not change careers.[6] It follows that the occupational structure evolves slowly as each group of new workers makes a different set of choices than the previous group had made.

Within this slow pace, the occupational trend among white men was the shift to white collar work. In the 1950 census 32 percent of white men were in white collar occupations. By 1980 the proportion had climbed to 43 percent.[7] It was a broad-based trend, and high-paying professional occupations like doctors and managers expanded as rapidly as lower-paying jobs in sales (Table 7.1).

In a few obvious cases—the growth of government—white collar employment came from the growth of the service sector. But in manufacturing industries, employment was becoming more white collar as well: more engineers, more managers, more accountants, and so on (Table 7.1). Bureau of Labor Statistics data (for men and women of all races) show that in durable goods manufacturing, nonproduction (white collar) workers as a proportion of all workers rose from 17 percent in 1948 to 31 percent by 1980.[8]

As the proportion of white men in white collar jobs expanded, the proportion in agriculture and blue collar jobs declined. Again, the process did not rely so much on career changes (though people did move from agriculture into blue collar work) but on young people who responded to financial incentives.

---

[6] Recent work suggests that most men, after an initial period of job shopping, spend the bulk of their career in two or three long-term jobs. See George A. Akerlof and Brian M. Main, "Unemployment Spells and Job Tenures: Are They Long? Are They Short? Or, Are They Both?" working paper, Department of Economics, University of California, Berkeley, 1980.

[7] Tabulations by the author of the 1950 and 1980 Census Public Use Microdata Samples.

[8] U.S. Department of Labor, *Employment and Training Report*, table C-5.

White collar work typically requires high levels of education. The early postwar growth of white collar work put educated workers in high demand. In 1950 white men aged 25 to 34 with four or more years of college earned 27 percent more than white men who had only a high school diploma. In 1960 the gap was 30 percent. It was a clear signal to pursue higher education, and people responded accordingly. Among white men aged 25 to 29, the proportion who had completed four or more years of college rose from 6 percent in 1947 to 12 percent in 1959 and 27 percent in 1979.[9] As younger men were gaining education, older men were retiring at increasingly early ages (see Chapter 8) so that by 1980, 25 percent of *all* white male workers had completed four or more years of college while another 15 percent had one to three years of college.[10]

In the process the supply of educated workers overtook demand, particularly for professional and managerial jobs. Economist Richard Freeman illustrates the point. In 1952 Freeman calculates that there were 2.2 managerial and professional jobs for every college graduate (regardless of race and sex). After 1958 the ratio began to fall steadily, and by the early 1970s it had declined to about 1.6 to 1. Nevertheless, young college graduates retained a relative income advantage. Unemployment in the 1970s was high and as college-educated workers moved down the job ladder, they bumped less educated workers into still lower jobs or out of the labor force altogether. In the mid 1980s a 30-year-old man with a college diploma earned $23,000 a year (in 1984 dollars), one third more than a man with a high school diploma and twice as much as the $11,500 earned by the 30-year-old high school drop-out.[11]

But as these numbers indicate, a college degree no longer guaranteed a middle-class standard of living. Young college graduates, like all young workers, were members of the baby boom cohorts. Within the baby boom, the biggest cohorts were born after 1950 and it was during the 1970s that these young people began their careers.

---

[9] See Dave M. O'Neill and Peter Sepielli, *Education in the United States: 1940–1983*, U.S. Bureau of the Census, Special Demographic Analysis, CDS-85-1 (Washington, DC: U.S. Government Printing Office, 1985).

[10] See U.S. Bureau of the Census, *Earnings by Occupation and Education*, Report PC80-2-8B (Washington, DC: U.S. Government Printing Office, May 1984), table 3.

[11] See Freeman, *The Over-Educated American*, chap. 1; and U.S.Bureau of the Census, "Money Income of Households, Families and Persons in the United States: 1984," *Current Population Reports*, series P-60, no. 151 (Washington, DC: U.S. Government Printing Office, 1986), table 34.

TABLE 7.1

Occupational Distribution of Experienced White Male Workers,
1950 and 1980

Over the postwar period white men's occupational structure has shifted toward white collar work and away from blue collar work and farming, but this shift has been slow and has not radically affected the proportion of white men in goods-producing industries.

	Percentage of All White Men in Group	
Occupational Group	1950	1980
PROFESSIONAL AND MANAGERIAL WORKERS		
Executives, Administrators, and Managers	10.2%	10.1%
Management-Related Occupations	1.5	2.9
Engineers and Natural Scientists	1.8	3.6
Doctors, Dentists, and Other Health Diagnostic Occupations	.9	1.1
Elementary and Secondary School Teachers	.6	2.0
Post-Secondary School Teachers	.2	.6
Lawyers and Judges	.5	.9
Miscellaneous Professional Specialties (Ministers, Social Workers, and so on)	1.6	2.2
OTHER WHITE COLLAR WORKERS		
Health Aides and Technicians	.6	1.0
Technicians other than Health Technicians	.6	2.4
Sales-Related Occupations	6.9	9.1
Administrative Support Workers	6.8	6.6
BLUE COLLAR WORKERS		
Craftsmen and Precision Workers	21.6	20.6
Machine Operators	12.4	9.1
Transport Equipment Operators	5.8	6.9
Handlers, Laborers, and so on	6.9	6.5

TABLE 7.1 *(continued)*

	Percentage of All White Men in Group	
Occupational Group	1950	1980
SERVICE WORKERS		
Household Workers	.1	—
Protective Service Workers (Police, Fire, and so on)	1.7	2.4
Food Services, Building Services (Except Household), Childcare, Restaurant, and Personal Services Workers	3.7	6.3
FARMERS AND FARM-RELATED OCCUPATIONS	13.3	4.5
ARMED FORCES	2.0	2.0
Total	99.7%	100.8%

NOTE: The occupational classification is described in Appendix C. Data are restricted to men with positive earnings. Numbers may not total 100% due to rounding.

SOURCES: Author's tabulations of 1950 and 1980 Census Public Use Microdata Samples.

The number of white men aged 25 to 34 in the labor force totaled 10 million in 1960 and 10.9 million in 1970, but it grew to 16.3 million by 1980. In the context of supply and demand, this was increased supply with a vengeance. The result was a decline in the wages of young workers (of whatever education) relative to those of older workers. The income gap between 30-year-old and 50-year-old men opened from 19 percent in 1975 to 23 percent in 1979 and 36 percent in 1984 (Chapter 5, Figure 7.1).

The final blow was that most of these *relative* wage movements took place after 1973 when absolute wages were stagnating. The distinction is important. Had the baby boom come of age in a healthy economy, they would have still progressed slowly vis-à-vis older workers. But they would have seen steady *absolute* progress both in their own wages and against fixed reference points like memories of their parents' standard of living. The total stagnation of wages made these forms of progress impossible. For example, in the 1950s and 1960s a young man passing from age 25 to 35 saw his real income

FIGURE 7.1

Average Incomes of White Men Aged 25–34 and 45–54, 1947–1984 (in 1984 dollars)

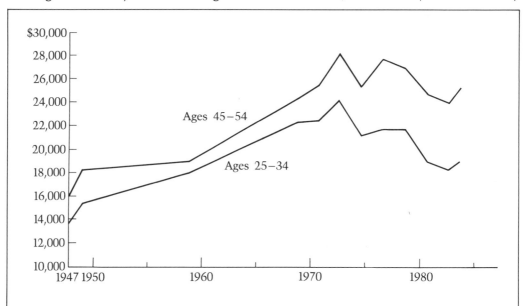

SOURCES: U.S. Bureau of the Census, *Current Population Reports*, series P-60, various numbers; and the 1950 census.

increase by about 110 percent, but a man aged 25 in 1973 saw his income over the next ten years—the period of his most rapid promotions—increase by only 16 percent.[12]

Public opinion data show many young people were sensitive to this turnaround. Since the late 1960s the American Council on Education has surveyed the attitudes of college freshmen. In their questionnaire students are asked to rank the importance of each of a series of values in their lives. Between 1968 and 1972 about half of all male freshmen felt that "being very well off financially" was "essential" or "very important," the highest and second highest possible ratings. In the fall of 1973, as the economy was going sour, this proportion jumped to 62 percent and it trended upward until it now stands in the low 70s. For freshmen women, the corresponding pro-

[12] See Frank Levy and Richard C. Michel, "An Economic Bust for the Baby Boom," *Challenge*, March–April 1986, figure 3 (p. 35), and see table 5.1, this volume.

portion jumped from 30 to 46 percent and then trended upward to 58 percent by 1980.[13]

There were other signs. One was the proportion of young persons who described themselves as middle class. Since the early 1950s the proportion had increased steadily, but after 1970 it began to decline modestly.[14] Still another was the choice of college major. In the mid 1960s, when all careers paid well (by historical standards), only 10 percent of freshmen majored in business administration. As the economy worsened, this proportion increased, and it stands at 25 percent today. Premed, prelaw, and, later, computers had a similar popularity.

This search for high-paying occupations was a natural reaction, but, as we saw earlier, there were limits to what it could accomplish. The first limit was the economy itself. When wages began to stagnate, they stagnated for *all* occupations (Table 7.2). The second limit was the slow grinding of supply and demand from which no occupation was safe. Two examples illustrate the point.

In the early 1970s becoming a lawyer appeared to be one sure way to make money. As Richard Freeman (1976) notes:

> Toward the end of the 1960's, the market for young lawyers underwent a significant economic boom. Expenditure on legal services increased from $3.9 billion to $9.3 billion in the period 1965 to 1973. The number of federal court cases increased by 73%; the fraction of national income spent on the legal industry rose from 0.7% to 0.9%. The increase in demand, coupled with the relatively slow growth in supply, produced a major boom in the market for young lawyers in the late 1960's. [p. 126]

Universities responded to this demand by rapidly increasing law school capacity. Between the 1970 and 1980 censuses the number of white male lawyers (including judges) grew from 293,000 to 434,000, with most of the growth in the younger ranks. Given the generally stagnant wages of the period, salaries fell absolutely. In 1979 the average 30-year-old white male lawyer earned $34,821, whereas his 1969 counterpart had earned $39,304. This decline was steep, even

[13] See the American Council on Education, Cooperative Institutional Research Program, *The American Freshman: National Norms* (Washington, DC: The American Council on Education, various editions).

[14] See Philip E. Converse et al., *American Social Attitudes Data Sourcebook, 1947–78* (Cambridge, MA: Harvard University Press, 1980), table 1.24.

TABLE 7.2

White Men's Average Earnings by Occupation and by Year
(in 1984 dollars)

Each entry is the result of two forces: economic growth, which pushed up *all* earnings through 1973, and supply and demand for particular occupations, which determined the distribution of relative earnings around the average.

	Mean Earnings			
	1949	1959	1969	1979
MEAN EARNINGS FOR ALL WHITE MALES	$11,514	$15,227	$19,619	$19,307
PROFESSIONAL AND MANAGERIAL WORKERS				
Executives, Administrators, and Managers	18,074	27,810	35,845	33,770
Management-Related Occupations	16,227	23,727	29,470	28,174
Engineers and Natural Scientists	19,677	27,188	34,833	30,530
Doctors, Dentists, and Other Health Diagnostic Occupations*	27,093	46,316	68,306	70,507
Teachers (all levels)	15,729	20,293	25,032	28,368
Lawyers and Judges*	27,326	37,099	55,734	52,574
Miscellaneous Professional Specialties (Ministers, Social Workers, and so on)	13,060	19,469	23,422	19,909
OTHER WHITE COLLAR WORKERS				
Health Aides and Technicians	13,301	15,191	20,736	16,989
Technicians other than Health Technicians	13,060	19,504	23,880	22,616
Sales-Related Occupations	13,407	19,239	24,529	24,003
Administrative Support Workers	12,353	15,384	18,306	17,821

TABLE 7.2 *(continued)*

	Mean Earnings			
	1949	1959	1969	1979
BLUE COLLAR WORKERS				
Craftsmen and Precision Workers	12,335	16,741	21,012	20,760
Machine Operators	10,965	14,367	17,884	17,729
Transport Equipment Operators	12,242	14,815	18,538	19,449
Handlers, Laborers, and so on	8,639	9,714	10,836	11,349
SERVICE WORKERS				
Household Workers	—	—	—	—
Protective Service Workers	11,568	15,249	19,897	17,888
Food Services, Building Services (Except Household), Childcare, Restaurant, and Personal Services Workers	8,691	8,865	10,257	9,429
FARMERS AND FARM-RELATED OCCUPATIONS	7,961	10,213	12,623	13,496
ARMED FORCES	10,443	10,539	12,451	13,193

*Estimates for occupations like doctors and lawyers are biased downward because census public use tapes "cap" individual income amounts at fixed levels—for example, $75,000 in 1979—for purposes of privacy. The occupational classification is described in Appendix C.
NOTE: Data restricted to men with positive earnings in the previous year.
SOURCES: Author's tabulations of 1950–80 Census Public Use Microdata Samples, inflation-adjusted using the Consumer Price Index.

for the 1970s, and as salary problems became known the next step of the market process was a decline in law school applications as students looked for greener pastures. Over the early 1980s the number of applications for 41,000 U.S. law school places fell from 73,000 to 58,000, and law school faculty were clearly worried.[15]

[15] This sounds hard to believe given the $68,000–$95,000 starting salaries being offered by some Wall Street firms "in order to compete with investment banking houses." But these salaries go to perhaps 300 graduates a year out of about 35,000. See Al Kamen, "Fewer Students Apply to Enter Law Schools," *Washington Post*, June 10, 1985, sect. A, p. 3.

This story is supply and demand with a twist. If demand increases in the market for chickens, farmers can increase supply very quickly (a chicken takes about sixty days from egg to supermarket), and so supply and demand are rarely much out of balance. Unlike chicken farms, the number of places in law schools changes slowly, which means that supply responds to demand slowly and the market is out of equilibrium most of the time. When demand increases, salaries rise rapidly (because high salaries can only call forth more lawyers three years after law schools increase in size). And when demand is sated, salaries fall rapidly (because the market has to absorb lawyers already in the pipeline). The market works, but it takes time.

In this respect, doctors go lawyers one better. A doctor requires several more years of training than a lawyer. And the medical profession, despite its protestations, has been fairly successful in limiting the number of medical school places. For both reasons, the supply of new doctors was extremely slow to respond to growing demand. Over the 1970s the number of white male doctors grew from 435,000 to 509,000, a 17 percent increase compared with an 48 percent increase among white male lawyers. The restricted supply explains why doctors are one of the few occupations in Table 7.2 whose average earnings actually rose over the 1970s. But the message of the American Medical Association report that opened this chapter is that the market is now working here, too. The growing supply of doctors makes it very difficult to establish a new practice, and young doctors increasingly have to take salaried positions with hospitals or health maintenance organizations. In focus group discussions they now say they would oppose *their* children becoming doctors.[16]

A Small Silver Lining

To this point we have seen how upward mobility broke down in the 1970s. It is a gloomy story and yet it contains a silver lining: the way in which demand, supply, and the flood of new practitioners put limits on doctors' and lawyers' salaries.

The issue is more general than doctors and lawyers per se. In recent years, some analysts have argued that we are being pushed

---

[16] Personal communication from Jack Hadley, a health economist at the Georgetown School of Medicine, who observed such focus groups.

toward a two-tier job market not through the growing service sector, but through the advance of high technology and computers. The issue is one of degree. Computers are certainly part of the shift toward white collar work in which uneducated workers are at an increasing disadvantage. But critics of computerization hold that even among educated workers occupations will fall into two groups: those that design and control technology and those that are controlled by it. The first group will form a highly paid elite while those who are controlled will become drones.

Given the nature of both technology and occupational markets, the view is not very plausible. Begin with the idea of drones. We can quickly think of jobs where computers have downgraded required skills. Today's cash registers, for example, no longer require fast food clerks to know how to add and subtract.[17] But how do we classify stockbrokers, real estate agents, and other "market-makers" who rely heavily on computers. They do not design the technology but neither are they drones: To the contrary, computers have extended their reach. If the airlines had to revert to a system where reservations were made without computers, the airline industry would collapse.

Computerization, like other mechanization, is not totally benign. The mechanization of agriculture reduced the number of farmers, and computer-assisted design will reduce the future need for draftsmen while word processing will reduce the need for secretaries. Plant automation will reduce the need for certain types of craftsmen and machine operators, but it is increasingly helping manufacturers deal with the problems of the 1970s: slow-growing markets and short product cycles (see Chapter 5).[18]

Most important, the picture of a small number of highly paid "controllers" jobs ignores the lesson of the lawyers and the doctors. By the early 1980s computer science departments on college campuses were overflowing with enrollments. As these graduates complete their training it is reasonable to assume that computer-related

---

[17] Even this is a doubled-edged sword because while it holds down the wages that fast food stores have to pay, it also opens employment for low-skilled workers.

[18] For a discussion of the role of computerized manufacturing in dealing with short product cycles, see Michael J. Piore and Charles F. Sabel, *The Second Industrial Divide* (New York: Basic Books, 1984). For a discussion of the limited impact of "high technology" jobs on the occupational distribution, see Richard W. Riche, Daniel E. Hecker, and John U. Burgan, "High Technology Today and Tomorrow: A Small Slice of the Employment Pie," *Monthly Labor Review*, November 1983, pp. 50–58.

salaries will begin to resemble those of other occupations. In this sense, the limit of the market also helps to limit earnings inequality.

Evidence on this point is contained in the income distributions of prime-age white men for 1969 and 1984 in Figure 7.2. These distributions describe all money received by all white men between the ages of 25 and 55. Both earned and unearned income is included (but income received by other family members is not).[19] Had the 1970s been normal, incomes would have grown and the 1984 distribution would have moved to higher incomes. But wages were stagnant and the baby boom came of age; thus, the 1984 distribution has actually slipped down a little. Inequality has increased moderately but despite computerization, there is little evidence of extreme polarization among these prime-age white men.

Occupations and Earnings: Black Men

On the eve of World War II half of all black men worked in the rural South, the poorest part of the country (Chapter 3). Another quarter lived in southern cities. Only one third had gone beyond the seventh grade (compared with three quarters of whites). They were restricted to agriculture, service work, and low-level blue collar jobs. Their nationwide earnings averaged $3,300 (in 1984 dollars), about two fifths of the earnings of white men.

Beyond this was the pressure of legal and informal discrimination in the South but also in the North. Philly Joe Jones was a world-renowned jazz drummer who came to prominence in the Miles Davis quintet of the late 1950s.[20] In August 1944 Jones, then a World War II veteran, and seven other men were hired as the first black conductor-trainees for the Philadelphia Transportation Company (PTC). Six thousand white PTC conductors and motormen called a wildcat strike in protest. State liquor stores and bars were ordered closed to forestall racial violence. The strike was settled only after the secretary of war had ordered military personnel to take over the system.[21]

---

[19] The distributions use income, rather than earnings per se, because published data on the distribution of earnings by age was not available for 1969.

[20] This was the first Miles Davis quintet to record on a major label (Columbia) and to reach large white audiences.

[21] See Francis David, "The Stories They Can Tell on Philly Joe," *Philadelphia Inquirer*, June 15, 1986, sect. H, p. 1.

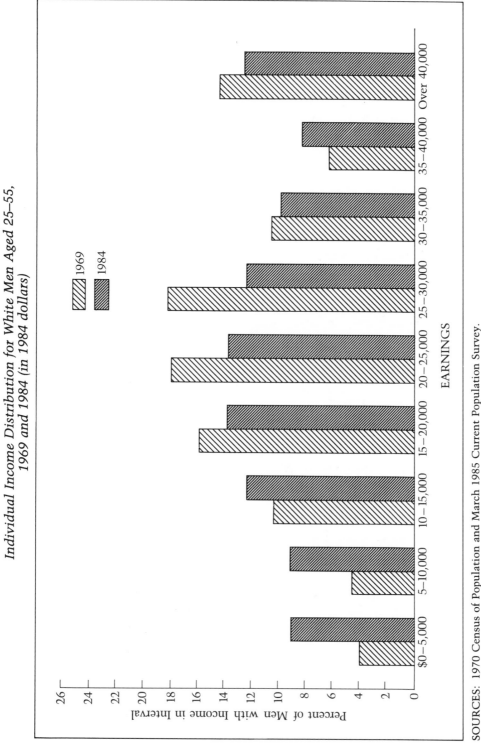

FIGURE 7.2

Individual Income Distribution for White Men Aged 25–55,
1969 and 1984 (in 1984 dollars)

SOURCES: 1970 Census of Population and March 1985 Current Population Survey.

TABLE 7.3

Occupational Distribution of Experienced Black Male Workers,
1950 and 1980

Throughout the postwar period black men remained more concentrated in agriculture and in blue collar jobs than white men. By 1980, despite significant strides, about 25 percent of black men were in white collar occupations compared with 43 percent for white men.

Occupational Group	Percentage of All Black Men in Group		All White Men (included for reference) 1980
	1950	1980	
PROFESSIONAL AND MANAGERIAL WORKERS			
Executives, Administrators, and Managers	.7 %	3.4 %	10.1%
Management-Related Occupations	.2	1.4	2.9
Engineers and Natural Scientists	.7	1.3	3.6
Doctors, Dentists, and other Health Diagnostic Occupations	.4	.2	1.1
Elementary and Secondary School Teachers	.8	1.4	2.0
Post-Secondary School Teachers	—	.4	.6
Lawyers and Judges	—	.1	.9
Miscellaneous Professional Specialties (Ministers, Social Workers, and so on)	.5	1.6	2.2
OTHER WHITE COLLAR WORKERS			
Health Aides and Technicians	.7	1.4	1.0
Technicians other than Health Technicians	—	1.3	2.4
Sales-Related Occupations	1.5	3.7	9.1
Administrative Support Workers	3.9	8.5	6.6
BLUE COLLAR WORKERS			
Craftsmen and Precision Workers	9.8	13.9	20.6
Machine Operators	13.1	14.5	9.1
Transport Equipment Operators	8.1	10.2	6.9
Handlers, Laborers and so on	18.7	12.0	6.9

TABLE 7.3 *(continued)*

Occupational Group	Percentage of All Black Men in Group		All White Men (included for reference)
	1950	1980	1980
SERVICE WORKERS			
Household Workers	.8	.2	—
Protective Service Workers	.8	2.8	2.4
Food Services, Building Services (Except Household), Childcare, Restaurant, and Personal Services Workers	12.1	13.4	6.3
FARMERS AND FARM-RELATED OCCUPATIONS	25.9	3.4	4.5
ARMED FORCES	1.5	4.3	2.0
Total	100.2%	99.4%	100.8%

NOTE: Data are restricted to men with positive earnings in the previous year. Numbers may not total 100% due to rounding. The occupational classification is described in Appendix C.

SOURCES: Author's tabulations of 1950 and 1980 Census Public Use Microdata Samples.

In the years since then, black men's progress has been substantial but uneven—uneven across persons and uneven over time (Table 7.3). The civil rights movement and the breakdown of discrimination have both been important in this progress, but equally important was traditional upward mobility. Children acquired more education than their parents had, they become better acclimated to urban life than their parents were, and in this way they achieved some of those things that their parents could not. This is a hard process in which a "group" improves its position by a slow and painful change of membership. But occasionally an event occurs that advances the progress of most group members—not just the new ones. Over the postwar period, two such events affected black men.

The first was the movement out of southern agriculture in the 1940s and 1950s. It was during that time that black men faced both the pull of manufacturing jobs in the North and the push of declining farm employment (Chapter 6). Over the two decades one third of the southern black population migrated to cities in the North and, to a lesser extent, the Far West.

Migration did not mean enormous occupational mobility. There was movement out of agriculture and into blue collar jobs and service worker jobs, but white collar jobs were out of reach. In 1960, 12 percent of black men held such jobs. This was one third of the rate for white men, and the disparity was in some sense greater because few of the black jobs came from the private sector. Most were in teaching, administrative support personnel, and other government positions.[22]

Nevertheless, migration substantially increased black male incomes because southern agriculture paid so little. In 1950 a black man in rural Georgia earned about $1,750 (in 1984 dollars), $3,000 less than black workers in Georgia cities. If a man could move from agriculture to almost any blue collar or service work job, it would be a big step up. Many men successfully made such moves, but others did not. The U.S. Department of Labor began keeping separate unemployment rates for black adult males in 1954. Over the late 1950s black men averaged 10 percent unemployment while white men averaged 4 percent.

Black men who obtained full-time work were closing the gap with whites: By 1960 full-time black workers had incomes (from all sources) 58 percent of those of full-time white workers. But *all* black men (including men who worked less than full time) had incomes 47 percent of those of white men (Figure 7.3). This 47 percent figure was lower than it had been in 1948 and reflected particularly high black unemployment in the 1958–60 recession.[23]

The migration out of agriculture could boost black incomes, but the process had obvious limits. By 1960 the proportion of black men in agriculture had fallen to 11 percent, and there were few men left to continue the process. At this point a second event boosted black progress—the 1960s economic boom.

The boom came at a good time. In Chapter 6 we saw that during the 1950s and 1960s manufacturing jobs were rapidly leaving central cities, and the exodus of jobs left many black men stranded. By 1963 the national economy had recovered from the 1958–60 recession, but the unemployment rate for black adult men still stood at 8 percent,

---

[22] Based on tabulations by the author of the 1960 Census Public Use Microdata Sample file.

[23] See U.S. Bureau of the Census, "Money Income of Households, Families and Persons in the United States: 1983," *Current Population Reports*, series P-60, no. 146 (Washington, DC: U.S. Government Printing Office, 1985), table 40.

FIGURE 7.3

Median Individual Income of Black and White Men, 1948–1984 (in 1984 dollars)

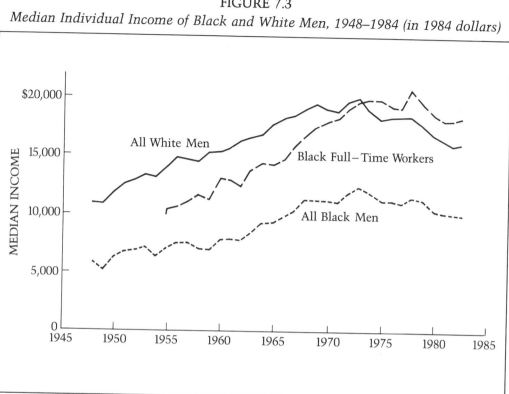

NOTE: Data include males aged 14 years and over. Data for blacks include other nonwhite races. Data for year-round, full-time workers were collected only after 1954.

SOURCES: U.S. Bureau of the Census, *Current Population Reports*, series P-60, various numbers.

more than twice the rate for white men. Then Keynesian tax cuts and Vietnam deficits began to stimulate the economy. As high demand exhausted the white labor pool, increased demand focused on blacks.

Relative to earlier years black men did well. In the last half of the 1960s, black men averaged 4.5 percent of unemployment, their best experience since unemployment statistics were collected by race. And low unemployment translated into big relative income gains. By 1969 the black-white income ratio for full-time workers stood at .69 (up from .58 in 1959), while the income ratio for all men stood at .59 (up from .47 in 1959). (See Figure 7.3.)

Tight labor markets also led to modest occupational mobility. By 1969, 17 percent of black men were in white collar jobs (up from

12 percent in 1960). Movements were still confined to the lower tier of white collar jobs (administrative support positions, public school teachers); employment still relied disproportionately on the public sector; and the proportion of black men in white collar jobs was still one half that of white men. Nonetheless, progress was being made.

In Chapter 6 we saw that the 1960s were also a time when the number of black families headed by women increased rapidly. How does this picture fit with the black progress just described? The answer involved a growing split within the black male population. Many men were making substantial progress. But other men, trapped by the loss of manufacturing jobs and the isolation of the ghetto, were falling further behind. A sense of this split is contained in Figure 7.3, which shows a widening gap between the median incomes of *all* black men and black men who work full time. But even these medians obscure the circumstances of the bottom of the distribution.[24] In 1969, a banner year for low unemployment, 5 percent of 25-to-55-year-old black men reported no earned income, while 25 percent reported total income below the federal poverty standard for a family of four.[25]

The many black men who did progress in the 1960s benefited from more than tight labor markets. Discrimination was slowly eroding (in part under government pressure) and young blacks were closing the educational gap with whites.[26] But low unemployment enhanced these processes, and when labor markets went slack in the 1970s the process began to slow. At the top of the distribution, fur-

[24] Median income is defined by the fact that half of all people have more than that income and half of all people have less. This definition says nothing about "how much less" income the lower half has, and so the lower tail of the distribution can deteriorate substantially without affecting the median.

[25] On the proportion of black men who report no earned income, see Frank Levy, "Changes in the Employment Prospects for Black Males," *Brookings Papers on Economic Activity*, no. 2 (1980), pp. 513–37. This work is an outgrowth of the work of Butler and Heckman, who argued that traditional comparisons of black-white earnings ratios overstated black progress because published earnings statistics were based on persons who had at least one dollar of earnings. Thus, they potentially obscured those black men who were out of the labor market altogether. See Richard Butler and James J. Heckman, "The Government's Impact on the Labor Market Status of Black Americans: A Critical Review," in Leonard J. Hausman et al., eds, *Equal Rights and Industrial Relations* (Ithaca, NY: Industrial Research Association, 1977). On the distribution of black men's incomes in 1969, see U.S. Bureau of the Census, "Income in 1969 of Families and Persons in the United States," *Current Population Reports*, series P-60, no. 75 (Washington, DC: U.S. Government Printing Office, 1970), table 45.

[26] These gains are summarized in Richard B. Freeman, "Changes in the Labor Market for Black Americans, 1948–72," *Brookings Papers on Economic Activity*, no. 1 (1973), pp. 67–132.

ther mobility was minimal. In the early 1980s black men who worked full time had incomes 75 percent of their white counter-parts—up only modestly from the late 1960s (69 percent). At the bottom of the distribution a growing number of poorly educated black men faced intense competition for jobs from the baby boom cohorts and dropped out of the labor market altogether. In 1978, a fairly good year, 11 percent of prime-age (25–55) black men reported no earned income from any source. This figure was twice what it had been in the late 1960s and three times the figure for whites. While some of these men may have actually had earnings from the underground economy, many were living from public assistance or, more often, from the income of other family members. The recession of 1980–82 exacerbated the trend.[27] (We examine the underground economy in Appendix B.)

At several earlier points we examined the propositions that the service sector or high technology was creating a "two-tier" job market. In those cases, we found little evidence that structural trends were pulling the broad job market apart. But when we come to the particular position of black men, the polarization of incomes has much more force.

Large numbers of black men are doing better than ever. In the 1980 census, black men aged 25 to 34 with at least some college earned 80–85 percent as much as their white counterparts. For these men, the old yardstick—a black man with a college degree earns less than a white man with a high school diploma—had finally been broken.[28]

These men represented the upper one third of their age group. At the other end were the one quarter of black men aged 25 to 34 who had not finished high school and could not compete in the oversupply of labor in the 1970s. This split is evident in the development of the distribution of individual incomes for prime-age black men. (See Figure 7.4.) Recall that the comparable figure for white men showed that between 1969 and 1984 the distribution generally slid lower as individual incomes generally declined (Figure 7.2). But in the case of blacks, the distribution became more polarized and the

---

[27] See U.S. Bureau of the Census, "Money Income of Households, Families and Persons in the United States: 1983," table 40; and Levy, "Changes in the Employment Prospects for Black Males."

[28] See U.S. Bureau of the Census, *Earnings by Occupation,* table 4. James Morgan points out to me that progress may be deceptive because while black workers are *starting out* on a greater parity with whites, the income gap widens as both groups age.

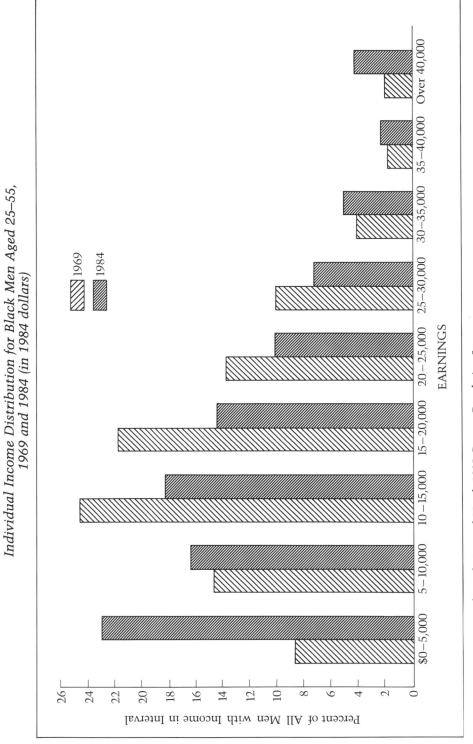

FIGURE 7.4

Individual Income Distribution for Black Men Aged 25–55, 1969 and 1984 (in 1984 dollars)

SOURCES: 1970 Census of Population and March 1985 Current Population Survey.

proportion of black men aged 25 to 55 with incomes over $25,000 and incomes less than $5,000 both increased.

More precisely, in 1984, a relatively good year, nearly one quarter of all black men aged 25 to 55 reported incomes of less than $5,000 per year. If this figure were adjusted for the 10 percent of black men not counted by the census, the proportion would be slightly larger.[29] Even after correcting for the underground economy, many of these men are now part of an equilibrium involving economically isolated neighborhoods and families headed by women. We discuss the last piece of the equilibrium—welfare payments—in Chapter 8.

Occupations and Earnings: White Women

If simple averages are insufficient to describe the position of black men, they are equally inadequate to describe the position of white women. Anyone can see that there are many more women lawyers, doctors, and managers than there were thirty years ago. Yet in 1984 white women who worked full time earned an average of $14,677, 35 percent less than white men who worked full time (Figure 7.5). The gap is almost unchanged from its value in 1955, the first year it was published.[30]

Three facts reconcile this paradox:

- Over the postwar period, white women increased in the labor force far more rapidly than white men.

- The rapid increase in working women meant not only more women lawyers and executives, but also more women teachers and sales clerks and secretaries. Thus, the overall occupational distribution of white women did not change very much.

- Within most occupations, women still earn about 20–30 percent less than men, even when age, education, and hours worked are held constant.

The story surrounding these facts begins with the increase in women's labor force participation. Recall from Chapter 3 that even

---

[29] U.S. Bureau of the Census, "Money Income of Households, Families and Persons in the United States: 1984," *Current Population Reports*, series P-60, no. 151 (Washington, DC: U.S. Government Printing Office, 1986), table 32.

[30] See U.S. Bureau of the Census, "Money Income," table 29.

FIGURE 7.5

*Median Income of Black and White Women and White Men
Who Worked Year Round and Full Time, 1955–1984 (in 1984 dollars)*

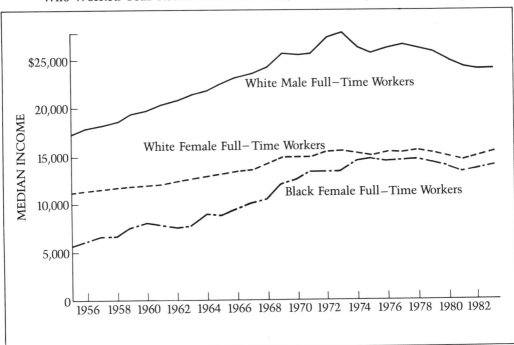

NOTE: White men are included for reference. Data for black women include other nonwhite races. Data for year-round, full-time workers were collected only after 1954.

SOURCES: U.S. Bureau of the Census, *Current Population Reports*, series P-60, various numbers.

during World War II working women were the exception. In 1944, at the peak of the war, about 35 percent of all women over age 16 were employed. It was a high rate for its time but far less than today's rate (54 percent).

The low postwar labor force participation rate reflected a straightforward career pattern: work for pay (if you work at all) before marriage. Then stop. Among young white women (aged 18 to 24), about one half worked. Among older white women (aged 25 to 54) one third worked, and women showed little tendency to return to work after their children were grown. This would soon change. By the late 1950s almost half of all white women aged 45 to 54 were working, and women in their late 30s were returning to work as well. But the women most likely to have young children—those aged 25 to 34—still remained out of the labor market in large numbers.[31]

During the 1960s labor force participation grew moderately among women of all ages, but during the 1970s it exploded particularly among women in the traditional child-raising years (aged 25 to 34). Among these women, about half worked in 1973. By 1983 the proportion exceeded two thirds. In total, white women's labor force participation increased faster over 1973–83 than it had over the previous twenty-six years.

The huge number of women workers helped reshape the labor force. Between 1955 and 1984 the number of adult white men workers grew by 12.5 million while the number of adult white women workers increased by 20 million.[32] The influx led to an illusion of white women's rapid progress. Consider two questions:

- Among all white women, what proportion are executives, administrators, and managers (first category in Table 7.4)?

- Among all executives, administrators, and managers, what proportion are white women?

Despite appearances, the proportion of white women who are executives is quite small—about 5 percent—and it has not grown appreciably since World War II. To the contrary, three traditional occupations—clerical positions (administrative support), sales, and elementary school teachers—have absorbed almost half of all white women throughout the postwar years. In this sense, white women's occupational distribution changed no more quickly than the occupational distributions of white and black men.

The proportion of executives who are white women is a different issue. Because the number of white women in the job market has grown so rapidly, women have become more numerous and visible in every occupational category even without significant occupational mobility. Thus, the proportion of all executives who are white women has risen from about 15 percent in 1950 to nearly 30 percent today.[33] In this way white women could appear to be *making giant*

---

[31] For early data on women's labor force participation, see U.S. Bureau of the Census, *Historical Statistics of the United States: Colonial Times to 1970* (1975), series D49-62. For later data, see U.S. Department of Labor, *Employment and Training Report*, table A-3. For an excellent discussion of trends, see Suzanne M. Bianchi and Daphne G. Spain, *American Women in Transition*, The Population of the United States in the 1980s: A Census Monograph Series (New York: Russell Sage Foundation, 1986).

[32] See U.S. Department of Labor, *Employment and Training Report*, table A-5.

[33] See U.S. Bureau of the Census, *Earnings by Occupation*, table 3.

TABLE 7.4

Occupational Distribution of Experienced White Female Workers,
1950 and 1980

The occupational distribution of white women has not changed very much over the postwar period. The sense of their progress reflects their increased labor force participation, which has meant more white women in almost every occupation.

Occupational Group	Proportion of All White Women in Group		All White Men (included for reference) 1980
	1950	1980	
PROFESSIONAL AND MANAGERIAL WORKERS			
Executives, Administrators, and Managers	4.0%	4.9%	10.1%
Management-Related Occupations	.6	2.4	2.9
Engineers and Natural Scientists	.3	.7	3.6
Health Diagnostic Occupations	.1	.3	1.1
Elementary and Secondary School Teachers	6.8	7.4	2.0
Post-Secondary School Teachers	.2	.6	.6
Lawyers and Judges	—	.2	.9
Miscellaneous Professional Specialties (Ministers, Social Workers, and so on)	2.2	2.3	2.2
OTHER WHITE COLLAR WORKERS			
Health Aides and Technicians	5.9	8.4	1.0
Technicians other than Health Technicians	.3	.9	2.4
Sales-Related Occupations	9.8	12.2	9.4
Administrative Support Workers	31.8	31.0	6.6
BLUE COLLAR WORKERS			
Craftsmen and Precision Workers	2.1	2.1	20.6
Machine Operators	20.1	8.1	9.1
Transport Equipment Operators	.1	.8	6.9
Handlers, Laborers and so on	.6	2.2	6.5

TABLE 7.4 *(continued)*

Occupational Group	Proportion of All White Women in Group		All White Men (included for reference)
	1950	1980	1980
SERVICE WORKERS			
Household Workers	3.7	.9	—
Protective Service Workers	—	.4	2.4
Food Services, Building Services (Except Household), Childcare, Restaurant, and Personal Services Workers	9.7	12.4	6.3
FARMERS AND FARM-RELATED OCCUPATIONS	1.5	1.0	4.5
ARMED FORCES	.1	.2	2.0
Total	99.9%	99.4%	100.8%

NOTE: The occupational classification is described in Appendix C. Data are restricted to women with positive earnings in the previous year. Numbers may not total 100% due to rounding.

SOURCES: Author's tabulations of 1950 and 1980 Census Public Use Microdata Samples.

strides even as their occupational distribution improved only very gradually.

Slow change in the occupational distribution helps explain why the incomes of white women and white men have remained in a roughly constant ratio over time. Equally important are female-male earnings differences *within* occupations. In the 1980 census white women who worked full time earned 20–30 percent less than white men of the same age, education, and occupational category.[34] Some of the gap has a basis in economics. Women classified as year-round, full-time workers actually work 10 percent fewer hours than men in a similar classification.[35] Similarly, the rapid growth in working women means that many women (especially above age 30) were relatively new on the job and so their wages suffered much as the wages

[34] See U.S. Bureau of the Census, *Earnings by Occupation*, table 3.

[35] See June O'Neill, "The Trend in the Male-Female Wage Gap in the United States," working paper (Washington, DC: Urban Institute, revised March 1984).

of baby boom males suffered.[36] But together these factors cannot fully explain male-female pay differences, and researchers are left to look elsewhere, including the way in which women are concentrated in smaller, lower-paying firms. Some of this concentration reflects worker choice since small firms are more likely to permit flexible work schedules which many mothers require, but a part of the concentration reflects residual discrimination.[37]

Over time, the economic causes of wage differences should mitigate. The enormous surge in white women's labor force participation is over, and so the composition of white women workers will shift away from new entrants and toward more experienced workers with longer job tenures. As this happens wage differences within occupations should close, but the concentration of even young white women in traditional "women's occupations" means that full income parity with men will be very slow in coming.

Occupations and Earnings: Black Women

The postwar occupational distributions of white men, black men, and white women have all changed very slowly. Black women are the exception to this pattern. Over the postwar period, their occupational status has improved very rapidly, so that today black and white women workers are essentially on a par.

Unlike white women, black women have always worked in large numbers, a reflection of economic necessity; and in the early postwar period nearly half of all black women worked (compared with one third of white women). In the labor market, they shared many of the disadvantages of black men: geographic concentration in the South, lack of education, and official and informal discrimination.

In 1950 two fifths of black women worked as household domestics and another fifth worked as cafeteria personnel, custodians, and similar low-rung service workers (Table 7.5). Low-rung occupations translated into low earnings. In the mid-1950s a black woman who

---

[36] See O'Neill, "The Trend in the Male-Female Wage Gap"; and James P. Smith and Michael P. Ward, *Women's Wages and Work in the Twentieth Century* (Santa Monica, CA: Rand Corporation, October 1984).

[37] See Francine D. Blau, *Equal Pay in the Office* (Lexington, MA: Heath, 1977); and Bianchi and Spain, *American Women in Transition*.

worked full time had an income of $5,700, about one half the income of her white counterpart (Figure 7.5).

Over the next twenty years, migration out of the South, more education, and the rapidly growing service sector would radically change this condition. In 1950 the average young white woman had a high school diploma, but the average young black woman had not completed the ninth grade. By 1970 young women from both groups averaged better than a high school diploma, and the educational gap was less than three tenths of a year.[38]

Improved education and a general decline in discrimination left black women in a position to benefit from the rapid expansion of service employment. By the 1980 census black women had shifted dramatically into clerical and health care occupations. The proportion of black women in domestic work had declined to less than 5 percent, while the proportion in clerical work, health care, and sales grew from 7–43 percent (Table 7.5).

Through the 1960s the number of black families headed by a woman was growing quickly but this trend had little effect on black women's labor force participation. Fifty percent of black female family heads were in the labor force, a figure only slightly below the 58 percent of married black women. Thus, relatively large numbers of female household heads worked. But for those who did not work, the economic consequences for their families were severe; in 1969, at the peak of the economic boom, 70 percent were in poverty.[39]

Improved occupational standing meant improved earnings. By the mid-1970s black and white women of similar age and education had similar earnings,[40] a parity that continues to the present (Figure 7.5). These statistics seem to say that black women have progressed further than black men, and it is worth asking why.

Much of the difference involves the way we have structured the comparison. We expect all prime-age men to work, and so Figures

---

[38] See U.S. Bureau of the Census, *Historical Statistics* (1975), series H623-647.

[39] On the labor force participation and poverty rates of black female household heads, see U.S. Bureau of the Census, "24 Million Americans—Poverty in the United States: 1969," *Current Population Reports*, series P-60, no. 76, table 11. For the labor force participation rate of black wives, "Income in 1970 of Families and Persons in the United States," *Current Population Reports*, series P-60, no. 80, table 17. Among black female family heads who were in the labor force, 37 percent were in poverty, about one half the rate of those who were in the labor force.

[40] See, for example, Freeman, "Changes in the Labor Market."

TABLE 7.5

Occupational Distribution of Experienced Black Women Workers,
1950 and 1980

Unlike other groups, black women showed rapid change in their occupational distribution. Over the postwar period the proportion of black women in domestic work fell from 40 percent to almost nothing while the proportion in clerical and nursing work grew from 5 percent to over 40 percent.

Occupational Group	Proportion of All Black Women in Group		All White Men (included for reference) 1980
	1950	1980	
PROFESSIONAL AND MANAGERIAL WORKERS			
Executives, Administrators, and Managers	.9%	2.8%	10.1%
Management-Related Occupations	—	1.7	2.9
Engineers and Natural Scientists	—	.6	3.6
Doctors, Dentists, and other Health Diagnostic Occupations	—	.2	1.1
Elementary and Secondary School Teachers	4.3	6.3	2.0
Post-Secondary School Teachers	—	.3	.6
Lawyers and Judges	—	.1	.9
Miscellaneous Professional Specialties (Ministers, Social Workers, and so on)	1.3	2.2	2.2
OTHER WHITE COLLAR WORKERS			
Health Aides and Technicians	2.6	12.2	1.0
Technicians other than Health Technicians	—	.7	2.4
Sales-Related Occupations	.9	6.4	9.1
Administrative Support Workers	3.8	24.6	6.6
BLUE COLLAR WORKERS			
Craftsmen and Precision Workers	.9	2.3	20.6
Machine Operators	14.4	11.5	9.1
Transport Equipment Operators	1.7	.9	6.9
Handlers, Laborers and so on	—	3.3	6.5

TABLE 7.5 *(continued)*

Occupational Group	Proportion of All Black Women in Group		All White Men (included for reference)
	1950	1980	1980
SERVICE WORKERS			
Household Workers	39.7	4.6	—
Protective Service Workers	—	.8	2.4
Food Services, Building Services (Except Household), Childcare, Restaurant, and Personal Services Workers	19.2	17.2	6.3
FARMERS AND FARM-RELATED OCCUPATIONS	9.8	.6	4.5
ARMED FORCES	.4	.5	2.0
Total	100.5%	100.7%	100.8%

NOTE: Data are restricted to women with positive earnings in the previous year. The occupational classification is described in Appendix C.

SOURCES: Author's tabulations of 1950 and 1980 Census Public Use Microdata Samples.

7.2 and 7.4 are based on the distribution of all (prime-aged) men's incomes. As more black men dropped out of the labor force, these distributions made it obvious. Conversely, we know that many women choose to stay at home, and so in comparing black and white women we limit the data to women who work and, in the case of Figure 7.5, women who work full time. To the extent that nonworking women are in deteriorating circumstances, our comparison does not capture that fact. Thus, the comparison is an artifact of the data because black men without jobs and poor black families headed by women are, in many cases, two sides of the same coin.

Conflicting Trends

When we look at total labor force numbers, few big changes appear. In the late 1940s, 59 percent of all persons aged 20 and older were in the labor force. In 1984, 66 percent of all persons aged 20 and older were in the labor force. But the trends beneath these aggregates are sharper. The number of working women has risen enormously, men are retiring at earlier ages, and a significant minority of black men are out of the labor force altogether.

Certain of these trends have implications for inequality. The growing earnings gap between younger and older workers is one; the convergence of black and white women's earnings is another. To assess the full impacts on inequality, we have to understand how these individuals combine (or do not combine) themselves into families. In family income statistics, low baby boomer wages can be offset if both husband and wife are working. Conversely, many unemployed black men do not appear in the family income distribution at all, but their presence is felt through more families headed by women. We turn to the subject of families in Chapter 8.

HOUSEHOLDS, FAMILIES, AND THE GOVERNMENT

Units of Measurement

THE FAMILY income distribution is based on family incomes. The point seems obvious, but it is important because family incomes vary substantially by family arrangement. Consider some 1984 averages:

- Husband-wife families aged 45–54, with both spouses working $42,100
- Husband-wife families aged 25–34, with only the husband working $23,450
- Families headed by women aged 25 or under $ 5,200
- Husband-wife families aged 65 and over $18,600[1]

In earlier chapters we saw that *individual* incomes vary across occupations, regions, and industrial sectors. But these *family* income

[1] U.S. Bureau of the Census, "Money Income of Households, Families and Persons in the United States: 1984," *Current Population Reports*, series P-60, no. 151 (Washington, DC: U.S. Government Printing Office, 1986), table 16.

variations are typically larger and they raise a note of caution. We are using the family income distribution as a framework to describe the postwar economy, but as the economy changed family arrangements changed, too, and we need to take account of this fact.

Changing arrangements involve more than just families. They include increasing number of persons who live outside families, like young singles and divorced men and women. These people affect the income distribution of unrelated individuals, but they also affect the family income distribution through the families that are *not* formed.

At the end of World War II this variety was of little concern because 94 percent of the population lived in families (Chapter 3). Of those families, 80 percent had a husband and a wife under age 65, and in most of those families the wife did not work.

Since that time family arrangements have changed in a number of ways. Young men and women now stay single longer, married women are more likely to work, older men and women retire earlier, and more families are headed by unmarried women.

At the same time, more families rely on the government for income. Over the postwar period government payments to individuals have grown from 5 to 12 percent of Gross National Product and totaled $437 billion in 1984. One fifth of this sum ($83 billion) were means-tested programs aimed specifically at the poor. The rest were social insurance expenditures, including Social Security benefits, unemployment benefits, veterans benefits, pensions for retired government workers and other programs in which eligibility is established through contributions.[2]

In earlier chapters we saw that many trends within the income distribution worked in offsetting directions. Family arrangements and government benefits are another example. We know that throughout the postwar period family income inequality has remained fairly constant. Could this have happened without, say, Social Security? If large numbers of older families had retired without Social Security, income inequality certainly would have grown. But of course without Social Security, many older families would not have retired at all. This leads to an important question: To what extent did government payments *cause* changing family arrangements? In some cases that is what the payments were designed to

---

[2] See U.S. Department of Commerce, Bureau of Economic Analysis, *National Income and Product Accounts of the United States, 1929–76* (Washington, DC: U.S. Government Printing Office, 1981), table 3.11; and "National Income and Product Account Tables, 1982–85," *Survey of Current Business* 66, no. 3 (March 1986): table 3.11.

do. Social Security was intended to encourage people to retire by age 65. But Aid to Families with Dependent Children was not intended to encourage more female-headed families. To the extent that it has, it creates a situation proposed by social scientists Nathan Glazer, Charles Murray,[3] and others, in which antipoverty programs perpetuate dependence and poverty. We shall discuss this hypothesis as the chapter progresses.

The Growth of Independent Households

The census defines a household as "all the persons who occupy a housing unit."[4] Households encompass both families and unrelated individuals, but at the end of World War II households and families were, *de facto*, close in meaning. Together 36 million families and 9 million unrelated individuals constituted only 39 million households. The housing shortage of the Great Depression and World War II had forced people to double up. In Chapter 3 we saw that:

- One family in fourteen was living in a household headed by another person or family, typically a relative.

- Seven unmarried adults in ten lived with other adults or families.

- About one quarter of the population age 65 and over (2.8 million persons) lived in households headed by their children.[5]

Privacy is expensive. The Bureau of Labor Statistics estimates that if a young adult moves out of her parents' home, minimum living expenditures for all persons involved increase by one quarter.[6]

---

[3] See Nathan Glazer, "The Limits of Social Policy," *Commentary*, September 1971, pp. 51–58; and Charles Murray, *Losing Ground* (New York: Basic Books, 1984). Also see George Gilder, *Wealth and Poverty* (New York: Basic Books, 1980); and Lawrence Mead, *Beyond Entitlement* (New York: Free Press, 1986).

[4] See, for example, U.S. Bureau of the Census, "Money Income of Households, Families and Persons in the United States: 1983," *Current Population Reports*, series P-60, no. 146 (Washington, DC: U.S. Government Printing Office, 1985), p. 210. In census terminology, a family is two or more people who are living together and who are related by blood, marriage, or adoption.

[5] See Robert J. Lampman and Timothy M. Smeeding, "Interfamily Transfers as Alternatives to Government Transfers to Persons," *Review of Income and Wealth*, March 1983, pp. 45–66.

[6] For example, in 1983 the federal poverty standard for a four-person family, including one child over age 18, was $10,437. But the sum of the poverty standards for a three-person family and a fourth person living alone totaled $13,195, a 26 percent increase. See U.S. Bureau of the Census, "Characteristics of the Population Below the Poverty Level: 1983," *Current Population Reports*, series P-60, no. 147 (Washington, DC: U.S. Government Printing Office, 1985), table A-2.

Nevertheless, as postwar incomes rose, people purchased privacy in abundance. The move to the suburbs, the move of northern retired persons to Florida, and the increasing numbers of young singles in cities were all part of the breakup of the extended family. By 1970 the extent of doubling up had declined substantially:

- The proportion of families living in other persons' households had declined from one in fourteen (in 1950) to one in forty.

- Among unmarried adults, the proportion who lived alone had risen from three in ten (in 1950) to six in ten.

- The number of persons aged 65 and over increased from 13 million to 20 million, but the number of elderly parents who lived in their children's households declined from 2.8 million to 2.3 million.[7]

Through the late 1960s this drive for privacy stopped at the edge of the nuclear family.[8] The same rising incomes that undermined the extended family permitted young men and women to marry at earlier ages and, once married, to have large numbers of children. This was the baby boom, and in historical context it came as a great surprise. Since the beginning of the nineteenth century, birthrates had been falling steadily. In 1800 there were approximately 280 births per year for every 1,000 women aged 15 to 44, or about 7 to 8 children for the average mother over her lifetime. For more than a century the birthrate fell steadily, reaching 103 in the mid 1920s (Figure 8.1). It fell still further to 76–78 during the 1930s; this was due in part to the Great Depression's low incomes, and some small postwar increase was expected. In fact, the postwar increase was enormous. The birthrate climbed to 107 in 1950 and 123 in 1957, as high as it had been in the early 1900s.[9]

As demographer Andrew Cherlin writes, these high birthrates did not reflect many 5- and 6-children families but rather a growing number of women who had 2 or 3 children rather than 1.[10] Many of

---

[7] Lampman and Smeeding, "Interfamily Transfers."

[8] Eugene Smolensky reminds me that this is not quite correct. The drive for privacy within the nuclear family took the form of increasingly large homes. Smolensky suggests (and I agree) that the development of multiple-bathroom homes has substantially reduced the level of violent conflict between the hours of 7:00 A.M. and 9:00 A.M.

[9] See, for example, U.S. Bureau of the Census, *Historical Statistics of the United States: Colonial Times to 1970* (Washington, DC: U.S. Government Printing Office, 1975), series B5-10.

[10] See Andrew J. Cherlin, *Marriage, Divorce, Remarriage* (Cambridge, MA: Harvard University Press, 1981), chap. 1.

FIGURE 8.1

The United States Birthrate, 1900–1984

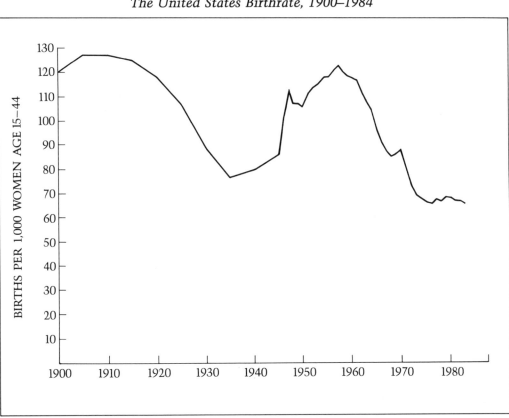

SOURCES: U.S. Bureau of the Census, *Historical Statistics of the United States;* and *Statistical Abstract of the United States,* various years.

these women had been raised in the Great Depression and began their families in the mid-1940s, at a time of rapidly expanding opportunity (Chapter 4).

These opposing trends—the shrinking extended family and the growing nuclear family—appear in Figure 8.2. During the 1950s and mid-1960s average *household* size fell steadily but average *family* size continued to grow. The missing link was the increasing number of single persons of all ages who moved out of families to form households of their own.

There was one exception to the flourishing nuclear family—the continuing increase in black families headed by women. Over the

FIGURE 8.2

Average Household Size and Average Family Size, 1947–1984

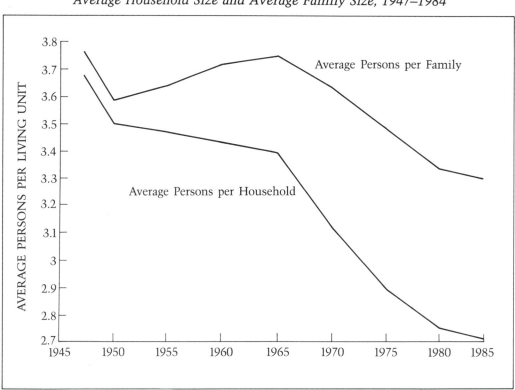

SOURCES: U.S. Bureau of the Census, *Current Population Reports*, series P-20 and P-60, various numbers.

1950s the proportion of black families headed by women increased from 15 to 22 percent (Chapter 6).

The baby boom continued through the early 1960s and then abruptly ended. The birthrate declined from 123 in 1957 to 109 in 1963 and then fell to 88 in 1967 (Figure 8.1). Young men and women continued to marry early, but they postponed and reduced the numbers of children. Some of this drop was predictable. If birthrates of the 1930s had been below long-run trends, the birthrates of the 1950s had been far above trend and some decline was natural. But the speed of the decline was surprising, particularly since the economy in the late 1960s was so good.

Rapid falls in the birthrate are historically associated with bad times (like the Great Depression) when money is tight. In the late

1960s this pattern changed. The strong economy expanded women's options. While women's earnings were not improving vis-à-vis men's, they were rapidly growing in absolute terms, and we can assume that declining birthrates, at least in part, reflected women's increased opportunities.[11]

After 1973 women's career interests and the bad economy reinforced one another. Women's labor force participation continued to increase while birthrates continued to decline. And now the baby boomers who were coming of age began to postpone marriage as well. Between 1973 and 1984 the average age of first marriage for both men and women each rose by two years (to 25.4 and 23.0 years, respectively) and were the highest they had been since about 1900. Now household size continued to shrink because the nuclear family was shrinking. Families were having fewer children and people were staying single longer before they formed families.

Changed aspirations and the stagnant economy were not the only causes of these trends. The sexual revolution was clearly important and baby boomers may have also taken caution from the increasing divorce rates among their parents. But whatever the causes, the economic effects were clear. Consumption *per capita* among younger families could continue to rise despite the bad economy, because there were more workers and fewer children in each family.

Relevant census data combines families between ages 25 and 44, but these data are still sufficient to illustrate the point. Recall that between 1973 and 1984 the median income of both 30- and 40-year-old *men* declined significantly (Table 5.1); but because of increased earnings of wives, the average income of husband-wife *families* aged 25 to 44 only fell from $32,800 to $31,400. And because of the postponement and reduction in the number of children, average family size dropped from 4.12 to 3.56. Together these factors permitted income *per capita* in these families to grow by 11 percent.[12]

High consumption led to false impressions. By the early 1980s the popular press had developed a fascination with Yuppies: young,

---

[11] See William P. Butz and Michael P. Ward, "The Emergence of Countercyclical U.S. Fertility," *American Economic Review*, 69 (June 1979):318–28.

[12] These calculations are based on data from U.S. Bureau of the Census, "Money Income in 1973 of Families and Persons in the United States," *Current Population Reports*, series P-60, no. 97 (Washington, DC: U.S. Government Printing Office, 1975); U.S. Bureau of the Census, "Money Income of Households, Families, and Persons in the United States: 1984," *Current Population Reports*, series P-60, no. 151 (Washington, DC: U.S. Government Printing Office, 1986).

two-income professional families who consumed conspicuously and who were taken as a symbol of the baby boom's success. In marketing terms the emphasis was sensible. Because of the baby boom's size, the number of high-income young families had grown substantially (just as numbers of every kind of young family had grown substantially). There were, in addition, the new young singles who could buy balsamic vinegar, despite low earnings, because they didn't have a family to support. But as a symbol, Yuppies were misleading. The proportion of young married couples with combined income over $35,000 was no different in 1984 than it had been in 1973 (adjusted for inflation), and in 1973 more of the couples had achieved this income on one paycheck.[13]

By coincidence or design, aspiring middle-class families were adjusting to tighter circumstances, which sharpened the contrast with families headed by women. Recall from Chapter 6 that despite the 1960s economic boom the proportion of black families headed by women grew from 22 percent in 1960 to 31 percent in 1970. In the bad economy of the 1970s this proportion continued to increase, so that by 1984, 43 percent of all black families were headed by a woman. The proportion of white families headed by a woman rose as well from 9 percent in 1964 to 13 percent in 1984.

Among black families this trend had a second dimension. In earlier decades female-headed families were the product of desertion or divorce. By the early 1980s an increasing number of female-headed families were headed by women who had never married and who had often had their first child as a teenager. During this time the birthrate among black unmarried teenagers actually *fell* but this was offset by the fact that fewer black teenagers were getting married. In 1984 half of all black families under age 35 were headed by a woman, and of these women, three quarters had never been married.[14] These were not all "underclass" families in a strict sense but most were at an enormous disadvantage (Chapter 9).

Viewed in terms of children (of all races) rather than families,

---

[13] The paradigm treatment of the Yuppie was the December 31, 1985, cover story in *Newsweek*, which proclaimed 1986 "the Year of the Yuppie." For a different view, see Frank Levy and Richard C. Michel, "Are Baby Boomers Selfish?" *American Demographics*, April 1985, pp. 38–41. The calculations in the paragraph are from the sources cited in footnote 12.

[14] See U.S. Bureau of the Census, "Household and Family Characteristics: March 1984," *Current Population Reports*, series P-20, no. 398 (Washington, DC: U.S. Government Printing Office, 1986).

the shift toward female-headed families was steeper. While the number of female-headed families was increasing, two-parent families were lowering their childbearing rate and so the proportion of children in female-headed families grew sharply. In 1970, 10 percent of all children were in female-headed families. By 1984, 21 percent of all children and 54 percent of black children were in families headed by a woman.[15]

Family Arrangements and Inequality

Table 8.1 summarizes postwar changes in households and families. When all persons are considered, regardless of race, only moderate changes have occurred. Among all households, the importance of unrelated individuals has grown. Particularly among younger persons, more husband-wife families have two earners. But husband-wife families under age 65 are still dominant, accounting for 80 percent of all families in 1950 and 70 percent in 1984. Families with a head aged 65 or over gradually grew in importance while families headed by a single woman grew more quickly. When household statistics are separated by race the increase in black families headed by women emerges clearly (Table 8.2). Potentially, we might have expected another change among families: a growing proportion of younger husband-wife families (the baby boomers). But because of the sharp rise in age of first marriage the relative importance of young families did not increase.

How did these changes affect family income inequality? At first glance the answer requires an elaborate controlled experiment in which everything but family structure is held constant. The question is not really this complex. In Chapter 5 we saw that the earnings distribution of full-time male workers (including most husbands) remained remarkably stable through 1979 and only then split along age lines. Chapter 6 showed that central city incomes slid down in the distribution, but much of this slide reflected increasing numbers of families headed by women. In Chapter 7 we saw the growing polarization of individual incomes of black men, but the low incomes of many black men correspond to black families headed by women. It follows that the most important factors affecting family income in-

---

[15] U.S. Bureau of the Census, "Household and Family Characteristics."

TABLE 8.1

Characteristics of Families and Unrelated Individuals, 1949 and 1984

During the postwar period the major changes in family structure involved a growing number of persons who lived outside families and, within families, a growing reliance on working wives. The proportions of families headed by someone aged 65 or over or a woman under age 65 grew moderately. Because baby boomers postponed marriage, baby boom families did not come to dominate family structure.

Age	1949	1984
Total Number of Families	39,929,000	62,706,000
Head Aged 65 or Over (Male or Female)	12%	16%
Husband-Wife Family Aged 35–64		
Wife Works	12	26
Wife Does not Work	41	21
Husband-Wife Family Aged 34 or Under		
Wife Works	6	14
Wife Does not Work	19	9
Female Head Aged 64 or Under	10	14
Total	100%	100%
Total Number of Unrelated Individuals	8,995,000	30,268,000
Persons Aged 65 or Over	23%	30%
Males		
Aged 35–64	21	14
Aged 34 or Under	21	23
Females		
Aged 35–64	22	16
Aged 34 or Under	13	17
Total	100%	100%

SOURCES: U.S. Bureau of Census, *Current Population Reports*, series P-60, no. 151; and author's tabulations of the 1950 Census Public Use Microdata Samples.

equality have ultimately worked through family arrangements, and so it is reasonable to directly assess the impact of family arrangements on inequality.

The numbers in Table 8.1 make clear that if family arrangements did affect income inequality, they did so in three ways:

- The effects of relatively more two-earner couples

- The effects of relatively more families headed by someone aged 65 or over

TABLE 8.2

Characteristics of Families and Individuals by Race, 1984

When families are divided by race, sharper demographic trends emerge. In 1984 families headed by a woman under age 65 accounted for 14 percent of all families, but they accounted for 39 percent of black families. (Families headed by a woman of any age accounted for 43 percent of all black families.)

Age	White	Black	All Races
Total Number of Families (thousands)	54,400	6,778	62,706
Head Aged 65 or Over (male or female)	16%	13%	16%
Husband-Wife Family Aged 35–64			
Wife Works	27	20	26
Wife Does not Work	22	12	21
Husband-Wife Family Aged 34 or Under			
Wife Works	15	11	14
Wife Does not Work	9	5	9
Female Head Aged 64 or Under	11	39	14
Total	100%	100%	100%
Total Number of Unrelated Individuals (thousands)	26,094	3,501	30,268
Persons Aged 65 or Over	31%	23%	29%
Male			
Aged 35–64	15	22	16
Aged 34 or Under	23	22	23
Females			
Aged 35–64	15	19	16
Aged 34 or Under	17	14	16
Total	100%	100%	100%

NOTE: "Husband without working wife" includes about 2% of all families with a male head and no wife.

SOURCES: U.S. Bureau of the Census, *Current Population Reports*, series P-60, no. 151; series P-20, no. 299.

- The effects of more families headed by women

We discuss each effect in turn.

Two-earner couples have been a topic of some confusion. In the early 1980s popular articles focused on "supercouples" (a subspecies of Yuppies). Both husbands and wives in these couples had high-paying careers, and the resulting high family incomes were supposed to pull the income distribution apart. But in reality, two-earner couples come from a far wider range of situations. Many working wives do not have high-paying jobs, and some wives work not out of career interests but to help support low family incomes.

Both situations—two-career couples and economic necessity— are apparent in the data. *Among wives who work*, higher-earning wives are married to higher-earning husbands. If all else were equal, this correlation would increase family income inequality. But other things are not equal because the range of wives' earnings is smaller than the range of husbands' earnings and because women married to men with high earnings are less likely to work.

The net result is an increase in equality, as the following example shows. Begin by considering women married to men who earned over $35,000 per year in 1984. Among these women, 58 percent worked and those who worked averaged $12,600 per year. Thus, the "average" woman in this group (including nonworkers) earned $7,300, or about 15 percent of her husband's earnings. Next consider women married to men who earned $7,000–$15,000 per year. Among these women, a higher 68 percent worked but these working women averaged $8,500 per year. The "average" woman in this group (including nonworkers) earned $5,100, an amount equivalent to about 40 percent of her husband's earnings. In this way, women's earnings had greater relative impacts in lower-income families, and so they tended to reduce family income inequality (Figure 8.3).

What about female-headed families and the elderly? Other things being equal, the growing number of female-headed families should have increased income inequality. In Chapter 7 we saw that only half of all black women heading families worked (the proportion for white women was comparable), and so more female-headed families mean more families without earnings. Even those women who worked full time earned about 40 percent less than men (Figure 7.5). Moreover, as wages stagnated during the 1970s, an increasing proportion of husband-wife families came to rely on two earners, an option female-headed families did not have. For all of these reasons, more families headed by women should have meant greater income inequality.

Men and women aged 65 and over also have relatively low earnings and, unlike female household heads, their labor force participation has been declining over time. Chapter 3 showed that in 1947 one half of all men aged 65 and over still worked. But the practice of retirement grew steadily, and by the early 1980s labor force participation among men aged 65 and over fell to less than 20 percent. Over

FIGURE 8.3

Wives' Average Earnings as a Percentage of Husbands' Earnings, 1984
(data arranged by husbands' earnings)

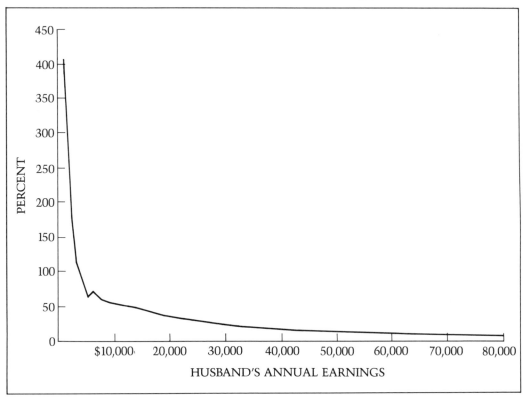

SOURCE: U.S. Department of the Census, "Money Income of Households, Families and Persons in the United States: 1984," *Current Population Reports*, series P-60, no. 151 table 22.

the same period labor force participation among men aged 55 to 65 also fell from 90 to 70 percent. This also should have increased the number of families without earnings, and so should have increased income inequality.

Has income inequality actually grown since World War II? To explain what happened, we look at three measures:

(a) the inequality of *earned* income across all families (includ-ing families with no earnings)

(b) the inequality of earned income across families who have at least a dollar of earned income

(c)   the inequality of total income (including unearned income) across all families

The first measure is self-explanatory, and we will shortly see that inequality of *earned* income across families has increased substantially over the postwar period. But this growing inequality of earned income can come from two quite different sources. One is through the growing number of families headed by women and retired families who have no earnings at all.[16] The other source is through growing inequality among families who do have earnings: the female head who works part time, the two-earner couple, and so on. A comparison of (a) and (b) will help separate these factors. Note, however, that demographics are not the only influence on (b). Since World War II the proportion of all families working in low-wage agriculture has declined significantly. This should have worked to substantially decrease earnings inequality (among families with earnings), but changing demographics may have offset this effect.

Measure (c) is an old friend, the Gini coefficient for the census-defined family income distribution (Table 2.1). We already know what it says—that family income inequality has not changed very much since World War II—but we include it here to make an important point. While the inequality of *earned* income has grown, it is possible for other kinds of income—including Social Security, private pensions, and welfare—to increase in ways that leave the inequality of *total* income (earned and unearned) relatively constant.[17] A comparison of (a) and (c) shows the extent to which this was happening.

The statistics contained in Table 8.3 tell an uncommonly clear story:

- Among families with at least some earned income, inequality of earned income has declined slightly. This means that the movement of families out of low-wage agriculture has more than offset the declining position of baby boom families, more female-headed families, and other demographic factors (b).

- The proportion of families with no one working rose from 5.4 percent in 1947 to 15.1 percent in 1984, a reflection of in-

[16] Earnings here refer to wages, salaries, and income from self-employment. They do not include Social Security benefits, private pension payments, interest, or dividends even though it is fair to say such payments are "earned."

[17] Rather than compensation for unequal earnings, these payments may have helped to create unequal earnings by encouraging people to retire earlier, and so on. We explore this issue below.

TABLE 8.3

Three Measures of Family Income Inequality, 1949 and 1984

During the postwar period the distribution of earnings across all families became substantially less equal, a reflection of the growing number of families
with no one in the labor force. Despite this, the distribution of total income
across all families remained relatively constant because other income sources—
largely government benefits—took up the slack.

	1949	1984
Proportion of all Families with no one in the Labor Force	5.4%	15.1%
Gini Coefficient of the Distribution of Earnings Across *all* Families (a)	.415	.460
Gini Coefficient of the Distribution of Earnings Across Families with at least a Dollar of Earnings (b)	.383	.360
Gini Coefficient of the Income Distribution Across all Families (Including Earnings and all other Money Income) (c)	.378	.385

NOTE: Earnings refer to income from wages, salaries, and self-employment. Measures "a"
and "c" include some families with no earnings. Measures "a" and "b" are calculated by
the author using grouped data.

SOURCES: U.S. Bureau of the Census, *Current Population Reports*, series P-60, nos. 7
and 151; and calculations by the author.

creasing rates of retirement and the increasing number of
families headed by women.

- Because more families have *no* earner, inequality of earned
  income across *all* families has increased sharply (a).

- Despite the growing inequality of *earned* income across all
  families, the inequality of *total* income across all families has
  remained relatively constant, indicating that unearned income has taken up much of the difference (c).

*In sum, family income inequality remained roughly constant
over the postwar period, even though a declining number of families
had earnings, because other income sources grew enough to take up
the slack.*[18]

[18] Lester Thurow and Joseph Pechman also conclude that earnings have become less
equally distributed across all families and that growing welfare state benefits have helped
keep this in check. Both have also conjectured in conversation that earnings have become
less equal across families with positive earnings and that does not seem to be the case.
See Lester C. Thurow, *The Zero-Sum Society* (New York: Basic Books, 1980); and Joseph
A. Pechman, *Who Paid the Taxes, 1966–85* (Washington, DC: Brookings Institution,
1985).

Critiques of the Welfare State

What is this "other income"? As counted by the census, something over one half of it now comes from government benefits (Table 8.4). Recall from Chapter 3 that in 1947 government payments made up perhaps 3 percent of all census-reported family income. By 1984 it made up over 8 percent. In the National Income Accounts (which include both money income and nonmoney income like food stamps and Medicare), government payments to individuals rose from 5.4 percent to 12 percent of all gross national product (Figure 8.4) and these payments rose from 21 percent to 33 percent of all government spending.[19]

We have just seen how these payments compensated for the growing inequality of earnings. Why didn't the payments do more? How could government payments more than double as a percent of GNP without reducing family income inequality or without increasing the constant 4.5–5.5 percent of all family income received by the poorest one fifth of families (Table 2.1)?

TABLE 8.4
Sources of Family Money Income, 1984

In census tabulations, government payments account for about one half of all income other than earnings. When we consider income not counted by the census—food stamps, Medicare, Medicaid—the proportion grows.

Source	Percentage
Wages, Salaries, and Income from Self-Employment	81%
Other Income	
Interest, Dividends, and Income from Property	6
Social Security, Railroad Retirement, and Other Social Insurance	6
Aid to Families with Dependent Children, General Assistance, and Supplemental Security Income	1
All Other Income, Including Pensions for Government Workers, Private Pensions and Annuities, Alimony, Child Support, etc.	6
	100%

SOURCE: U.S. Bureau of the Census, *Current Population Reports*, series P-60, no. 151, table 20.

[19] See the sources cited in footnote 2, this chapter.

FIGURE 8.4

Government Payments to Individuals as a Percentage of GNP, 1949–1984

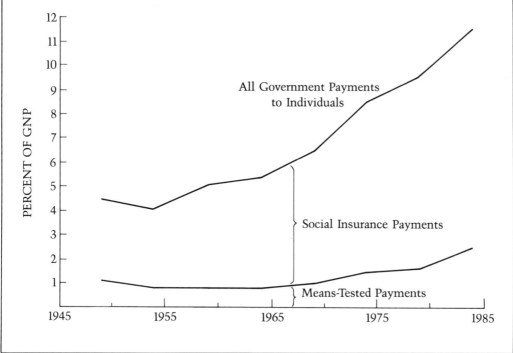

SOURCES: U.S. Department of Commerce, Bureau of Economic Analysis, *National Income and Product Accounts of the United States*, various years. Data include nonmoney benefits like Medicare.

The question has several answers, and the first one involves definitions. The census income definition, which counts only pretax
money payments, understates redistribution by not subtracting taxes
at the top of the distribution and not adding nonmoney benefits at
the bottom. In Chapter 9 we correct for these problems (as well as
employee fringe benefits) and find that postwar income equality has
improved marginally.

The second answer involves the nature of the welfare state itself. As we have seen, one fifth of all government benefits are means-
tested programs aimed specifically at the poor. The rest are social
insurance programs—Social Security, unemployment insurance, government workers' pensions, veterans' benefits, Medicare—paid to
persons who have established eligibility through prior contributions.

167

While many recipients of social insurance have low incomes, many others do not, and there is no sense in which these benefits are focused on the poorest one fifth of families.[20]

The third and most important answer is that growing benefits did not just go to the same people: Growing benefits went to a growing number of people. Increased expenditures were part and parcel of the growing number of families without a working member. We have called this picking up the slack, but presumably some of the "slack" was created by the programs themselves. We know that without Social Security many older workers would have kept working longer and we can speculate that without means-tested programs fewer female-headed families would have formed.

It is a short leap from this speculation to an attack on the welfare state, an attack that takes two forms:

- The simplest criticism is that the welfare state costs too much. Between 1970 and 1984 alone, government payments to individuals (including Medicare, and so on) have risen from 8.5 percent to 12.0 percent of gross national product. Researcher Phillip Longman argues that most of this increase represents too-generous benefits for the elderly, which must be financed largely by struggling baby boomers. Journalist Maxwell Newton argues more simply that we have become "Handout America."[21]

- A second criticism made by Nathan Glazer, Charles Murray, and others is that means-tested programs in particular are self-defeating. By providing assistance to the poor, we are creating incentives to become poor and so are not reducing inequality.[22]

In sum, government programs may have kept income inequality from growing, but at great cost to society and, in some cases, to the beneficiaries themselves.

[20] Economist Daniel Weinberg calculates that in 1979, 64 percent of Social Security and Medicare went to persons who, without these payments, would have had incomes below the poverty line. Daniel H. Weinberg, "Filling the 'Poverty Gap': Multiple Transfer Program Participation," *Journal of Human Resources* 20, no. 1 (Winter 1985): 64–89.

[21] On the poor position of children, see Samuel H. Preston, "Children and the Elderly: Divergent Paths for America's Dependents," *Demography* 21, no. 4 (November 1984):435–57. On one estimate of the burden this implies for baby boom workers, see Phillip Longman, "Justice Between Generations," *Atlantic*, June 1985, pp. 73–81. Maxwell Newton is the chief financial columnist for the *New York Post*.

[22] See Glazer, "The Limits of Social Policy"; and Murray, *Losing Ground*.

To make sense of these critiques, we need some historical perspective because important aspects of today's welfare state are not the intended result of policy. They are the result of a collision between policies predicated on economic growth and an economy that suddenly went stagnant. We can see this by briefly recounting the development of two major benefit programs: Aid to Families with Dependent Children and Social Security.

Aid to Families with Dependent Children Through 1973

When people talk about welfare, they usually mean Aid to Families with Dependent Children (AFDC), the main source of cash assistance for low-income, female-headed families. AFDC and Social Security had quite different purposes, but both were part of the Social Security Act of 1935. AFDC was a federal attempt to aid states' widows and orphans programs. Initial plans had included a minimum national benefit, but southern legislators were concerned that too high a benefit could disrupt the South's wage structure. Proposals for a national minimum benefit were defeated, and benefit levels and other aspects of the program were left to each state individually, with the federal government sharing in program costs.

The legislative record indicates Congress' expectation that the AFDC program would wither away as the economy improved and such programs as Social Security (which included survivors' benefits for widows) became established.[23] In fact, AFDC did not wither away but rather grew at a moderate rate. In 1940 it paid benefits to 372,000 families, about one family in 83 families with children. By 1960 it was paying benefits to 803,000 families, one family in 38.[24]

A look at census statistics suggests that the growth could have been much larger. While the 1960 AFDC caseload stood at 803,000, there were 4.6 million female-headed families (of all ages), half of whom had incomes below $10,400 (in 1984 dollars). A good guess is that many of these families were technically eligible for AFDC ben-

---

[23] For a brief history of the early AFDC program and subsequent reform attempts see, Vincent J. and Vee Burke, *Nixon's Good Deed* (New York: Columbia University Press, 1974).

[24] U.S. Bureau of the Census, *Historical Statistics of the United States: Colonial Times to 1970*, series A 292 and H 358 (Washington, DC: U.S. Government Printing Office, 1975).

efits but their own attitudes, the stigma of welfare, and restrictive administration were keeping them from applying.[25]

In the early 1960s the United States rediscovered poverty. The discovery built on both the civil rights movement and such events as Edward R. Murrow's television documentary on migrant labor, "The Harvest of Shame" (1960), and Michael Harrington's *The Other America* (1962). Equally important was an economic optimism which suggested that poverty was a residual, manageable problem.

The optimism was appropriate. As the federal government developed antipoverty policies, a first step was to define a poverty-level living standard. The work was directed by Mollie Orshansky, an economist with the Social Security Administration, who settled on a 1963 poverty line of $3,200 for a family of four (or $10,178 in 1984), with comparable incomes for other family sizes.[26] When this standard was projected backward (with adjustments for inflation), it showed that the proportion of the population in poverty had declined from 32 percent in 1949 to 22 percent in 1960, through a process sketched in Figure 8.5. As shown in the figure, the poverty standard was adjusted for inflation and so was constant in real dollars.[27] In the late 1940s real incomes were still low enough that the standard fell in the second quintile of the family income distribution. As real incomes grew, the income distribution shifted to higher levels, and by 1960 only the lowest quintile remained below the poverty line.[28] If real incomes could keep growing in this way, the proportion of families with below-poverty incomes would continue to shrink automatically and government policies could help those persons whom the economy bypassed. Lyndon Johnson's War on Poverty was an

[25] Income statistics come from 1960 census. The figure includes female-headed families without children who would be ineligible for AFDC.

[26] For a detailed description of the poverty line, see U.S. Department of Health, Education, and Welfare, *The Measure of Poverty: A Report to Congress as Mandated by the Education Amendments of 1974* (Washington, DC: U.S. Government Printing Office, April 1976).

[27] That is, the poverty line was adjusted each year only for inflation as measured by the Consumer Price Index. This meant that if real incomes rose enough, the poverty rate would fall close to zero. Economist Victor Fuchs, among others, has argued that poverty should be defined on a *relative* rather than an absolute basis at perhaps one half of median family income in each year.

[28] This description oversimplifies in two ways. First, it ignores the way in which the official poverty standard is different for different family sizes. Thus, some two-person families in the lowest quintile were not poor while some five- and six-person families in the second quintile were poor. Second, it ignores the companion calculation that had to be made for unrelated individuals. (The poverty line for an unrelated individual living alone was $1,555 in 1963, or $5,282 in 1984 dollars.)

FIGURE 8.5

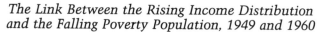

*The Link Between the Rising Income Distribution
and the Falling Poverty Population, 1949 and 1960*

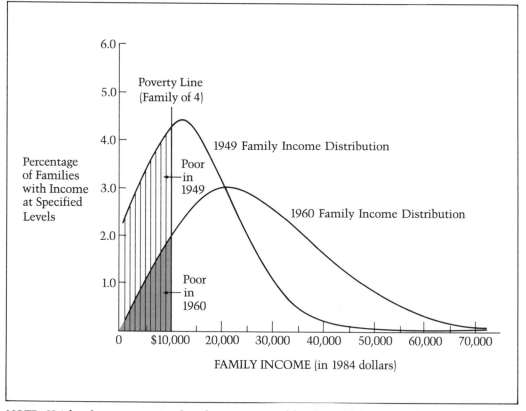

NOTE: Height of curve at a point describes proportion of families with income within a $1,000 interval of the point.

SOURCES: Income distribution statistics taken from U.S. Bureau of the Census, *Current Population Reports*, series P-60, various numbers.

attempt to establish these policies: expanded manpower training, the funding of community action programs, compensatory education programs for disadvantaged children, and so on.[29]

How did AFDC fit into these efforts? In a highly ambivalent way. A war on poverty meant a war for self-sufficiency and in this sense administrators still hoped that the AFDC rolls would wither

---

[29] For a good sense of policy-makers' perceptions of poverty in this period, see Daniel P. Moynihan, ed., *On Understanding Poverty: Perspectives from the Social Sciences* (New York: Basic Books, 1969); and James L. Sundquist, ed., *On Fighting Poverty: Perspectives from Experience* (New York: Basic Books, 1969).

away. But a war on poverty also meant raising people's incomes and in this AFDC might help.

AFDC policy reflected this ambivalence. During the 1960s the federal government instructed states to initiate several AFDC changes to help states move families off the rolls. The first was an intensive, federally funded program of social services and counseling advanced by former Senator Abraham Ribicoff, President Kennedy's Secretary of Health, Education, and Welfare. The AFDC rolls continued to grow, however, and in 1967 Congress tried to increase recipients' work incentives by establishing the "$30 + 1/3" rule. This rule permitted recipients to keep part of any money they earned rather than have it deducted, dollar for dollar, from their benefits.[30] In 1968 Congress passed "separation" legislation which required states to take the jobs of determining eligibility and calculating budgets away from social workers and give them to eligibility technicians would handle only these tasks. The separation was supposed to keep overly sympathetic social workers from further expanding the rolls.[31]

Simultaneously, other policies made AFDC more attractive. Throughout the 1960s many states raised AFDC benefits. In 1965 Congress passed the Medicaid program, medical insurance for low-income persons. Like AFDC, Medicaid was a joint federal-state program with substantial state control. In many states Medicaid benefits could be received only by AFDC recipients (and a few other groups),[32] which further increased AFDC's attractiveness. After the first big city riots many states reduced administrative barriers for applicants. Some tried a "declaration" AFDC application, which reduced the need for applicants to complete lengthy forms and produce

---

[30] Though it was not recognized at the time, the "$30 + 1/3" rule had ambiguous effects. By allowing recipients to keep part of their earnings, it gave them an incentive to work. But a by-product of these incentives was to bring AFDC eligibility "within reach" of persons who had low levels of earnings and who had previously been off the rolls. In practice, such persons appear to have been drawn onto the rolls in sufficient numbers to offset the work incentive's purpose. See Frank Levy, "The Labor Supply of Female Household Heads, or AFDC Work Incentives Don't Work Too Well," *Journal of Human Resources* 14, no. 1 (winter 1979):76–97.

[31] For a good discussion of these policies, see Burke and Burke, *Nixon's Good Deed.*

[32] All states also extended Medicaid benefits to recipients of what is now known as Supplemental Security Income (SSI). SSI was formally created in 1971 and represented a substantially increased federal role in state income programs for the indigent aged, the blind, and the disabled. In addition, some states extended Medicaid benefits to the "medically indigent"—families who received neither AFDC nor SSI but whose income, less medical expenses, fell below eligibility level. Today about half of all Medicaid expenditures cover the low-income elderly persons in nursing homes.

documentation.[33] In 1971 Richard Nixon and Congress took the experimental concept of food stamps and expanded it to a full national program. Food stamps were available to all low-income persons—not just AFDC recipients—but it further increased the income that came with AFDC.

The temper of the times was as important as policy liberalizations. The booming economy and government rhetoric had significantly raised expectations that poverty would soon be eliminated. At the same time, the Vietnam war and the civil rights revolution had made antigovernment protest commonplace, so that the big city riots were often discussed in political terms. Together, these forces helped transform AFDC from a program of emergency assistance. It became, depending on one's view, a kind of government patronage or an entitlement that all eligible families should receive (even if they could somehow make do without it). The political scientists Richard A. Cloward and Frances Fox Piven (1971) give a sense of this outlook:

> That a demand for information about welfare entitlements had been created is not difficult to show. The Southern California chapter of the ACLU prepared a manual in the summer of 1968, and within a short time, 8,000 copies were sold to many different local organizations which had contact with the poor. Requests for more than one thousand copies were also received from public and private agencies elsewhere in the country. Indeed, even relief officials showed interest for "state welfare departments as far away as South Carolina ordered [sample] copies." After 1964, in other words, there was truly an information explosion, and that had much to do with the explosion of applications for welfare which followed. [p. 302]

The increase in AFDC cases was dramatic and went far beyond the urban ghettos. The AFDC caseload grew from 803,000 families in 1960 to 1.3 million in 1967 and 3.2 million by 1973, with white families composing half of the increase. In 1973 AFDC was received by one white child in fifteen and two black children in five nationwide.[34]

---

[33] For a realistic picture of one big city welfare system during this time, see the Harvard Business School teaching case, *Public Assistance (B)*, case 9-373-239 (Boston: Intercollegiate Case Clearing House, 1973).

[34] U.S. Bureau of the Census, *Statistical Abstract of the United States: 1978* (Washington, DC: U.S. Government Printing Office, 1978), table 562.

Even officials favoring expanded benefits had not expected anything like this, and they spent substantial effort searching for explanations. One theory held that AFDC itself was causing the problem because it was largely restricted to female-headed families.[35] According to this theory, an unemployed father might desert his wife and children so that they could apply for benefits. The theory implied that an extension of AFDC to two-parent families might reverse the process.

We have seen that the theory was far too optimistic. AFDC did not transform husband-wife families into families headed by women: Significant numbers of low-income, female-headed families both black and white, were there all along. What was changing was the willingness of these families to sign up for AFDC benefits and the willingness of state programs to accept them.[36] (See Figure 8.6.) When large numbers of families came on the case rolls, they also came to public attention and that is what made the theory plausible.

Extending benefits to two-parent families would not have helped this situation appreciably, but restricting eligibility would not have done much more, particularly among blacks. In 1969, at the height of the economic boom, AFDC benefits across the nation averaged $7,704 in 1984 dollars. This was about three quarters of the poverty standard for a family of four. Yet in that year 46 percent of black men aged 20 to 24 and 17 percent of black men aged 25 to 34 reported earning a lesser amount. (See Chapter 7.) Even allowing for the presence of the underground economy, these figures suggest a shortage of black male breadwinners.[37]

If AFDC did not create female-headed families in the late 1960s it helped to perpetuate such families during the 1970s. The effect was clearest among blacks in depressed big city neighborhoods

---

[35] In 1960 Congress had permitted states to offer AFDC-"UP", a program which extended AFDC benefits to two-parent families. But the program was adopted by only half of the states, and it contained a number of eligibility restrictions which caused caseloads to be about one tenth the size of AFDC.

[36] Barbara Boland, "Participation in the Aid to Families with Dependent Children Program (AFDC)," in U.S. Congress, Joint Economic Committee, *The Family, Poverty and Welfare Programs: Factors Influencing Family Instability,* Studies in Public Welfare Paper no. 12 (part 1) (Washington, DC: U.S. Government Printing Office, 1973).

[37] See Frank Levy and Richard C. Michel, "Work for Welfare: How Much Good Will It Do?" *American Economic Review* 76 (May 1986): 399–404; and William Julius Wilson and Katherine M. Neckerman, "Poverty and Family Structure: The Widening Gap Between Evidence and Public Policy Issues," paper presented at the Institute for Research on Poverty Conference on Poverty and Policy: Retrospect and Prospects, Williamsburg, Virginia, December 6–9, 1984.

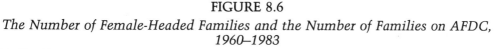

FIGURE 8.6

*The Number of Female-Headed Families and the Number of Families on AFDC,
1960–1983*

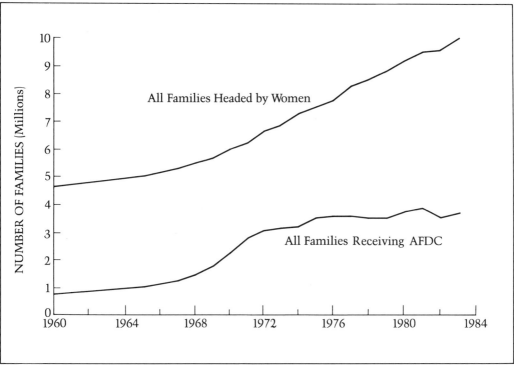

SOURCES: U.S. Bureau of the Census, *Current Population Reports*, series P-60, various numbers; and
Statistical Abstract of the United States, various years.

where AFDC served as the third leg of a three-legged stool—jobless
men, families headed by women, and income from welfare—in
which life was increasingly cut off from the larger economy. But the
number of black families receiving welfare was far larger than this
special group. Census statistics on this point contain some problems
but in 1973 a good guess at the number of black families with children would have been 4.0 million, including:

- 2.1 million husband-wife families

- .3 million female-headed families who were not receiving
  AFDC

- 1.6 million female-headed families who were receiving
  AFDC.

In the same year, there were about 27 million white families with children, including:

- 23.7 million husband-wife families

- 2.0 million female-headed families who were not receiving AFDC

- 1.6 million female-headed families who were receiving AFDC.[38]

From the perspective of AFDC, black and white families were of equal numerical importance. But in relative terms welfare receipt was far more important among blacks and the near term prospects of these families were not good. Sociologist Mary Jo Bane and economist David Ellwood estimate that during the 1970s the average black family entering AFDC would stay on the rolls 5.3 years.[39]

Social Security Through 1973

As a social insurance program, Social Security differed fundamentally from the means-tested AFDC. AFDC was funded by general tax revenues and was restricted to low-income families (primarily headed by women). Social Security was funded by worker and employer contributions, and a recipient could understandably feel that he or she was merely collecting what they had already paid for. If the two funding concepts became blurred, it was because of Social Security's financing.

When in 1935 Congress created Social Security, it had two fi-

---

[38] These estimates (which include subfamilies) were obtained through discussions with Patricia Ruggles of the Urban Institute, formerly with the Congressional Budget Office. Ruggles emphasizes the difficulty in meshing data from various sources—in particular, the annual Current Population Survey and the biannual Department of Health and Human Services Survey of AFDC Recipients' Characteristics.

[39] See Mary Jo Bane and David Ellwood, "The Dynamics of Dependence: The Routes to Self-Sufficiency," report prepared for the Department of Health and Human Services by Urban Systems Research and Engineering, 1983, table 10. Estimating an individual's duration on AFDC or in poverty is particularly sensitive to the way in which the question is posed. The 5.3 year figure refers to all persons who *begin* to receive AFDC at a particular point in time. This group includes people with temporary problems who get off the rolls quickly and people with serious problems who are on the rolls for a long time. It follows that if we look at a second group—all persons who *receive* AFDC at a point in time (including those whose cases started earlier)—this group will be more dominated by families with serious problems. Bane and Ellwood estimate the average duration on welfare for this group to be 10.2 years.

nancing options. One involved establishing a savings program in which people deposited money in interest-bearing accounts and retired on the money they had accumulated. The other was a pay-as-you-go program in which today's beneficiaries are paid directly by today's workers. Congress chose the latter option. The choice in part was motivated by the nature of the Great Depression: High unemployment reflected the fact that people had little money to spend, and it seemed a poor time to build up a large reserve of savings which had to be invested in a slack economy.[40]

The economics of a pay-as-you-go system can be summarized in three equations:

1. Real Revenues = (Number of Covered Workers) × (Real Wages per Worker) × (Social Security Tax Rate)
2. Real Expenditures = (Number of Recipients) × (Real Benefits per Recipient)
3. Real Revenues ≥ Real Expenditures

The government is happiest when it can run such a system without increasing the tax rate, and two conditions facilitate this: when, *ceteris paribus*, the number of covered workers is growing faster than the number of recipients and when real earnings per worker are growing faster than real benefits.

If these conditions are not present—if recipients are increasing faster than workers or benefits are growing faster than wages—the government is faced with two choices. It can raise the tax rate on wages or it can let real benefits decline. Declining benefits need not be politically explosive. In the original Social Security legislation, recipients' benefits were fixed in dollar terms (rather than real terms) and were increased only by congressional vote. Congress could, if it chose, increase dollar benefits more slowly than the rate of inflation, which would cause real benefits to decline (much as young workers' real wages declined in the late 1970s) without highly visible dollar reductions.

In the early years of Social Security it cost very little. While it covered a majority of the work force, few workers had been in the system long enough to qualify for benefits. In the late 1940s there

---

[40] For an excellent history of the Social Security program, see Martha Derthick, *Policy Making for Social Security* (Washington, DC: Brookings Institution, 1979), p. 2.

were 12.5 million persons aged 65 and over while only 3 million persons received Social Security checks. These 3 million recipients were being supported by 39 million covered workers—a ratio of 13 workers per recipient—and so taxes could remain low.[41]

Through the 1950s and 1960s the program continued to run smoothly. Workers' real wages were growing, Congress was steadily expanding the proportion of workers covered by the program, and both of these factors increased revenue growth. When this revenue growth was projected forward, the system would show great surpluses and Congress would respond by raising benefits. Congress passed a 14 percent benefit increase in 1952 and a 15 percent benefit increase in 1960, each with only minor tax increases.[42]

Beginning in 1965, several pieces of legislation laid the groundwork for future cost pressures. The first was the passage of Medicare, health insurance for the elderly. In one sense, Medicare simply redressed a growing imbalance in access to health care. Since the end of World War II the proportion of all *workers* covered by employer-provided health insurance had grown dramatically. In this way, Medicare (and the previously discussed Medicaid for certain low-income families) put working and nonworking families on an equal footing. But the growth in public and private insurance dramatically increased the demand for health care, while the supply of doctors was relatively slow to expand (Chapter 7). The result was a rapid inflation in medical prices. By 1973 Medicare was costing $22.5 billion (in 1984 dollars), an amount equal to one fifth of Social Security itself.

Equally important was the 1972 legislation linking Social Security benefits to the Consumer Price Index. The link was proposed by the Nixon Administration and at the time was seen as a prudent reform. From 1947 to 1972 the economy had produced twenty-five years of almost unbroken growth in real wages. Since living standards were steadily rising, the indexing of Social Security benefits to keep purchasing power constant seemed an equitable thing to do. Moreover, it undercut election year pressures to vote even bigger increases. Like the rest of us, Congress had no idea that the nation was about to enter a decade of real wage stagnation and decline.

---

[41] On the number of recipients, see *Historical Statistics of the United States* (1975), series H187, 198, and 199.

[42] See Derthick, *Policy Making*, chap. 17.

The Welfare State in 1973

By 1973 government payments to individuals had grown to equal 9.5 percent of gross national product (GNP) (up from 5 percent in 1947). (See Figure 8.4). These payments, together with rising real wages, were reshaping the bottom of the income distribution. The lowest quintile of the family income distribution contained, as always, the poorest one fifth of all families, but the nature of these families was changing as were the sources of their income.

Recall from Chapter 3 that in the late 1940s two fifths of all families in the bottom quintile were aged 65 and over or headed by a woman under age 65. By the early 1970s the proportion had risen to two thirds (Figure 8.7). Half of the increase represented newly formed female-headed families. The other half were elderly families whose retirement incomes had not kept up with rapidly growing real wages. The quintile's reliance on government benefits grew even more quickly. In the late 1940s both Social Security and AFDC were very small programs. Most families (including many elderly families) had a working member, and even in the lowest quintile about 80 percent of all income came from earnings. By 1973 only 55 percent of income in the lowest quintile came from earnings, which reflected higher retirement rates among the elderly, more female-headed families, and greater AFDC participation.[43]

Equally sharp changes occurred in the poverty population *per se.* Unlike the lowest quintile, the poverty population had no set size but rather counted all families whose incomes fell below the fixed real value of the poverty standard. As real wages continued to rise, the proportion of the population in poverty continued to fall from 22 percent in 1959 to 11 percent in 1973.[44]

Not surprisingly, the fall in poverty was quickest among husband-wife families under age 65, families best able to enter the booming economy. As a result of their success, the composition of the poverty population was shifting. Between 1959 and 1973 the proportion of the poverty population who were elderly stayed constant at about 15 percent, but the proportion who lived in female-headed

---

[43] Author's estimates based on data from the 1950 census and *Current Population Reports.*

[44] See, for example, U.S. Bureau of the Census, "Characteristics of the Population Below the Poverty Level: 1983," *Current Population Reports,* series P-60, no. 147 (Washington, DC: U.S. Government Printing Office, 1985), table 1.

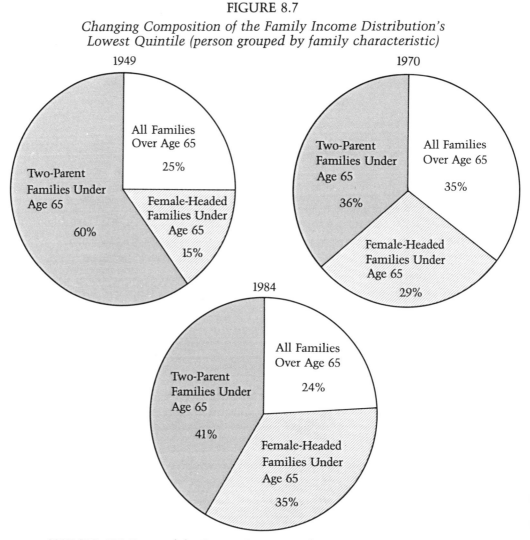

FIGURE 8.7

*Changing Composition of the Family Income Distribution's
Lowest Quintile (person grouped by family characteristic)*

1949

All Families
Over Age 65

25%

Two-Parent
Families Under
Age 65

60%

Female-Headed
Families Under
Age 65

15%

1970

Two-Parent
Families Under
Age 65

36%

All Families
Over Age 65

35%

Female-Headed
Families Under
Age 65

29%

1984

Two-Parent
Families Under
Age 65

41%

All Families
Over Age 65

24%

Female-Headed
Families Under
Age 65

35%

SOURCES: U.S. Bureau of the Census, *Current Population Reports*, series P-60, various numbers, and the 1950 census.

families (under age 65) rose from 21 to 41 percent in a trend termed the feminization of poverty.[45]

These figures seem to say that neither the elderly nor female-headed families were progressing, but that was not the case. The el-

[45] If we add to this figure persons in families headed by a woman over age 65 and female unrelated individuals, the sum of these statistics—the sum of all persons living in households headed by a woman—totaled 50.2 percent of the poverty population.

TABLE 8.5

Composition of the Poverty Population, 1959, 1973, and 1984
(in millions)

Between 1959 and 1973 rising real incomes substantially reduced the size of the poverty population both as a proportion of the population and in absolute numbers. The reduction was greatest among nonelderly husband-wife families, but there was a strong reduction among elderly families as well. The proportion of female-headed families who were poor declined as well, but this was offset by the rapid increase in the number of female-headed families. Between 1973 and 1984 stagnant wages, deep recessions, and reduced welfare benefits increased the size of the poverty population, but indexed Social Security benefits and rising private pensions protected the elderly from this trend.

Characteristics of Population	1959	1973	1979	1984
All Persons Aged 65 or Over	5.5	3.4	3.7	3.3
Husband-Wife Families Aged 64 or Under (all persons)	24.5	9.3	9.5	14.3
Female-Headed Families Aged 64 or Under (all persons)	6.4	7.6	9.3	11.6
Male Unrelated Individuals Aged 64 or Under	1.2	1.1	1.8	2.2
Female Unrelated Individuals Aged 64 or Under	1.9	1.6	1.8	2.3
Total	39.5	23.0	26.1	33.7
Proportion of the Population in Poverty	22.4%	11.1%	11.7%	14.4%
Proportion of the Poverty Population who are Black	25.1%	32.1%	30.9%	28.2%

NOTE: All persons aged 65 and over are included in the first line even if they live in a family whose head is aged 64 or under.

SOURCES: U.S. Bureau of the Census, *Current Population Reports*, series, P-60, nos. 98, 147, 149, and 152.

derly were 15 percent of a *declining poverty population*, and it follows that the number of elderly poor was declining as well (Table 8.5). The principal reason was Social Security. Real Social Security benefits had risen over the 1960s, and the proportion of the elderly who qualified for benefits also rose from 62 percent in 1960 to 88 percent in 1973.[46] Through these increases (and growing private pen-

---

[46] See U.S. Council of Economic Advisors, *Economic Report to the President* (Washington, DC: U.S. Government Printing Office, 1985), chap. 5, table 5-6.

sions) the proportion of elderly persons in poverty declined from 35 percent in 1959 to 16 percent in 1973.

Even female-headed families made some progress. Recall that before 1973 real wages rose for women as well as for men (Figure 7.5). Recall also that half of all female family heads work, and as real wages rose over the 1960s the poverty rate among all female-headed families fell from 50 to 36 percent (and from 70 to 56 percent for blacks).[47] Thus, any individual female-headed family was less likely to be poor. But this progress did not appear in aggregate statistics because the *total number* of female-headed families was increasing rapidly (Table 8.5).

As the composition of the poverty population changed, so did its sources of income. By 1973 only half of all poverty families were headed by an employed person while 30 percent had no working member at all. In the census definition of income (where the value of Medicare, Medicaid, and food stamps are excluded) 50 percent of all income for poverty families came from government payments. The welfare state had assumed a big responsibility. It would become bigger when the economy went bad.

The Welfare State After 1973

By 1973 the welfare state was linked to rising wages through two major assumptions. The first involved indexing Social Security benefits to the rate of inflation. Recall that Congress passed indexation under the assumption that workers' real wages would keep rising. If that happened, indexed Social Security benefits could be financed with little strain. But if real wages began to fall, maintaining indexed benefits would require increasing taxes.[48]

In the case of AFDC and other means-tested programs, the assumption was that rising real wages would keep shrinking the poverty population. To be sure, the AFDC caseload had grown rapidly in the late 1960s and early 1970s. But this growth reflected, at least in part, benefit liberalizations. For some women these added benefits made AFDC more attractive than work, living with relatives, or

[47] U.S. Bureau of the Census, "Characteristics of the Population Below the Poverty Level," table 5.

[48] Specifically, increasing the payroll tax. The problem was exacerbated because the payroll tax also financed Medicare, which was driven in part by the very high rate of medical cost inflation.

other alternatives.[49] If AFDC benefits could be now held in place, rising real wages would automatically make AFDC less attractive and restore equilibrium in a benign manner. This view ignored the possibility that some groups were cut off, by geography and behavior, from the mainstream economy.

After 1973 the decline in real wages undermined both assumptions, but the official reactions to the two situations were quite different. In the case of Social Security (and Medicare), the response was simply to pay the bill. Published data on average benefits must be interpreted with caution because they combine two effects: cost-of-living increases and the fact that each year's new recipients retired at higher dollar salaries and so were entitled to higher benefits.[50] With this in mind, the data show that between 1973 and 1984 the average benefits of a retired worker grew from $3,782 to $5,520 per year (in 1984 dollars), an increase of 46 percent (Figure 8.8). Over this same period the cost of Medicare per eligible person increased from $775 to $1,475 and the program now cost two fifths as much as Social Security.[51]

AFDC policy was quite different. By 1973 most administrators agreed that the rolls had expanded too much, and many states were already tightening eligibility. The worsening economy reinforced this decision. Recall from Chapter 4 that the 1973–74 OPEC price increase produced both inflation and unemployment. States constrained by law to have balanced budgets were pulled in two ways: Inflation pointed toward increased expenditures while unemployment meant falling revenues. In the resulting scramble for funds, AFDC received very low priority, and dollar benefits were eroded by inflation. After the 1979–80 OPEC price increase, the process was repeated, accentuated this time by federal eligibility restrictions that were part of the Reagan Administration's economic program.[52] Between 1975 and 1984 real AFDC benefits per recipient declined from

---

[49] See, for example, Levy and Michel, "Work for Welfare."

[50] There was the additional problem that the initial indexation formula *over*adjusted benefits for inflation. See Derthick, *Policy Making*, chap. 19. This overadjustment was subsequently corrected.

[51] See U.S. Bureau of the Census, *Statistical Abstract of the United States, 1986* (Washington, DC: U.S. Government Printing Office, 1986), tables 605, 612.

[52] Reagan's AFDC changes were very similar to those made while he was governor of California—the so-called Reagan Welfare Reforms. See Frank Levy, "What Ronald Reagan Can Teach the U.S. About Welfare Reform?" in Martha Wagner Weinberg and Walter Dean Burnham, eds., *American Politics and Public Policy* (Cambridge, MA: MIT Press, 1978), pp. 336–63.

FIGURE 8.8

Average AFDC Benefit per Recipient and Average Social Security Benefit per Retired Worker, 1969–1984 (in 1984 dollars)

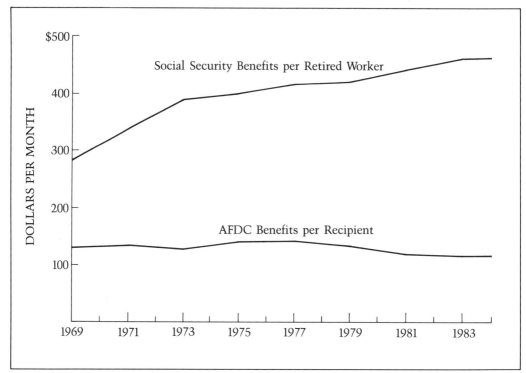

NOTE: The average monthly income of 40-year-old men is included for reference.

SOURCES: U.S. Bureau of the Census, *Current Population Reports*, various numbers; and *Statistical Abstract of the United States*, various years.

$139 to $115, or 18 percent.[53] Unlike AFDC, food stamp benefits were largely tied to the rate of inflation, but when food stamps and AFDC were added average benefits still declined in real terms.

Tightened restrictions and declining benefits helped to limit the program. Between 1973 and 1984 the number of female-headed families with children grew from 4.3 million to 7.0 million, but the number of AFDC cases increased only from 3.2 million to 3.7 million (Figure 8.6).

---

[53] Benefit levels and recipient numbers come from U.S. Bureau of the Census, *Statistical Abstract of the United States*, various years.

By the end of the 1970s then, four forces were at work:

- Real wages were stagnant or declining.
- Real Social Security benefits for the elderly were increasing.
- The number of families headed by women was increasing.
- Means-tested cash benefits were declining.

These forces continued to reshape the bottom of the income distribution. In the lowest quintile of the family income distribution, the biggest development was the exodus of the elderly. Rising Social Security benefits and, in some cases, private pensions kept elderly incomes growing while the rest of the income distribution was sinking around them. Thus, many elderly families moved up from the first to the second quintile, and their place was taken by newly formed female-headed families (Figure 8.7). Accompanying this shift was a further growth in the reliance on government payments such that in 1984 earnings represented only 42 percent of all money income in the lowest quintile.

The poverty population changed in similar ways. The decline in real wages together with the growing number of female-headed households led to an increase in officially measured poverty. Between 1973 and 1984 the number of persons in poverty increased by 10.5 million, and the poverty rate for the population increased from 11.1 to 14.5 percent, with half of this increase representing newly formed female-headed families (Table 8.5). The other half were husband-wife families under age 65, pulled into poverty by the severity of the 1980–82 recession. Through all of this, the number of poor elderly persons increased very little, a tribute to Social Security.

These movements reversed traditional economic status across generations. Recall that during the 1970s and early 1980s the proportion of all children in female-headed households had risen from 10 to 21 percent. This increase, combined with stagnant wages and falling AFDC benefits, caused the proportion of all children in poverty to increase sharply (Figure 8.9). At the same time, the elderly benefited from indexed Social Security benefits and rising private pensions, which kept their poverty rate in check. Traditionally the elderly had been disproportionately poor. But by 1984 the poverty rate among the elderly was slightly below the rate for the whole population and three fifths of the rate for children. We will return to the issue of children in poverty in Chapter 9.

FIGURE 8.9

Rate of Poverty Among Children and the Elderly, 1959–1984

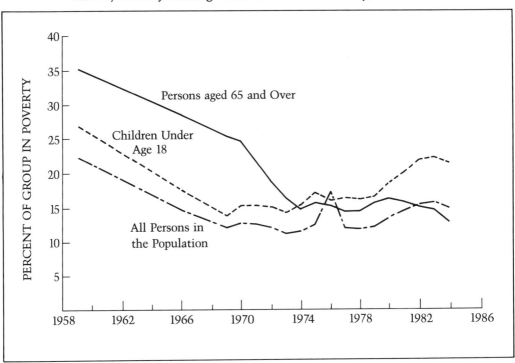

SOURCES: U.S. Bureau of the Census, *Current Population Reports*, series P-60, no. 150.

The Critiques Reconsidered

The preceding history helps put welfare state critiques into perspective. Begin with the criticism that the welfare state is too big. There is no objective way to judge this issue, but it is surely correct that today's welfare state is relatively bigger than most people had intended. In 1984 government payments to individuals (including such nonmoney payments as Medicare) equaled 12 percent of GNP, up from 8.5 percent in 1973. The increase in this percentage represents not only the fast growth of payments but the slow growth of GNP. If productivity growth after 1973 had not collapsed, 1984 government payments would have stood at about 10 percent of GNP, a significantly lower figure.[54]

---

[54] Two percent may not seem like very much, but most economists would give their eye teeth to see the current low U.S. savings rate rise an amount equivalent to 2 percent of GNP.

In this growth means-tested programs played a minimal role; the biggest increases came from Social Security and Medicare.[55] This helps explain the charge that the welfare state tilts too heavily toward toward the elderly, but much of this tilt was also unintended. When Social Security was indexed in 1972, it was seen as a way of defusing election year pressures to have benefits rise faster than real wages. When real wages began to stagnate, indexation had the opposite effect, but it was now part of the law and too politically costly to remove. Without indexation we can be certain that post-1973 real Social Security benefits would not have increased as much as they did.

It follows that the future of Social Security depends critically on future economic growth. Through benefit indexation and private pensions, average income per person among the elderly is now on a par with income per person in younger families.[56] If real wages continue to stagnate, a Social Security program that continues to raise the incomes of all elderly (as distinct from the poorest elderly) will be economically untenable. The fact that Congress has now partially taxed Social Security benefits and has occasionally postponed cost-of-living adjustments underlines the point. But if real wages begin to grow again, the issue will be moot. Younger families will simply have suffered from a spell of bad times much as today's elderly themselves suffered from far worse times in the Great Depression. In Chapter 9 we assess the likelihood that growth will return.

The economy also plays a role in assessing the critique of Charles Murray and others that means-tested programs are ultimately self-defeating. As Murray (1984) wrote:

> My conclusion is that social programs in a democratic society tend to produce net harm in dealing with the most difficult problems. They will inherently tend to have enough of an inducement to produce bad behavior and not enough of a solution to stimulate good behavior; and the more difficult the problem, the more likely it is that this relationship will prevail. The lesson is not that we can do no good at all, but that we must pick our shots. [p. 218]

---

[55] Between 1973 and 1984 all government payments to individuals rose by $188 billion (in 1984 dollars). Of this increase, $102 billion represented Social Security and Medicare.

[56] See Council of Economic Advisors, *Economic Report to the President*, table 5-2.

This might have been a modest thesis which held that aid to the poor had negative effects and was one of several causes of our current poverty problem. In practice, Murray pursued a more ambitious thesis in which aid to the poor was the main cause of our poverty problem. This broad view is implicit in Murray's "poverty-spending paradox" (reproduced as Figure 8.10) in which the number of poor rose

FIGURE 8.10
Murray's Poverty-Spending Paradox

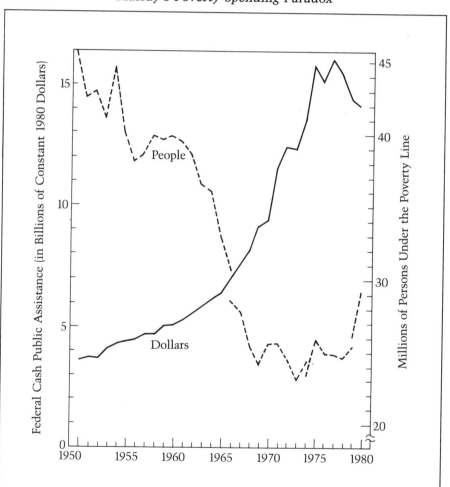

SOURCE: Charles Murray, *Losing Ground: American Social Policy 1950–1980.* Copyright © 1984 by Charles Murray. Reprinted by permission of Basic Books, Inc.

in the 1970s despite big increases in means-tested assistance. To wit: welfare payments induced more female households and idle men, which explained the increase in poverty.

In broad form, Murray's argument is too simple. To see this, it is again useful to distinguish between time periods. AFDC was liberalized in the mid-1960s at a time when the black community was already polarizing. Already one quarter of all black men were reporting very low incomes, while almost one quarter of black families were headed by women. The movement of black middle- and working-class families out of traditional ghettos accelerated the split. From the mid-1960s through the early 1970s Murray's story rings true. In those years the liberalization of AFDC in a precarious situation changed the program from emergency assistance into an entitlement and made it less difficult to have and raise children without a husband.

More than welfare was involved, however, because the liberalization of AFDC stopped in the early 1970s while the number of female-headed households continued to grow. Between 1973 and 1984 the number of female-headed families with children (all races) grew by 1.5 million, the number of poor female-headed families with children grew by 1.1 million, but the number of AFDC cases grew by only .5 million.[57] Among blacks, at least, the reason is not hard to find: AFDC benefits were tightening, but due in part to the bad economy, the lower end of the black male income distribution was deteriorating, too (Figure 7.4). In 1984 an average family on AFDC received cash and food stamp benefits totaling $5,244, about one third less (adjusted for inflation) than in 1973. As low as this figure was, 57 percent of young black men aged 20 to 24 and 27 percent of black men aged 25 to 34 reported incomes that were lower. AFDC was too restrictive and paid too little to encourage many new cases, but the circumstances of about one quarter of black men were so bad that many new black female-headed families were formed nonetheless.[58]

Because female-headed families are so frequent among blacks, it is easy to think of poor female-headed families as a black problem. The actual picture is more complex. Between 1973 and 1983 the

[57] See U.S. Bureau of the Census, "Money Income and Poverty Status of Families and Persons in the United States, 1984," *Current Population Reports*, series P-60, no. 149 (Washington, DC: U.S. Government Printing Office, 1986), table 15.

[58] See Levy and Michel, "Work for Welfare."

number of poor black female-headed families with children increased by 450,000, but the number of poor white female-headed families with children increased by 620,000.[59] These white families constitute a relatively small proportion of the white population, but in each case the data suggest a growing number of families (and a growing number of children) who may lie outside any economic recovery. We return to this point in Chapter 9.

The weak economy can account for only a part of the growth in female-headed families. It does a far better job in explaining Murray's poverty-spending paradox. Between 1973 and 1984 the poverty population increased by 10.7 million persons. (See Table 8.5.) But only one quarter were people in female-headed households. Another quarter were unrelated individuals while one half were people in husband-wife families under age 65. The stagnation of wages and the 1980-82 recession had clearly taken a toll.

Murray discounts this and argues that the 1970s were actually quite good:

> Even after holding both population change and inflation constant, per capita GNP increased only a little less rapidly in the seventies than it had in the booming sixties, and much faster than during the fifties. Growth did not stop. But, for some reason, the benefits of economic growth stopped trickling down to the poor. [p. 59]

In this description, Murray misreads the data we first encountered in Chapter 4. During the 1970s and early 1980s the labor force rose from 41 to 49 percent of the whole population, a reflection of declining birthrates and increased labor force participation among women. Income per capita (that is, per man, woman, and child) could continue to grow even though income per *worker* was not doing well. This meant a great deal for a husband-wife couple that opted for two incomes, but it meant little for a single woman and her children.

---

[59] See U.S. Bureau of the Census, "Characteristics of the Population Below the Poverty Level: 1983," and "Characteristics of the Low Income Population: 1973," *Current Population Reports*, series P-60, nos. 98 and 147 (Washington, DC: U.S. Government Printing Office, 1985 and 1975).

A Summing Up

As a source of income inequality, changes in family structure have potentially more importance than any other factor we have examined. We have not experienced this inequality to date because growing welfare state benefits have largely offset (and, to a certain extent, caused) the growing inequality of earnings. But beneath the income distribution the potential for increased inequality is still there. For at least twenty years, the proportion of families with two or more earners and the proportion of families with no earners have both grown. In Chapter 9 we discuss the implication of this fact.

THE ECONOMY IN THE MID-1980s

Good Times, Bad Times

SINCE 1973 most of us have been touched by the bad economy, and yet we can be excused for overlooking the point. Productivity growth is a subtle idea. Before 1973 its relative steadiness obscured it further.[1] As purchasing power rose, we took it as our due and failed to give credit to a basically healthy economy. We saw ourselves climbing a flight of stairs when we were really climbing an escalator, rising from its progress as well as our own.

When bad times came their nature was equally obscure. Unlike 1932, there was little mass unemployment and few people were forced to take money wage cuts. To the contrary, *money* wages were rising briskly, but prices were rising, too, and few people gained ground.

We knew that something was wrong, but we lacked the language to describe it. Conflict among regions, industrial sectors, and gener-

---

[1] As we saw in Chapter 4, productivity growth slowed from an average of 3.3 percent per year in 1947–66 to 2.5 percent per year in 1966–73. This lower rate was in line with long-run historical trends and, in particular, was about three times as large as the average .8 percent per year in 1974–82.

ations was clearly on the rise, and we spoke of growing inequality as if census statistics would show the income distribution splitting apart. But official income inequality increased only modestly, and the real change in inequality was harder to measure. It involved a mixture of family arrangements, when people bought their homes, and how established they were in their careers. It involved their current income but also their outlook for the future and the likelihood of attaining their aspirations. It was an inequality of prospects in which many people who had attained the middle-class dream could ride out the period while people who aspired to the dream—people who were banking on rising living standards—saw the future shrink.

The episode is not yet over and this should not surprise us. Ending the Great Depression required the stimulus of government policy including, ultimately, expenditures for World War II. An end to our current situation also requires government intervention and a change in national outlook. For more than a decade, we have postponed stagnation's effects by borrowing heavily from the future. The nation's financial position and the proportion of children in poverty both reflect this. Putting our house in order will require measurable short-term sacrifices.

Two issues are on the table. One is the future of the middle class. The other is the future of the poor and, within the poor, the underclass. The future of the middle class depends critically on our ability to revive real wage growth. If growth revives, the future of inequality depends on our ability to draw the poor back into the economy.

We begin this chapter by describing the income distribution as it existed in 1984. We then address the middle class and the poor in turn.

The Income Distribution in 1984

Census statistics describe the 1984 family income distribution as the most unequal in the postwar years, if not by much. Its Gini coefficient (.385) is well above the .348 of 1967–68 and slightly above those in the late 1940s (Table 2.1).

We must interpret these statistics with caution. As we saw in Chapters 2 and 3, the census counts only pretax money income and so contains important omissions. Incomes are not reduced for taxes paid, nor are they increased for the receipt of nonmoney income including Medicare, Medicaid, food stamps, and employer-provided health insurance.[2] Since the late 1940s each of these omitted items has grown larger. Taxes have more than doubled. The cost of employer-provided fringe benefits has increased from 2 to 10 percent of all wages. Medicare, Medicaid, and food stamps have grown from nothing to almost 3 percent of GNP.[3]

When census statistics are corrected for these omissions, the family income distribution moves moderately toward equality. In 1984 census statistics showed that the lowest quintile of families received 4.7 percent of all family income, but corrected estimates suggest that they received 6.7 percent of income and 7.3 percent after adjustments for family size. Similarly, the share of the top quintile drops from a census estimate of 42.9 percent of all family income to 39.1 percent, and then to 36.8 percent adjusted for family size (Table 9.1)

The extent of family income inequality is less than census statistics suggest, but what about inequality trends?[4] We do not know with certainty, but a combination of evidence and speculation suggests that even with corrections, the trends shown in census figures are correct (Table 2.1): The family income distribution moved mod-

---

[2] In the calculations that follow, we value a nonmoney benefit like employer-provided health insurance according to its cost per eligible (covered) person, but this technique raises some questions. It is clearly more sensible than looking at actual dollar payments since that would mean that the sicker a person is, the richer he is. But when we count a $2,000 insurance policy as if it were $2,000 of income, it implies that a family given $2,000 in cash would run out and buy the insurance. In the case of employer-provided health insurance, the implication may be reasonable, but when we talk about Medicaid for low-income families, the implication is probably wrong. For a detailed discussion of these problems, see Timothy M. Smeeding, "Alternative Methods for Valuing Selected In-Kind Transfer Benefits and Measuring Their Effect on Poverty," U.S. Bureau of the Census, Technical Paper no. 50 (Washington, DC: U.S. Government Printing Office, March 1982).

[3] Data taken from the National Income and Product Accounts. See U.S. Department of Commerce, Bureau of Economic Analysis, *The National Income and Product Accounts of the United States, 1929–76* (1981), tables 1.11 and 3.11; and "National Income and Product Accounts Tables, 1982–85," *Survey of Current Business*, 66, no. 3 (March 1986): tables 1.11 and 3.11 (Washington, DC: U.S. Government Printing Office).

[4] As we noted in Chapter 3, one could take our corrected estimates and modify them in a number of additional ways to incorporate the income implicit in subsidized student loans, parks, public schools, and a variety of other government programs. As we move into these areas, however, inputing the distribution of benefits becomes particularly difficult. See, for example, Morgan Reynolds and Eugene Smolensky, *Public Expenditures, Taxes, and the Distribution of Income* (New York: Academic Press, 1977).

TABLE 9.1

Corrected Family Income Distribution, 1984

When 1984 census income statistics are corrected for taxes, in-kind government and private benefits, and family size, the family income distribution becomes moderately more equal.

	Share of Income Received by Each Quintile of Families				
	1st Quintile (poorest)	2nd Quintile	3rd Quintile	4th Quintile	5th Quintile (richest)
Current Population Survey Definition (Pretax, Cash Only)	4.7%	11.0%	17.0%	24.4%	42.9%
Current Population Survey Definition less Taxes	5.8	12.3	17.8	24.1	40.0
Current Population Survey Definition less Taxes plus Medicare, Medicaid, and Food Stamps	7.2	12.2	17.7	24.3	38.7
Current Population Survey Definition less Taxes plus Medicare, Medicaid, Food Stamps, and Employer Fringe Benefits	6.7	12.3	17.6	24.3	39.1
Line above Adjusted for Differences in Family Sizes across Quintiles	7.3	13.4	18.1	24.4	36.8

SOURCE: See Appendix D.

erately toward equality through the early 1970s and moved toward inequality thereafter.

The argument has gaps because estimates of corrected family income distributions are not available for most years, but three pieces of data do exist: the corrected estimate for 1984 (Table 9.1), a similar estimate for 1979 constructed by economist Richard Michel and the author, and the "upper bound" estimate of 1949 family income equality contained in Chapter 3 (Table 3.5).[5] These estimates are displayed in Table 9.2 and lead to two conclusions.

[5] The Levy-Michel estimate appears in Frank Levy and Richard C. Michel, "The Way We'll Be in 1984: Recent Changes in the Level and Distribution of Disposable Income," working paper (Washington, DC: Urban Institute, November 1983), App. C.

TABLE 9.2

The Corrected Family Income Distribution Over Time

Estimates of the family income distribution corrected for taxes paid and nonmoney benefits received do not exist for most years, but such evidence as exists suggests that corrected family income inequality in 1984 was less than in 1949 but greater than in the 1970s.

	Share of "Corrected" Income Received by Each Quintile of Families				
	1st Quintile (poorest)	2nd Quintile	3rd Quintile	4th Quintile	5th Quintile (richest)
1949 Upper Bound Estimate Table	5.8%	13.1%	18.6%	23.2%	39.3%
1979 Corrected Estimate	8.7	14.5	18.0	24.8	34.0
1984 Corrected Estimate	7.3	13.4	18.1	24.4	36.8

NOTE: Figures include adjustment for family size.

SOURCE: See Appendix D.

The first is that the family income distribution in 1984 is slightly more equal than it was in 1949. This shift reflects both higher taxes (which take bigger bites out of the top of the income distribution) and the growing importance of such nonmoney benefits as food stamps and Medicaid—programs which, in their redistributive impact, more than offset the growth of nonmoney fringe benefits for middle-income families.

The second conclusion is that the family income distribution was less equal in 1984 than in 1979. We saw in earlier chapters how the deep 1980–82 recession and budget cuts lowered incomes at the bottom of the distribution. During this period the tax system became less progressive as well. The large tax reductions of 1981 that were part of the Reagan Administration's economic program focused on reducing *tax rates*, and left exemptions and deductions unchanged. From 1978 through 1984 inflation totaled 48 percent, and during this time many low-wage workers began paying taxes because their incomes now exceeded their fixed exemptions and deductions.[6] Together these factors lowered the share of "corrected" family income

[6] See Levy and Michel, "The Way We'll Be in 1984," sect. 4.

in the lowest quintile from 8.7 to 7.3 percent while the top quintile's share grew correspondingly (Table 9.2).

We lack estimates of the corrected income distribution for the late 1960s and early 1970s, but a good guess is that incomes were even more equally distributed in those years than in 1979. The speculation is based on three pieces of evidence.

- Census income distribution statistics—the starting point for all corrected distributions—was moderately more equal in 1968–70 than in 1979 or 1984 (Table 2.1).

- Over the 1970s the overall tax system became less progressive, a result demonstrated by economists Joseph Pechman and others.[7]

- Over the 1970s differences in family size across quintiles narrowed. The bottom quintile came to contain more female-headed households with children and fewer elderly couples, while the average number of children among middle- and upper-income families declined. It follows that adjusting quintile shares for differences in family size had a greater equalizing impact in the late 1960s than it did in 1979.

For all of these reasons the inequality trends in the census numbers appear essentially correct: The income distribution became moderately more equal through the late 1960s and early 1970s but became less equal thereafter. Much of the growing inequality was due to the continued increase in female-headed families, a trend which redefined the nature of the lowest quintile. But after 1979, inequality was reinforced by the deep recession and declining means-tested benefits, both of which undermined the lower quintiles.

As we turn to the content of income distribution it is useful to summarize trends we have observed in preceding chapters:

- *Age*: If we compare the late 1940s with the early 1980s, the income gap between older and younger men increased substantially. This increase reflected both the size of the baby boom cohorts and the fact that younger workers no longer had a substantial educational edge over older ones. *Ceteris paribus*, this concentrates middle-aged families in higher quintiles.

---

[7] On growing regressivity over the 1970s, see Joseph A. Pechman, *Who Pays the Taxes, 1966–85* (Washington, DC: Brookings Institution, 1985).

- *Occupation*: For men, the occupational distribution has changed slowly away from agricultural work and toward professional, managerial, and other white collar occupations. For women, the occupational distribution has been heavily white collar throughout the postwar period. When the income distribution is viewed through the occupation of the family head, it becomes increasingly white collar, particularly in the upper quintiles.

- *Geography*: On a regional basis, incomes in the Southeast began to approach the national average and regional variations declined. At the same time, central city-suburban differences grew markedly, a reflection of the increasing number of families in cities headed by women.

- *Family arrangements*: Both the proportion of families with no earner and those with two earners have grown. Families with no earner reflected increasing retirement rates and the growing number of families headed by women. Families with two earners reflected the rapid increase in women's labor force participation. Government payments increased in importance as a source of income.

These trends appear when the 1949 and 1984 income distributions are displayed side by side (Table 9.3 and Figure 9.1). The most striking development is in families' connections to the economy, a development that has worked in two directions. In the top two quintiles, 60 percent of all families now have two earners. In the bottom quintile 44 percent of families now have no earner. Both figures represent sharp changes from the late 1940s when most families had a single earner.

The quintiles have become stratified in other dimensions as well. Family heads in the top quintile have tended more toward professional and managerial occupations, while families in the bottom quintile have not. Families in the top quintile have become increasingly middle-aged couples (35 to 64) while younger couples have drifted down in the distribution. Some trends worked to diminish stratification—the narrowing of regional income differentials—but such trends are in the minority.

Within the distribution, the dimensions of age and race also stand out. The elderly have improved their status, and a significant share of the elderly have moved from the bottom to the second quintile. Children have moved in the opposite direction and are now more likely to be in the bottom quintile than any other part of the distribution. These movements come from quite different sources. The improved position of the elderly reflects rising Social Security benefits and increased pension coverage. The downward slide of children reflects the increasing proportion of children who live in families headed by a woman (Chapter 8). The downward movement of children may seem modest compared with the increased child poverty rates (Figure 8.9), but this poverty rate reflects both children's position within the income distribution and the fact that most of the distribution has moved to lower ground since 1973 (Figure 2.2).

With respect to race, the *average* position of blacks has changed little between 1947 and 1984, but still change has taken place. In 1947 blacks at the bottom of the income distribution were concentrated in poor, husband-wife families in agriculture. Since that time many blacks have made substantial progress, and three quarters of all black husband-wife families have incomes in the top three quintiles (over $21,700). In the aggregate this has been offset by the increasing proportion of black families headed by women. Most of these families have very low incomes and they have kept the average black position in the income distribution as low as it was at the end of the war.

When all these movements are taken together, they have not dramatically changed the inequality of current income (Table 2.1). But they have almost surely increased the inequality of "permanent" income, a family's average income over its lifetime.[8] We can imagine, for example, a young husband and wife who begin married life with an income below median family income. As time passes and their earnings increase relative to other families, they move toward the top of the income distribution. When they retire, they drop to the bottom of the distribution. If all families traced this cycle, income inequality among families in a single year would have less meaning. Even in the 1950s and 1960s mobility within the distribution was not this strong, but the data in Table 9.3 suggest that mobility is now diminishing. For example, in 1949 two fifths of all black families were in the income distribution's bottom quintile, heavily concentrated in the rural Southeast. They were desperately poor and faced enormous discrimination but the migration to the

---

[8] On permanent income, see Milton Friedman, *A Theory of the Consumption Function* (Princeton, NJ: Princeton University Press, 1957).

TABLE 9.3

*Composition of the Family Income Distribution
by Type of Family and Occupation of Family Head, 1949 and 1984*

Over the postwar period elderly families have moved up in the income distribution while "mature" (aged 35–64) couples have moved up substantially. The position of younger couples (under age 34) has remained unchanged while the growing number of female-headed families has become important in the bottom of the income distribution.

Family Type	1st Quintile (poorest)		2nd Quintile		3rd Quintile		4th Quintile		5th Quintile (richest)	
	1949	1984	1949	1984	1949	1984	1949	1984	1949	1984
Head Aged 65 or Over (Male and Female)	25%	24%	11%	23%	7%	11%	6%	7%	8%	7%
Husband-Wife Family Aged 35–64	42%	25	48	36	61	47	58	60	71	74

	1st Quintile		2nd Quintile		3rd Quintile		4th Quintile		5th Quintile	
	1949	1984	1949	1984	1949	1984	1949	1984	1949	1984
Husband-Wife Family Aged 34 or Under	18	16	33	25	28	32	32	30	17	15
Female Head Aged 64 or Under	15	35	8	16	4	10	4	3	4	4
Total	100%	100%	100%	100%	100%	100%	100%	100%	100%	100%
Addendum										
Proportion of All Families in Quintile with Working Wife	11%	15%	15%	30%	16%	49%	26%	57%	26%	67%

Over the postwar period the occupational distribution became moderately more stratified. The growth of professional, managerial, and other white collar jobs increased the concentration of these jobs in the top two quintiles. Conversely, the lower quintile became increasingly dominated by families whose head did not work, including many families with no working member.

Occupation of Family Head	1st Quintile (poorest)		2nd Quintile		3rd Quintile		4th Quintile		5th Quintile (richest)	
	1949	1984	1949	1984	1949	1984	1949	1984	1949	1984
Professional and Managerial	7%	4%	11%	10%	12%	16%	20%	25%	36%	45%
Other White Collar	3	10	9	16	10	18	12	22	12	21
Blue Collar	15	18	39	32	41	38	46	35	34	25
Service and Agricultural	37	19	16	13	17	10	12	7	10	5
Head Does Not Work	38	49	25	29	20	18	9	11	8	4
Total	100%	99%	100%	100%	100%	100%	100%	100%	100%	100%
Addendum										
Proportion of All Families with No Working Member	25%	44%	8%	16%	2%	8%	1%	4%	1%	3%

SOURCES: U.S. Bureau of the Census, *Historical Statistics of the United States; Current Population Reports*, series P-60, various numbers; and author's tabulations of the 1950 Census Public Use Microdata Samples.

FIGURE 9.1

Distribution of Families Across Quintiles
by Race, Age, and Residence, 1949 and 1984

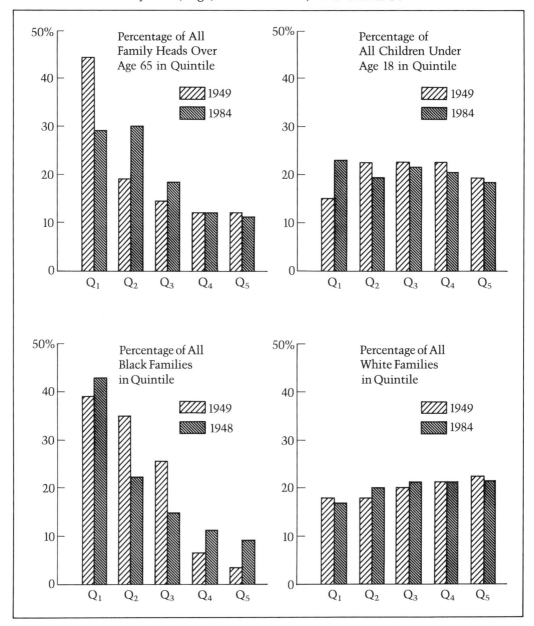

FIGURE 9.1 *(continued)*

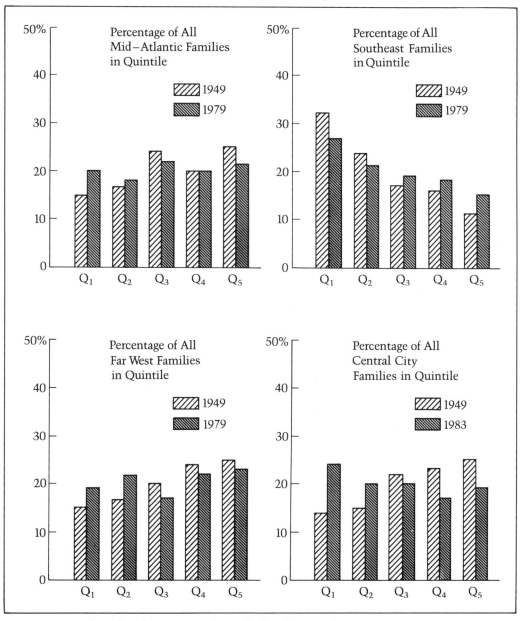

NOTES: Regional graphs refer to 1949 and 1979 (rather than1984) because they require the detail of the Decennial Census rather than the smaller, annual Current Population Survey. The central city graph refers to 1949 and 1983 (rather than 1984) because the Bureau of the Census is adjusting its definitions of Standard Metropolitan Statistical Areas and so the 1984 Current Population Survey does not classify data by central city residence. A set of bars for a single year sums to 100%.

SOURCES: U.S. Bureau of the Census, *Historical Statistics of the United States; Current Population Reports,* series P-60, various numbers; and author's tabulations of the 1950 and 1980 Public Use Microdata Samples.

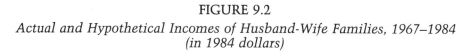

FIGURE 9.2

Actual and Hypothetical Incomes of Husband-Wife Families, 1967–1984
(in 1984 dollars)

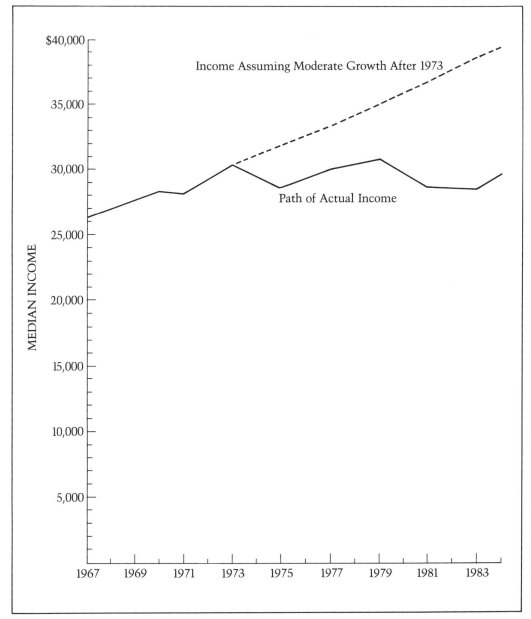

cities and the possibility of better jobs was still ahead of them. To-day, black families in the bottom of the income distribution are largely urban families headed by women with weak prospects for fu-ture income growth. Conversely, middle-class families now retire with pensions and indexed Social Security benefits, and so do not fall so far down in the distribution. For these and other families, their current position in the income distribution corresponds more closely to their past and future position. In this sense, long-run in-equality has increased.

Declining mobility within the income distribution has been reinforced by economic stagnation. In 1949 a 30-year-old man was earning about $12,600 (in 1984 dollars), but his earnings had risen sharply since the war and he could expect more increases in the fu-ture. In 1984 a 35-year-old man was earning about $23,000, but over the last ten years he had largely been treading water (Table 5.1). His future—including his chances of attaining his parents' living stan-dard—looked increasingly uncertain.

The point is not that inequality is unimportant. Rather, it is that people care not only about where they are but where they are going. A lack of growth makes long-run inequality greater than single-year statistics measure. This inequality of prospects is the real cost of stagnation, and it leads to the two issues that opened this chapter: the future of the middle class and the future of the poor and the underclass.

The Future of the Middle Class

Being middle class in America has at least two meanings. The first involves attitudes: an emphasis on formal education, a prefer-ence for reasoning over physical violence, an expectation of a stable career with a period of retirement.[9] The second meaning involves being somewhere in the middle of the income distribution. For those who see a vanishing middle class, it is the second meaning that is important:

> If our conventional wisdom is right and the middle class is really the social glue that holds society together, then America is in the process of becoming unglued. . . . a bipolar income distribu-

[9] See, for example, the definition synthesized by Edward C. Banfield, *The Unheav-enly City Revisited* (Boston: Little, Brown, 1974), chap. 3.

tion, composed of rich and poor, is replacing the wide expanse of the middle class. [Thurow 1984]

Most businessmen don't realize it yet, but the middle class—the principal market for much of what they make—is gradually being pulled apart. Economic forces are propelling one family after another toward the high or low end of the income spectrum. [Steinberg, 1983, p. 76]

The description is jarring for, as we know, census statistics say something quite different. Suppose that we define the "middle class" as the middle three quintiles of the family income distribution—that is, the middle 60 percent of all families. In 1947 this group received 52 percent of all family income. By 1969 this had increased to 53.8 percent, and by 1984 it had deteriorated to 52.4 percent. (See Table 2.1.) This movement follows the general trend of inequality we have observed, but it is not "bi-polarization."[10]

If the proposition is overdrawn, why has it received so much attention? One answer involves the changing types of families in the bottom of the distribution (Chapter 8). Since the early 1970s, income inequality among prime age families (including the growing number of female-headed families) *has* increased. But in the shape of the distribution, this increase has been masked by the rising incomes of the elderly.

The proposition also receives attention because being middle class has a third meaning: having an income sufficient to purchase a middle-class standard of living. When incomes were rising, this purchasing power definition was indistinguishable from being in the middle of the income distribution. After 1973 the two definitions began to diverge, and being in the middle of the distribution no longer guaranteed a middle-class income.

Any definition of a "middle-class income" is highly arbitrary, but suppose we assume that in 1984 the middle-class dream required an income of at least $30,000. The proportion of husband-wife families making incomes over $30,000 has declined from 51 percent in 1973 to 45 percent in 1984, despite the increase in wives who worked and the postponement of marriage among young workers (Figure 9.2).

[10] Several authors have made just this point. See, for example, Robert J. Samuelson, "Middle-Class Media Myth," *National Journal*, December 31, 1983, pp. 2673–78; and Sar A. Levitan and Peter E. Carlson, "The Eroding Middle Class: A New Idea?" mimeographed, Center for Social Policy Studies, George Washington University, June 25, 1984.

If the 1973–84 period had been one of normal postwar growth, *median* family income in 1984 would have stood at $36,000 and 60 percent of husband-wife families (rather than 45 percent) would have had incomes in excess of $30,000. This kind of growth was implicit in our expectations, and by comparison actual 1984 incomes represented a substantial drop (Figure 9.2).

Stagnation of incomes explains why many people felt that they were not doing well. It does not explain why other people seemed to be doing very well. Some of this, too, influenced demographics—two earners, few children—but it also involved housing costs and mortgages.

In Chapter 4 we saw that housing prices in the 1970s increased far more rapidly than the prices of most other goods. For families who had already purchased their homes, the price of housing made little difference. Their mortgage payments were fixed in nominal dollar terms, which did not increase with inflation. To the contrary, they provided a kind of inflation cushion. During the decade many workers received "cost-of-living" salary adjustments. Usually, these adjustments lagged behind the overall cost of living, but an important part of the homeowner's expenses—housing costs—did not increase at all. This left more money for other things.

An example underlines the point. Suppose that a 40-year-old couple now lives in a house they bought in 1973. The annual mortgage payments on the typical home sold in 1973 totaled $2,200 (in 1973 dollars) and of course those payments did not increase with inflation. Today, a 30-year-old couple buying a similar home would face mortgage payments of about $8,400. The difference is $6,200 and even after adjusting for the tax treatment of mortgage interest, this income difference is substantial. In the 1950s and 1960s we could not have constructed a similar example because neither decade had the sustained inflation of the 1970s. It is an economic axiom that debtors benefit in inflationary times, and during the 1970s mortgage holders benefited in exactly this way.

The census looks at income rather than expenditure;[11] thus, this inequality in purchasing power is something we can see but something census statistics do not capture.

---

[11] In fact, the Bureau of the Census has begun to explore after-shelter, after-tax income jointly with economists from the Conference Board. See Fabian Linden, Gordon W. Green, Jr., and John F. Coder, *A Marketer's Guide to Discretionary Income*, a joint study of the Consumer Research Center of the Conference Board and the U.S. Bureau of the Census (New York: Conference Board, 1985).

The Prospects for Growth

If wages begin to grow again, the issue of the vanishing middle class will itself vanish. How likely is such growth?

An answer begins with productivity. The post-1973 productivity slowdown, to the extent it is understood, is explained by a short list of factors: rapid increases in energy prices, a rapidly growing labor force, and the high inflation and slow market growth of the post-OPEC economy (Chapter 4).

By the mid-1980s some of these factors had turned sharply better. Conservation and recession had together sharply reduced the demand for oil. By 1982 it was clear that the 1979–80 oil price increase was not sustainable (in inflation-adjusted terms) and by early 1986 oil prices were falling rapidly.

Labor force growth had slowed. Most of the baby boom generation had now begun their careers. Most older women who had intended to return to work had now done so. The labor force, which had growth at 2.5 percent per year in the 1970s, was now growing at 1.5 percent per year in the 1980s and was projected to drop to 1 percent per year by the 1990s.[12]

Inflation was down, a result of the 1980–82 recession. Between 1982 and 1985 the Consumer Price Index increased at 3.5 percent per year, a performance not seen since the early 1960s.

Despite the good news, productivity growth remained weak. In 1983 and the first half of 1984 it grew smartly, as it usually does when the economy is emerging from recession. But over the second half of 1984 and all of 1985 it did not grow at all. Typical wage increases (adjusted for inflation) reflected this weak growth.[13]

Today, as in the 1970s, no one fully understands productivity's continued stagnation. But the search for an answer increasingly centers on financial debt. Recall from Chapter 4 how the decline in national savings (in particular, the federal budget deficit) helped keep consumption growing. A low savings rate required drawing in foreign capital, and this influx of capital kept the dollar relatively high. Exports were made expensive and imports were made cheap. Markets

---

[12] See Howard N. Fullerton, Jr., and John Tsehetter, "The 1995 Labor Force: A Second Look," *Monthly Labor Review*, November 1983, pp. 3–10.

[13] See Council of Economic Advisors, *Economic Report of the President, 1986* (Washington, DC: U.S. Government Printing Office, 1986), table B-42. In constant dollars, average gross weekly earnings for production workers showed essentially no growth from 1980 to 1985 and stood well below their levels in the 1970s.

for U.S. manufactured goods remained slack, with weak opportunities for expansion and investment (Chapter 5). In the mid-1980s manufacturing productivity was growing at 2.5 percent per year, but this growth reflected the closing of inefficient plants—not the building of new ones. If the goods-producing sector remains stagnant in this way, it is hard to imagine overall productivity growing at acceptable levels.

Wisdom begins by understanding that we have postponed stagnation's effects, but we have not avoided them. At the end of 1986 foreign investors will hold a net $300 billion of U.S. assets. Servicing this debt (without reducing the principal) will require about $25 billion a year. If GNP grows by 4 percent (an optimistic number) it increases by $160 billion, and so one dollar in every five of future growth is already claimed by our acquired debts. Living standards will suffer accordingly, and they will suffer even more if the situation is not soon reversed.

Reversing the situation requires short-run sacrifice. Reducing our reliance on foreign capital means, at the outset, reducing the federal deficit. Deficit reduction can come from higher taxes or reduced expenditures, but either strategy produces a near term loss in income. Closing a federal deficit of $220 billion absorbs the amount by which total personal income would grow in three good years.

Compared with other problems we have faced in the twentieth century—the Great Depression, World War II—our current problem is relatively modest. Because it is modest, it is tempting to ignore it until it becomes unmanageably large. If that should happen, the current episode of stagnation will become something much more serious. There will be no great crash (the English economy has had no great crash). Our economy will simply grind down, and we will have far less of the mobility and opportunity on which we have come to depend.

The Poor, the Underclass, and Inequality

If growth returns, we will still face the issue of reintegrating the poor into the economy. In previous chapters we have had little good to say about stagnation, but in a peculiar sense stagnation has kept inequality within bounds. Since World War II we have evolved from a nation of one-earner families to a nation in which about 60 percent of all families have two or more earners, while 15 percent have none. The post-1973 wage stagnation helped create this situation, but it also kept the resulting income differences across families smaller than they might have been. If wage growth returns, these income differences will grow, and it is possible that some part of the bottom of the income distribution may simply be left behind.

Not all the bottom quintile, or even all of the poor are at risk. In a healthy economy, the elderly will be increasingly protected by indexed Social Security benefits and growing pension coverage. Many of the new poor are in two-parent families who became poor in the 1980–82 recession. As the economy improves, their situation should improve as well.[14] But for about half of the poor, including the 12 million persons in poor female-headed families (under age 65), growth will have much less effect.

It is tempting to assert that these families are the American underclass, but the issue is more subtle. To anthropologists and sociologists, the term "underclass" has a very precise meaning.[15] Consider Oscar Lewis's 1965 description of a variant of the underclass, the culture of poverty:

> On the family level the major traits . . . are the absence of childhood as a specially prolonged and protected stage in the life cycle, early initiation into sex, free unions or consensual marriages, a relatively high incidence of the abandonment of wives and children, a trend toward female-or-mother-centered families and consequently a much greater knowledge of family relatives, a strong predisposition to authoritarianism. . . .
>
> On the level of the individual the major characteristics are a

---

[14] For example, between 1983 and 1984 the number of persons in poor, two-person families declined by 1.3 million (9 percent) while the number of persons in poor female-headed families declined by .27 million (2 percent). See U.S. Bureau of the Census, "Money Income and Poverty Status of Families and Persons in the United States: 1984," *Current Population Reports*, series P-60, no. 149 (Washington, DC: U.S. Government Printing Office, 1985), table 15.

[15] It is also a meaning many people wanted to ignore. See Lee Rainwater and William L. Yancy, *The Moynihan Report and the Politics of Controversy* (Cambridge, MA: MIT Press, 1967). At the time Moynihan was writing, the issue of the underclass was discussed largely in terms of blacks, which heightened its sensitivity. In relative terms, the issue remains critical for blacks, but from the point of the nation the issue of the underclass and the overlapping issue of female-headed families in poverty are by no means exclusively black issues. See, for example, Ken Auletta, *The Underclass* (New York: Random House, 1982).

strong feeling of marginality, of helplessness, of dependence and inferiority . . . [p. xlvii].

Today we would assume that most of these families are black and live in the economically isolated areas of big cities. But by this definition the underclass constitutes only a small percentage of the poor. Economist David Ellwood argues that even among poor female-headed families with children, only 12 percent live in the severe poverty areas of large and moderate-sized cities.[16] If this was the only group outside the economy, then poverty might indeed be a condition which a good economy could cure automatically.

Such a conclusion is too optimistic. If poor female-headed families are not all in an underclass, they are still at an enormous disadvantage in the economy. In 1984 one child in every nine in the nation was in a female-headed household in poverty.[17] Half were black, half were white, and the evidence suggests they will be poor for some time. Ellwood and Mary Jo Bane estimate that in the 1970s the typical poor child in a female-headed household was poor eight years or more.[18]

Moreover, recent studies suggest that the transmission of poverty status across generations is growing. Sociologists Sara McLanahan and Larry Bumpass estimate that white women raised in a two-parent family have a .05 chance of premarital birth, but white women raised in a female-headed family double the chance to .10. For young black women, the chances are .35 and .57, respectively.[19] The data in the study do not control for family income, but other work by McLanahan indicates that among low-income families per se, a young woman who comes from a female-headed family has an increased chance of forming her own female-headed family.[20] Other recent studies show that children raised in female-headed families

---

[16] See Ellwood's "Outside the Ghetto," in *The New Republic*, October 6, 1986, pp. 20–21.

[17] See U.S. Bureau of the Census, "Money Income and Poverty Status."

[18] See Mary Jo Bane and David T. Ellwood, "Slipping Into and Out of Poverty: The Dynamics of Spells," *Journal of Human Resources* 21, no. 1 (Winter 1986):1–23.

[19] Calculations based on data in Sara S. McLanahan and Larry Bumpass, "Intergenerational Consequences of Family Disruption," Working Paper no. 805-86, Institute for Research on Poverty, University of Wisconsin–Madison, May 1986.

[20] Sara S. McLanahan, "Family Structure and Dependency: Early Transitions to Female Household Headship," Working Paper no. 807–86, Institute for Research on Poverty, University of Wisconsin–Madison, March 1986.

have lower probabilities of completing high school and, for blacks, earlier initiation into sexual intercourse, both predictors of future poverty.[21]

Attempts in the early 1970s to measure the transmission of poverty status did not find such effects.[22] The contrast between the earlier and later studies may simply reflect improved statistical data and techniques. But they may also reflect changing behavioral norms. While today's poor, female-headed families may not exhibit all the attributes of an underclass, many may be beyond the reach of even a strong economy.

The Case of Massachusetts

To see these demographies at work, one need only go so far as Massachusetts.[23] In Chapter 6 we described Massachusetts' revival and its current economic boom. In 1984, the last year for which we have income statistics, the Massachusetts unemployment rate averaged 4.8 percent, something close to full employment. In the short run the effect of tight labor markets was to underline the gap between two-earner and female-headed families. Tight labor markets were sufficient to virtually eliminate poverty among two-parent families. Economist Andrew Sum and his colleagues estimate that in 1984 the poverty rate among two-parent families stood at 2.5 percent. But poverty among female-headed families stood at 27.6 percent, a rate below the national average but still quite high.[24] There is, moreover, little evidence that the situation is getting better. Despite the good economy, the rate of applications to the state's AFDC

[21] On educational performance, see Sara S. McLanahan, "Family Structure and the Reproduction of Poverty," *American Journal of Sociology* 90, no. 4 (1985):873–901. On early sexual initiation, see Dennis P. Hogan and Evelyn M. Kitagawa, "The Impact of Social Status, Family Structure, and Neighborhood on the Fertility of Black Adolescents," *American Journal of Sociology* 90, no. 4 (1985):823–55.

[22] One study which found relatively small intergenerational effects was Frank Levy, "Factors Affecting the Formation of Female-Headed Households on Welfare," chap. 4 in "The Intergenerational Transfer of Poverty," Working Paper no. 1231-02 (Washington, DC: Urban Institute, January 1980).

[23] These observations on Massachusetts come from work the author did with the Massachusetts Department of Public Welfare.

[24] See Andrew M. Sum et al., "Poverty Among Families in Massachusetts: Recent Trends and Their Implication for Future Anti-Poverty in the Commonwealth," paper prepared for the Massachusetts Division of Employment Security (Boston: Northeastern University, January 1986).

program has slightly increased in recent years. This is not an issue of race: Sixty percent of the Massachusetts AFDC caseload is white and only 18 percent is black.[25]

To bring these female-headed families (and the absent fathers) back into the economy is as difficult a problem as restoring wage growth. Unless we succeed, income inequality will increase substantially. In Massachusetts, despite the boom, one child in seven is poor, a proportion that reflects large numbers of female-headed families and low birthrates among the state's young middle class.[26] Department of Welfare researchers estimate that one child in four now born in the Commonwealth receives AFDC in the first eighteen months of his or her life.[27] These children will be coming of age when the labor force is growing slowly and labor is relatively scarce. This can mean nothing good for the country.

Epilogue

As I was beginning this book, I had a conversation with an old friend about his early career.[28] When he was young, his family moved several times and he twice repeated elementary school grades. "I always thought," he said, "that the two lost years hurt my early career."

By that time, I felt confident of all the numbers I had read and I challenged him on the point. "How much difference could two years make?" I asked. "You don't understand," he said. "I graduated college in 1932. In 1932 you couldn't find a job. The boys who got out in 1930 had a much easier time and by '32 they were far enough up the ladder to hang on." He was right, of course. Economic fluctuations have a great deal to say about any person's life.

My friend took some years to get settled, but things got better and in 1950 he could buy a good house for one year's salary. In the 1960s he put two children through college. In the 1970s he retired on Social Security and a reasonably good private pension. As his life progressed, he realized that bad times are not forever.

---

[25] Figures developed from the Massachusetts Department of Public Welfare monthly caseload bulletins.

[26] See Sum et al., "Poverty Among Families."

[27] See "Special Report on Recent Massachusetts Births," a supplement to an internal monthly caseload report prepared by the Department of the Budget, Massachusetts Department of Public Welfare, April 1985.

[28] Personal communication, 1982.

APPENDIX A:
THE INCOMES OF ASIANS
AND HISPANICS

IN PUBLISHED Bureau of the Census data, it is possible to trace black and white incomes back to the late 1940s, usually on an annual basis.[1] Comparable data for Hispanics and Asians are much more recent. Census publication of annual incomes for Hispanic families began only in the mid-1970s. Data for Asians are still largely restricted to the decennial census of population because the number of Asian families is too small to give a reliable sample in the smaller, annual census surveys.[2]

It follows that a consistent comparison of black, white, Hispanic, and Asian incomes must be drawn from the 1980 census of

[1] Annual census income data comes from the March edition of the Current Population Survey, the monthly household survey whose primary purpose is to estimate the monthly national unemployment rate. In March of each year, unemployment rate questions are supplemented by questions about the household's income in the previous calendar year. The census also collects income information through the decennial census. While the decennial census collects demographic information from the whole population, income information is only supplied by persons who receive the "long-form" questionnaire, a random sample equal to 20 percent of the U.S. population.

[2] The annual Current Population Survey consists of approximately 160,000 households on a national basis and so contains well under 5,000 Asian households, too small a number to construct accurate income estimates when subdivided by age, sex of household head, and other characteristics.

population, which surveyed incomes for 1979. In reviewing this data, several qualifications should be kept in mind.

First, each of the four "racial" groups is enormously diverse. Asians include Vietnamese, Cambodians, Chinese from various regions, Japanese, and Pacific Islanders, among other groups. Hispanics include persons with ancestors from Mexico, Colombia, Cuba, Puerto Rico, and so on. Blacks and whites, of course, have equal variation.

Second, the census does not consider Hispanics a racial group per se. A person is asked to specify his or her race in one set of questions. A second set of questions is then used to determine whether or not the person is of Hispanic ancestry. About 40 percent of Hispanics classify themselves as "white" while the remaining 60 percent classify themselves as "other." In practice, Hispanics who classify themselves as white constitute a relatively small portion of the entire white population (about 3 percent). These Hispanics are included in the income statistics for whites in Tables A.1 and A.2, but because of their small numbers their removal would not change the data appreciably.

Finally, 1979 was, in terms of incomes and wages, the best year since 1973. Median family income stood slightly above $28,000 (in 1984 dollars). It has since fallen by 6 percent, and the numbers should be judged correspondingly.

Table A.1 contains annual individual income data for persons who work full time in order to get a sense of wage differences. Among men in this group, Asians have a median income slightly below whites, while Hispanics and blacks have incomes about one quarter lower that whites. Actual group incomes depend both on

TABLE A.1

Incomes of Persons Aged 15 and Over Who Work Full Time, 1979
(in 1984 dollars)

	Asians	Hispanics	Blacks	Whites
Men	$24,903 (52%)	$18,560 (49%)	$17,983 (43%)	$25,731 (54%)
Women	$16,459 (36%)	$12,769 (29%)	$13,713 (29%)	$15,042 (24%)

NOTE: Numbers in parentheses are the proportion of all persons in the group who work full time.

216

TABLE A.2

Median Family Income by Family Type, 1979 (in 1984 dollars)

	Asians	Hispanics	Blacks	Whites
Two-Parent Families	$35,015 (88%)	$24,300 (80%)	$26,567 (64%)	$31,542 (89%)
Female-Headed Families	$17,481 (12%)	$ 9,927 (20%)	$10,535 (36%)	$16,934 (11%)
All Families	$32,502 (100%)	$21,065 (100%)	$18,028 (100%)	$29,815 (100%)
Percentage of all Persons in Poverty (1979)	7%	21%	27%	7%

NOTES: Numbers in parentheses are the proportion of all families of that race who are two-parent families (first row) or female-headed families (second row).

SOURCES: All data in these tables comes from U.S. Bureau of the Census, *1980 Decennial Census, General Social and Economic Characteristics, United States Summary*, vol. PC80-C1, pt. 1 (Washington, DC: U.S. Government Printing Office, 1983), tables 128, 131, 138, and 148.

these wage differences and on the proportion of the group who work full time. Here, too, Hispanics and blacks are 3–10 percentage points below Asians and whites. Income differences among women are relatively smaller than differences among men, with Asian women earning somewhat more than other racial groups.

Table A.2 contains data on 1979 family incomes. Because family income depends significantly on the proportions of two-parent and female-headed families, separate income statistics are presented for each type, along with an overall income statistic for the group.

APPENDIX B:
THE EFFECT
OF THE UNDERGROUND
ECONOMY

O VER the past decade, a growing number of authors have examined the underground economy, economic activity that
escapes official statistics.[1] Given their findings, it is reasonable to ask whether a better measurement of the underground economy would affect our general conclusions.

Two questions are at issue. First, we have argued that average
incomes rose steadily through 1973 and then stagnated. Would a
proper measurement of the underground economy have changed this
conclusion? Second, we have argued that the shape of the income
distribution has remained relatively constant (though the kinds of
families at the bottom of the distribution are quite different today
than they were at the end of World War II). Would a proper measurement of the underground economy have changed any part of this
conclusion? In both cases, the answer appears to be no.

[1] See, for example, Edward L. Feige, "How Big Is the Irregular Economy?" *Challenge*,
November–December 1979, pp. 5–13.

The Path of Incomes

A consistently large underground economy would mean that we have consistently understated actual income levels. This is a real possibility. But to affect our conclusion about income *growth*, it must be true that the underground economy was much larger after 1973 than before—that it grew fast enough after 1973 to offset the stagnation shown by official statistics. There is no evidence of this. A detailed study by the Internal Revenue Service suggests that unreported income and overstated expenses totaled 7.7 percent of gross national product (GNP) in 1973 and 9.1 percent of GNP in 1981.[2] Economist Ann Witte, using the IRS study and a variety of other sources, concludes that "(1) unrecorded activity was approximately 10 percent as large as recorded GNP in 1976/77, and (2) unrecorded activity grew at an average annual rate slightly (1 to 2 percent) greater than recorded GNP during the 1970's."[3]

To put these numbers in perspective, recall the example from Table 5.1: A man passing from age 40 to 50 saw his real earnings rise by 29 percent during the 1960s, but a similar man saw his real earnings decline by 14 percent from 1973 to 1984. Even though the underground economy grew slightly faster than measured GNP during the 1970s, the difference in growth rates was far too small to compensate for the stagnation we observe in census income statistics.

Income Inequality

If the underground economy does not affect observed trends in income growth, does it affect observed trends in income inequality? Again the answer seems to be no. Given the underground economy's modest size—currently about 12 percent of GNP—it would have to be concentrated in a single part of the income distribution to substantially affect the distribution's shape. Common observation suggests that it is not concentrated in this way. For every story of an unemployed young man who sells cocaine, there is a story of an

[2] U.S. Department of the Treasury, Internal Revenue Service, *Income Tax Compliance Research: Estimates for 1973–81* (Washington, DC, U.S. Department of the Treasury, 1983).

[3] Ann D. Witte, "The Nature and Extent of Unrecorded Activity: A Survey Concentrating on Recent U.S. Research," mimeographed, Wellesley College, April 1985, p. 26.

older opthamologist who collects most fees and pays for most purchases strictly in cash.

To the extent that distributional estimates exist, they come to a similar conclusion. In 1985 the underground economy accounted for about $439 billion. Witte estimates that about $90 billion of this number represents gambling, prostitution, and drugs (with drugs accounting for the lion's share). The remaining $349 billion represents the income from legal activities that are simply not reported: domestics and home remodelers who work off the books, small businesses that don't report all their business, and so on.[4] There is no reason to believe that the distribution of these monies is much different than the distribution of the income observed by the census.

A proper recording of these numbers might change certain specific figures—for example, the proportion of young black men who report no earnings during the year. But it would be unlikely to change the shape of the income distribution as a whole.

APPENDIX C:
CONSTRUCTING
AN OCCUPATIONAL
CLASSIFICATION

THE OCCUPATIONAL classification used in this book was designed to fulfill three functions:

- It had to be compact enough to be understood.
- It had to be applicable to the four censuses between 1940 and 1980.
- It had to highlight occupations of particular interest—for example, doctors and lawyers.

The classification began with the occupational coding used in the 1980 census. At its broadest level the 1980 census puts all occupations into fourteen major groups. In important respects these 1980 groups differ from the groups used in earlier censuses.[1] For example, in earlier years higher levels of white collar workers were divided into two broad classifications: "Professional, Technical and

---

[1] Compare the occupational classifications used in U.S. Bureau of the Census, *Occupational Characteristics*, 1970 Census of Population, Subject Report PC(2)-7A (Washington, DC: U.S. Government Printing Office, 1973), and *Occupation By Industry*, 1980 Census of Population, Subject Report PC80-2-7C (Washington, DC: U.S. Government Printing Office, 1984).

Kindred Workers," which contained 50 specific job titles, and "Managers and Administrators (except Farm Managers)," which contained 12 specific titles. In 1980 many (but not all) of the detailed occupations in these two groups fell under a single new classification: "Managerial and Professional Specialty Workers."

Fortunately, it was possible to map the specific job titles from one broad grouping to another, and thus to project the 1980 classification back through the 1950 census. Some meanings have changed. There were technicians in both 1950 and 1980, but few of the 1950 technicians repaired computers. Nevertheless the spirit of the detailed job titles remains intact. This conclusion is supported in work by Suzanne Bianchi and Nancy Rytina comparing the 1970 census and the 1980 census which suggests there was relatively little reclassification of persons among detailed titles.[2] It follows that reorganizing the specific titles under a consistent set of major groups provides a consistent picture.

Once the major groupings were complete, selected detailed titles were broken out because they were of particular interest. For example, health technicians were separated from other technicians and added to nurses to show the growth of employment in the health sector.

---

[2] See Suzanne M. Bianchi and Nancy Rytina, "Occupational Change, 1970–1980," paper presented at the annual meeting of the Population Association of America, Minneapolis, May 1984.

APPENDIX D:
CONSTRUCTING ESTIMATES OF THE
"TRUE" INCOME DISTRIBUTION

THERE are significant differences between the census definition of income and most people's definition of purchasing power. As we saw in Chapter 3, the census defines income to be gross money income. This definition overstates purchasing power by not removing taxes paid, and it understates purchasing power by not counting such nonmoney income as food stamps, Medicare (which can be thought of as a prepaid insurance plan), and employer provided fringe benefits.[1]

It is particularly hard to correct these problems in early postwar data. For example, assembling an accurate set of state and local taxes for the late 1940s is an almost impossible job. For this reason, Chapter 3 contained an "upper bound" estimate of income *equality* which corrected published census statistics only for federal income and payroll taxes. As noted in the chapter, the primary omissions—state

---

[1] There are, of course, other ways in which purchasing power can change, including the effect of a fixed payment mortgage in an inflationary period or the rising value of assets which have not yet been cashed in. Unfortunately, limited data sources make these issues too difficult to examine in this book.

and local taxes and employer-provided fringe benefits[2]—were both distributed relatively regressively. Their effect would have been to make an adjusted income distribution no more equal and probably less equal than the estimate we presented.

The "upper bound" estimate was constructed by applying federal income and Social Security tax estimates developed by Joseph Minarik[3] to published census estimates of the income distribution. Minarik's estimates were developed for 1954 and expressed as the percentage of income paid by a family of four at different income levels. These numbers were modified to fit the 1949 distribution and were applied to the published income shares of each quintile to obtain the estimates in Table 3.4.

For 1979 and 1984 it was possible to construct more systematic estimates using the Urban Institute's Transfer Income Model (TRIM2). TRIM2 is a microsimulation model which can use the Current Population Survey (CPS) as a data base. It simulates tax and transfer programs by organizing each person, family, and household data record from the CPS into the appropriate filing unit for the program being simulated. For example, income tax filing units are separately created within households on the basis of marriage status and dependency while food stamp filing units contain all household members irrespective of dependency and marriage status.

In Tables 9.1 and 9.2, TRIM2 estimates simulate the value of federal income and payroll taxes, state income taxes, state and local sales taxes, and state and local property taxes.[4] They also simulate the value of food stamps benefits, Medicare benefits, and Medicaid benefits. In the case of Medicare and Medicaid, members of the eligible population were assigned benefits equal to the program cost per eligible person. Thus, the benefit was treated as the dollar value of a prepaid insurance program. To do otherwise—to assign actual payments to recipients—would make it appear that the sickest people were the richest.

TRIM2 cannot yet simulate the effects of employer-provided fringe benefits. To deal with this problem, the model's estimates

---

[2] Medicaid, Medicare, and food stamps, of course, did not exist in the 1940s.

[3] See Joseph Minarik, *Making Tax Choices* (Washington, DC: Urban Institute, 1985), table 7.

[4] These simulations were done by Richard C. Michel of the Urban Institute and are detailed in Frank Levy and Richard C. Michel, "The Way We'll Be in 1984: Recent Changes in the Level and Distribution of Disposable Income," working paper, Urban Institute, Washington, DC, November 1983.

were adjusted using the figures developed by Timothy M. Smeeding (1982). Smeeding's work did not contain an estimate of fringe benefits for 1984, but his estimates for 1979 appeared to be the best adjustments available and so were applied to the 1984 estimates with slight modification.

One fact that emerged from these simulations was the way in which the tax system became more regressive in the early 1980s. Between 1978 and 1980 taxpayers at all levels had been pushed up into successively higher brackets by inflation. As noted in Chapter 9, the Reagan Administration's 1981 tax bill was designed to redress this situation, but it operated on tax rates while leaving the size of exemptions and deductions constant. The reduced rates benefited

TABLE D.1

Taxes as a Percentage of Cash Income plus Food Stamps

	Quintiles of the Family Income Distribution				
	1	2	3	4	5
1979 TAX RATES					
Payroll Taxes	2.6%	4.5%	5.4%	5.4%	4.4%
Federal Income Taxes	− .6	5.2	9.9	13.1	19.1
State Income Taxes	.2	1.0	1.7	2.3	3.1
State and Local Property Taxes	1.4	1.2	1.4	1.6	2.2
State and Local Sales Taxes	6.1	4.3	3.8	3.4	2.8
Cumulative Tax Rate	9.7	16.2	22.2	25.8	31.6
1984 TAX RATES					
Payroll Taxes	3.0%	4.7%	5.7%	6.0%	4.9%
Federal Income Taxes	.5	5.1	9.0	12.2	17.6
State Income Taxes	.4	1.4	2.2	2.8	3.6
State and Local Property Taxes	1.0	.9	1.1	1.3	2.4
State and Local Sales Taxes	7.0	4.4	3.8	3.4	2.6
Cumulative Tax Rate	11.9%	16.5%	21.8%	25.7%	31.1%
Change Since 1979	+2.2%	+.3%	−.4%	−.1%	−.5%

NOTE: The negative number in column 1 refers to a net tax refund under the Earned Income Tax Credit.

SOURCE: Simulations from the Urban Institute TRIM2 microsimulation model.

higher-income families who were already paying taxes before the inflation. But it did little to help poorer families who had moved from paying little or no federal taxes to positive federal taxes as inflation caused their incomes to exceed the exemptions and deductions. These results are summarized in Table D.1, in which taxes are expressed as a percentage of cash income *plus food stamps* to get a better sense of purchasing power.[5]

---

[5] These tables first appeared in Levy and Michel, "The Way We'll Be in 1984."

APPENDIX E:
DEFINING THE GINI COEFFICIENT

THE GINI coefficient, one of several measures of income inequality, is best described through a diagram.

To construct the diagram families are first ranked by order of increasing income. Incomes are then added across families, beginning with the poorest family, to answer the following questions:

- What percentage of all family income goes to the poorest 1 percent of families?
- What percentage of all family income goes to the poorest 5 percent of families?
- What percentage of all family income goes to the poorest 10 percent of families?

And so on.

If all families received equal incomes of, say, $27,000, the first 1 percent of families would receive 1 percent of all family income, the first 5 percent of families would receive 5 percent of all family income, and so on. This perfectly equal distribution is illustrated by the diagonal straight line in the figure.

In practice, the U.S. income distribution is far less equal than this. In Table 2.1, for example, we saw that the lowest 20 percent of families received about 5 percent of family income; the first 40 percent received 17 percent of income, and so on. This distribution is illustrated by the curved line, which lies below the straight line because the first 5, 10, and 15 percent of families receive less than 5, 10, and 15 percent of all family income. The greater income inequality, the lower the curve will be.

The Gini coeffient is defined as twice the size of the shaded area (between the diagonal line and the curve).

If income were distributed perfectly equally, the curve would *become* the straight line. There would be no shaded area and the Gini coefficient would be zero.

FIGURE E.1
Defining the Gini Coefficient

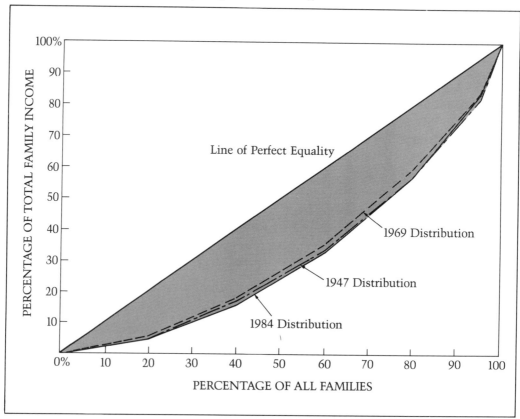

If all income were received by one family (perfect inequality) the "curve" would coincide with the bottom axis of the figure: the first 1, 2, . . . 99 percent of all families would receive nothing while the last family would receive 100 percent of income. In this case the shaded area would equal .5 (half of a 1.0 square), and the Gini coefficient would equal 1.0.

Ellwood, David "Outside the Ghetto." *New Republic* (October 6, 1986): 20–21.

Feige, Edward L. "How Big Is the Irregular Economy?" *Challenge* (November–December 1979):5–13.

Flaim, Paul O., and Ellen Sehgal "Displaced Workers of 1979–83: How Well Have They Fared?" *Monthly Labor Review* (July 1985): 3–16.

Freeman, Richard B. "Changes in the Labor Market for Black Americans, 1948–72." *Brookings Papers on Economic Activity*, no. 1 (1973): 67–132.

———— *The Over-Educated American.* New York: Academic Press, 1976.

Freudenheim, Milt "AMA Report Sees Too Many Doctors" *New York Times*, June 14, 1986, p. 1.

Friedman, Milton *A Theory of the Consumption Function.* Princeton, NJ: Princeton University Press, 1957.

Fuchs, Victor R. *Changes in the Location of Manufacturing in the United States Since 1929.* New Haven: Yale University Press, 1962.

———— *The Service Economy.* New York: National Bureau of Economic Research and Columbia University Press, 1968.

———— "Economic Growth and the Rise of Service Employment." In Herbert Giersch, ed. *Towards an Explanation of Economic Growth.* Tübingen: Mohr, 1981.

Fullerton, Howard N., Jr., and John Tsehetter "The 1995 Labor Force: A Second Look." *Monthly Labor Review* (November 1983): 3–10.

Gans, Herbert *The Levittowners.* New York: Pantheon Books, 1967.

Gilder, George *Wealth and Poverty.* New York: Basic Books, 1980.

Glazer, Nathan "The Limits of Social Policy." *Commentary* (September 1971): 51–58.

Gordon, Robert J. "Postwar Macroeconomics: The Evolution of Events and Ideas." In Martin Feldstein, ed. *The American Economy in Transition.* Chicago: University of Chicago Press, 1980, chap. 2.

Harrington, Michael *The Other America.* New York: Macmillan, 1962.

Harvard Business School *Public Assistance (B),* Teaching Case 9-373-239. Boston: Intercollegiate Case Clearing House, 1973.

Hathaway, Dale E. "Food Prices and Inflation." *Brookings Papers on Economic Activity*, no. 1 (1974): 63–116.

Heller, Walter *New Dimensions in Political Economy.* Cambridge, MA: Harvard University Press, 1960.

Henle, Peter, and Paul Ryscavage "The Distribution of Earned Income Among Men and Women, 1958–77." *Monthly Labor Review* (April 1980): 3–10.

Hirschman, Albert O. *Shifting Involvements.* Princeton, NJ: Princeton University Press, 1982.

Hogan, Dennis P., and Evelyn M. Kitagawa "The Impact of Social Status, Family Structure and Neighborhood on the Fertility of Black Adolescents." *American Journal of Sociology* 90, no. 4 (1985): 823–55.

Kain, John F. "The Distribution and Movement of Jobs and Industry." In James Q. Wilson, ed. *The Metropolitan Enigma.* Cambridge, MA: Harvard University Press, 1968, chap. 1.

Kamen, Al "Fewer Students Apply to Enter Law Schools." *Washington Post*, June 10, 1985, sect. A, p. 3.

Kendrick, John W. *Postwar Productivity Trends in the United States, 1948–69.* New York: National Bureau of Economic Research, 1974.

Kirkland, Richard I., Jr. "Are Service Jobs Good Jobs?" *Fortune* (June 10, 1985): 38–43.

Kuttner, Bob "The Declining Middle." *Atlantic* (July 1983): 60–72.

Lampman, Robert J., and Timothy M. Smeeding "Interfamily Transfers as Alternatives to Government Transfers to Persons." *Review of Income and Wealth*, series 29, no. 1 (March 1983): 45–66.

Lawrence, Robert Z. *Can America Compete.* Washington, DC: Brookings Institution, 1984, pp. 80–81.

Lebergott, Stanley *The American Economy: Income, Wealth and Want.* Princeton, NJ: Princeton University Press, 1976.

Lee, Joung Young Unpublished doctoral dissertation, Department of Economics, University of Maryland at College Park, April 1985.

Lemann, Nicholas "The Origins of the Underclass." *Atlantic* (June 1986): 31–55 (part 1); (July 1986): 54–68 (part 2).

Levitan, Sar A., and Peter E. Carlson "The Eroding Middle Class: A New Idea?" Mimeographed. Center for Social Policy Studies, George Washington University, June 25, 1984.

Levy, Frank "What Ronald Reagan Can Teach the United States About Welfare Reform." In Martha Wagner Weinberg and Walter Dean Burnham, eds. *American Politics and Public Policy.* Cambridge, MA: MIT Press, 1978, pp. 336–63.

—— "The Labor Supply of Female Household Heads or AFDC Work Incentives Don't Work Too Well." *Journal of Human Resources* 14, no. 1 (Winter 1979):76–97.

—— "Changes in the Employment Prospects for Black Males." *Brookings Papers in Economic Activity*, no. 2 (1980): 513–37.

—— "Factors Affecting the Formation of Female-Headed Households on Welfare." Chapter 4 in "The Intergenerational Transfer of Poverty." Working Paper no. 1231–02. Washington, DC: Urban Institute, 1980.

—— "Affluence, Altruism and Happiness in the Postwar Period." In Martin David and Timothy Smeeding, eds. *Horizontal Equity, Uncertainty and Economic Welfare.* Chicago: University of Chicago Press, 1985, chap. 1.

——, **and Richard C. Michel** "The Way We'll Be in 1984: Recent Changes in the Level and Distribution of Disposable Income." Working Paper. Washington, DC: Urban Institute, November 1983.

—— "Are Baby Boomers Selfish?" *American Demographics* 17 (April 1985): 38–41.

—— "An Economic Bust for the Baby Boom." *Challenge* (March–April 1986): 33–39.

—— "Work for Welfare: How Much Good Will It Do?" *American Economic Review* 76 (May 1986): 399–404.

Lewis, Oscar *La Vida.* New York: Random House, 1965.

Lillard, Lee; James P. Smith; and Finis Welch "What Do We Really Know About Wages" *Journal of Political Economy* 94, no. 3 (June 1986):489–506.

Linden, Fabian; Gordon W. Green, Jr.; and John F. Coder *A Marketer's Guide to Discretionary Income.* Joint study of the Consumer Research Center of the Conference Board and the U.S. Bureau of the Census. New York: Conference Board, 1985.

Long, Larry H. "Interregional Migration of the Poor: Some Recent Changes." U.S. Bureau of the Census, *Current Population Reports*, Special Studies series P-23, no. 73. Washington, DC: U.S. Government Printing Office, 1973.

—— *Migration and Residential Mobility in the United States.* The Population of the United States in the 1980s: A Census Monograph Series. New York: Russell Sage Foundation, 1987 (forthcoming).

————, and **Donald C. Dahmann** "The City-Suburb Income Gap: Is It Being Narrowed by a Back-to-the-City Movement?" U.S. Bureau of the Census, *Special Demographic Analyses*, CDS-80-1. Washington, DC: U.S. Government Printing Office, 1980.

Longman, Phillip "Justice Between Generations." *Atlantic* (June 1985): 73–81.

Loury, Glen C. "The Family as Context for Delinquency Prevention: Demographic Trends and Political Realities." Paper prepared for the Executive Session on Delinquency and the Family, J. F. Kennedy School of Government, Cambridge, Massachusetts, November 10–12, 1985.

Maraniss, David "For West Texans, It's Merely Boom and Bust, as Usual." *Washington Post*, February 11, 1986, p. 1.

Massachusetts Department of Public Welfare, Department of the Budget "Special Report on Recent Massachusetts Births." Xerox. Boston, Massachusetts, April 1985.

McLanahan, Sara S. "Family Structure and the Reproduction of Poverty." *American Journal of Sociology* 90, no. 4 (1985): 873–901.

———— "Family Structure and Dependency: Early Transitions to Female Household Headship." Working Paper no. 807-86. Institute for Research on Poverty, University of Wisconsin–Madison, March 1986.

————, and **Larry Bumpass** "Intergenerational Consequences of Family Disruption." Working Paper no. 805-86. Institute for Research on Poverty, University of Wisconsin–Madison, May 1986.

Mead, Lawrence *Beyond Entitlement.* New York: Free Press, 1986.

Mieszkowski, Peter "Recent Trends in Urban and Regional Development." in Peter Mieszkowski and Mahlon Strasheim, eds. *Current Issues in Urban Economics.* Baltimore: Johns Hopkins Press, 1979, pp. 3–34.

Minarik, Joseph J. *Making Tax Choices.* Washington, DC: Urban Institute, 1985.

Mitchell, Daniel J. B. "Recent Union Contract Concessions." *Brookings Papers on Economic Activity*, no. 1 (1982): 165–201.

Morrison, Peter A. "Current Demographic Change in Regions of the United States." Victor L. Arnold, ed. *Alternatives to Confrontation.* Lexington, MA: Heath, 1980, chap. 2.

Moynihan, Daniel P., ed. *On Understanding Poverty: Perspectives from the Social Sciences.* New York: Basic Books, 1969.

Mueller, Dennis *The Corporation: Growth, Diversification, and Mergers.* London: Gordon & Breach, 1987.

Murray, Charles *Losing Ground.* New York: Basic Books, 1984.

National Conference of Catholic Bishops, Ad Hoc Committee on Catholic Social Teaching and the U.S. Economy "First Draft Pastoral Letter on Catholic Social Teaching and the U.S. Economy." *National Catholic Reporter*, November 23, 1984.

Nixon, Richard *Six Crises.* New York: Doubleday, 1962.

Okun, Arthur M. *The Political Economy of Prosperity.* Washington, DC: Brookings Institution, 1969.

———— "Postwar Macroeconomic Performance." In Martin Feldstein, ed. *The American Economy in Transition.* Chicago: University of Chicago Press, 1980, pp. 168–69.

———— *Prices and Quantities.* Washington, DC: Brookings Institution, 1981.

O'Neill, Dave M., and Peter Sepielli *Education in the United States: 1940–1983.* U.S. Bureau of the Census, Special Demographic Analyses, CDS-85-1. Washington DC: U.S. Government Printing Office, 1985.

O'Neill, June "The Trend in the Male-Female Wage Gap in the United States." Mimeographed. Washington, DC: Urban Institute, revised March 1984.

Paige, Benjamin *Who Gets What from Government.* Berkeley: University of California Press, 1983.

Pechman, Joseph *Who Pays the Taxes, 1966–85.* Washington, DC: Brookings Institution, 1985.

Peterson, George E. "Finance" In William Gorham and Nathan Glazer, eds. *The Urban Predicament.* Washington, DC: Urban Institute, 1976, chap. 2.

———, **and Thomas Muller** "Regional Impact of Federal Tax and Spending Policies" In Victor L. Arnold, ed. *Alternatives to Confrontation.* Lexington, MA: Heath, 1980, chap. 6.

Piore, Michael J., and Charles F. Sabel *The Second Industrial Divide.* New York: Basic Books, 1984.

Piven, Frances Fox, and Richard A. Cloward *Regulating the Poor.* New York: Pantheon Books, 1971.

Preston, Samuel H. "Children and the Elderly: Divergent Paths for America's Dependents." *Demography* 21, no. 4 (November 1984):435–57.

Prudhomme, Paul *Paul Prudhomme's Louisiana Kitchen.* New York: Morrow, 1984.

Rainwater, Lee *What Money Buys.* New York: Basic Books, 1974.

———, **and William L. Yancy** *The Moynihan Report and the Politics of Controversy.* Cambridge, MA: MIT Press, 1967.

Reeves, Richard "Heartbreaker on Wheels." *New York Times,* December 29, 1985, sect. 6, p. 20.

Reynolds, Morgan, and Eugene Smolensky *Public Expenditures, Taxes and the Distribution of Income.* New York: Academic Press, 1977.

Riche, Richard W.; Daniel E. Hecker; and John U. Burgan "High Technology Today and Tomorrow: A Small Slice of the Employment Pie." *Monthly Labor Review* (November 1983): 50–58.

Rosenthal, Neal H. "The Shrinking Middle Class: Myth or Reality?" *Monthly Labor Review* (March 1985): 3–10.

Ruggles, Patricia, and Michael O'Higgins "The Distribution of Public Expenditure Among Households in the United States." *Review of Income and Wealth,* series 27, no. 2 (June 1981): 137–63.

Samuelson, Robert J. "Middle Class Media Myth." *National Journal* (December 31, 1983): 2673–78.

Schumpeter, Joseph *Capitalism, Socialism and Democracy.* New York: Harper, 1942.

Serrin, William "Growth in Jobs Since '80 is Sharp, But Pay and Quality Are Debated." *New York Times,* June 8, 1986, sect. 1, p. 1.

Smeeding, Timothy M. "Alternative Methods for Valuing Selected In-Kind Transfer Benefits and Measuring Their Effect on Poverty." U.S. Bureau of the Census, Technical Paper no. 50. Washington, DC: U.S. Government Printing Office, March 1982.

Smith, James P., and Finis Welch "Race Differences in Earnings: A Survey and New Evidence." In Peter Mieszkowski and Mahlon Straszheim, eds. *Current Issues in Urban Economics.* Baltimore: Johns Hopkins University Press, 1979, pp. 40–73.

Smith, James P., and Michael P. Ward *Women's Wages and Work in the Twentieth Century.* Santa Monica, CA: Rand Corporation, 1984.

Smith, Tom W. "America's Most Important Problem—a Trend Analysis, 1946–76." *Public Opinion Quarterly,* 44, no. 2 (1980):164–80.

Stanback, Thomas M. Jr., et al. *Services: The New Economy.* Totowa, NJ: Allanheld, Osmun, 1981.

Stein, Andrew "Children of Poverty—Crisis in New York." *New York Times,* June 8, 1986, sect. 6, pt. 1, pp. 38ff.

Stein, Herbert "Changes in Macroeconomic Conditions." In Martin Feldstein, ed. *The American Economy in Transition.* Chicago: University of Chicago Press, 1980, pp. 170–77.

Steinberg, Bruce "The Mass Market is Splitting Apart." *Fortune* (November 28, 1983): 76–82.

Sum, Andrew M., et al. "Poverty Among Families in Massachusetts: Recent Trends and Their Implication for Future Anti-Poverty in the Commonwealth." Paper prepared for the Massachusetts Department of Employment Security. Boston: Northeastern University, January 1986.

Sundquist, James L. *Politics and Policy, The Eisenhower, Kennedy, and Johnson Years.* Washington, DC: Brookings Institution, 1968.

———, ed. *On Fighting Poverty: Perspectives from Experience.* New York: Basic Books, 1969.

Terkel, Studs *Hard Times.* New York: Pantheon Books, 1970.

Thurow, Lester C. *The Zero-Sum Society.* New York: Basic Books, 1980.

——— "The Disappearance of the Middle Class." *New York Times,* February 5, 1984, sect. 3, p. 2.

——— *The Zero Sum Solution.* New York: Simon & Schuster, 1985.

Tocqueville, Alexis de *Democracy in America.* Translated by Henry Reeve. New York: Appleton, 1899.

Tucillo, John A. *Housing and Investment in an Inflationary World.* Washington, DC: Urban Institute, 1980.

U.S. Bureau of the Census "Income of Families and Persons in the United States: 1949." *Current Population Reports,* series P-60, no. 7. Washington, DC: U.S. Government Printing Office, 1951.

——— *County and City Data Book, 1949.* Washington, DC: U.S. Government Printing Office, 1952.

——— "Average Income of Families Up Slightly in 1960." *Current Population Reports,* series P-60, no. 36. Washington, DC: U.S. Government Printing Office, 1961.

——— "Income of Families and Persons in the United States: 1959." *Current Population Reports,* series P-60, no. 35. Washington, DC: U.S. Government Printing Office, 1961.

——— "Occupation by Earnings and Education." *U.S. Census of Population: 1960,* Final Report PC(2)-7B. Washington, DC: U.S. Government Printing Office, 1961.

——— *County and City Data Book: 1967.* Washington, DC: U.S. Government Printing Office, 1967.

——— "Income in 1969 of Families and Persons in the United States." *Current Population Reports,* Series P-60, no. 75. Washington, DC: U.S. Government Printing Office, 1970.

——— "24 Million Americans: Poverty in the United States: 1969." *Current Population Reports,* series P-60, no. 76. Washington, DC: U.S. Government Printing Office, 1970.

——— "Earnings by Occupation and Education." *1970 Census of Population.* Subject Report PC(2)-8B, 1973.

——— "Characteristics of the Low-Income Population: 1973." *Current Popula-*

tion Reports, series P-60, no. 98. Washington, DC: U.S. Government Printing Office, 1975.

—— Historical Statistics of the United States: Colonial Times to 1970. Washington, DC: U.S. Government Printing Office, 1975.

—— "Money Income in 1973 of Families and Persons in the United States." Current Population Reports, series P-60, no. 97. Washington, DC: U.S. Government Printing Office, 1975.

—— "Money Income in 1975 of Families and Persons in the United States." Current Population Reports, series P-60, no. 105. Washington, DC: U.S. Government Printing Office, 1977.

—— "Characteristics of the Population Below the Poverty Level: 1979." Current Population Reports, series P-60, no. 130. Washington, DC: U.S. Government Printing Office, 1981.

—— "Geographical Mobility: March 1975 to March 1980." Current Population Reports, series P-20, no. 368. Washington, DC: U.S. Government Printing Office, 1981.

—— "Money Income of Families and Persons in the United States: 1979." Current Population Reports, series P-60, no. 129. Washington, DC: U.S. Government Printing Office, 1981.

—— 1980 Census of Population and Housing, Earnings by Occupation and Education, Subject Report PC80-2-8B. Washington, DC: U.S. Government Printing Office, 1983.

—— 1980 Census of Population and Housing, General Social and Economic Characteristics: United States Summary, PC 80-C1, pt. 1. Washington, DC: U.S. Government Printing Office, 1983.

—— "Characteristics of the Population Below the Poverty Level: 1983." Current Population Reports Series P-60, no. 147, Washington, DC: U.S. Government Printing Office, 1985.

—— "Household and Family Characteristics: March 1984." Current Population Reports, series P-20, no. 398. Washington, DC: U.S. Government Printing Office, 1985.

—— "Marital Status and Living Arrangements: 1984." Current Population Reports, series P-20, no. 399. Washington, DC: U.S. Government Printing Office, 1985.

—— "Money Income of Households, Families and Persons in the United States, 1983." Current Population Reports, series P-60, no. 146. Washington, DC: U.S. Government Printing Office, 1985.

—— "Money Income of Households, Families and Persons in the United States: 1984." Current Population Reports, series P-60, no. 151. Washington, DC: U.S. Government Printing Office, 1986.

—— "Characteristics of the Population Below the Poverty Level: 1984." Current Population Reports, series P-60, no. 152. Washington, DC: U.S. Government Printing Office, 1986.

—— Statistical Abstract of the United States. Washington, DC: U.S. Government Printing Office, various years.

—— "Household Wealth and Asset Ownership." Current Population Reports, series P-70, no. 7. Washington, DC: U.S. Government Printing Office, 1986.

U.S. Council of Economic Advisors Economic Report of the President: 1985. Washington, DC: U.S. Government Printing Office, 1985.

—— Economic Report of the President: 1986. Washington, DC: U.S. Government Printing Office, 1986.

U.S. Department of Commerce Bureau of Economic Analysis *The National Income and Product Accounts of the United States, 1929–76.* Washington, DC: U.S. Government Printing Office, 1981.

—— "National Income and Product Accounts Tables, 1982–85." In *Survey of Current Business*, vol. 66, no. 3. Washington, DC: U.S. Government Printing Office, March 1986.

U.S. Department of Labor *Employment and Training Report of the President: 1982.* Washington, DC: U.S. Government Printing Office, 1982.

—— *Handbook of Labor Statistics.* Washington, DC: U.S. Government Printing Office, December 1983.

U.S. Department of Health, Education and Welfare *The Measure of Poverty: A Report to Congress as Mandated by the Education Amendments of 1974.* Washington, DC: U.S. Government Printing Office, April 1976.

U.S. Department of Treasury, Internal Revenue Service *Income Tax Compliance Research: Estimates for 1973–81.* Washington, DC: U.S. Department of the Treasury, 1983.

U.S. House of Representatives, Committee on Ways and Means *Children in Poverty* (committee print). Washington, DC: U.S. Government Printing Office, May 22, 1985.

U.S. Office of Management and Budget *America's New Beginning: A Program for Economic Recovery.* Washington, DC: U.S. Government Printing Office, 1981.

Vernon, Raymond *The Changing Economic Function of the Central City.* New York: Area Development Committee of the Committee for Economic Development, 1959.

—— "International Investment and International Trade in the Product Cycle." *Quarterly Journal of Economics*, 80 (May 1966): 190–207.

Weinberg, Daniel H. "Filling the 'Poverty Gap': Multiple Transfer Program Participation." *Journal of Human Resources* 20, no. 1 (Winter 1985): 64–89.

White, Theodore H. *The Making of the President, 1960.* New York: Atheneum, 1961.

Williamson, Jeffrey G. "Unbalanced Growth, Inequality and Regional Development: Some Lessons from United States History." In Victor L. Arnold, ed. *Alternatives to Confrontation.* Lexington, MA: Lexington Books, 1980, chap. 1.

Wilson, William Julius *The Declining Significance of Race.* Chicago: University of Chicago Press, 1978.

——, **and Katherine M. Neckerman** "Poverty and Family Structure: The Widening Gap Between Evidence and Public Policy Issues." Paper presented at the Institute for Research on Poverty Conference on Poverty and Policy: Retrospect and Prospects, Williamsburg, Virginia, December 6–9, 1984.

——, **and Robert Aponte** "Urban Poverty." *Annual Review of Sociology*, no. 11 (1985): 231–58.

Witte, Ann D. "The Nature and Extent of Unrecorded Activity: A Survey Concentrating on Recent United States Research." Mimeographed. Wellesley College, April 1985.

Name Index

Subject Index

A

accounting, 85, 85n, 86, 122

administrative support jobs, 33, 136, 138, 143

administrators, 30, 143

aerospace industry, 109

"Affluence, Altruism and Happiness in the Postwar Period" (Levy), 59n

age: and education, 30, 31n; and income, 30, 31, 31n, 39–41, 44, 97–99, 150, 197, 198–199; and income of men, 78–80, **79, 81,** 125–130, **126,** 197; and income of women, 141; and labor force participation of women, 33, 142–143; *see also* elderly; middle-aged couples; older workers; young

agriculture (farm), 8, **26,** 27, 44, 74, 75n, 87, 105, 164, 198; blacks in, 32, 132, **134,** 135, 136, 199; employment, 31, 32, **32,** 41, 49, 51, 78, 122, **124,** 135; mechanization of, 131; migrations, 49n, 103–104; productivity, 51, 83; white men in, 122

Aid to Families with Dependent Children (AFDC), 37, 38, 67, 153, 169–176, 169n, **175,** 176n, 179, 182–185, 183n; benefit decline, 183–184, **184;** as cause of poverty, 189–190; in Massachusetts, 212–213

air-conditioning, 25, 108

aircraft industry, 49, 97, 107, 109, 113

airlines, 82, 109, 131

air traffic controllers union, 65n

Alabama, 102, 107

Alaska, 109

"Alternative Methods for Valuing Selected In-Kind Transfer Benefits" (Smeeding), 194n

American Council on Education, 126, 127

American Medical Association (AMA), 120, 130

American Women in Transition (Bianchi and Spain), 143n

antipollution regulations, 63n

antipoverty programs, 10, 37, 57, 153, 153n, 170–172

Arab-Israeli War of 1973, 62, 62n

Arkansas, 104

armed forces, 32; *see also* military

arts, 84n

Asians, 11n, 215–217, 215n

assets, vs. income, 19–20

automation, 131

automobiles, 24, 49–50, 57, 90, 91, 111, 112; mechanics, 31; ownership, 8; workers' wages, 92n

B

baby boom, 2, 2n, 3, 5, 7, 10, 15, 50–51, 50n, 63, 68, 69, 90, 97, 97n, 99, 103, 105, 117, 154–155, 156, 208; incomes of, 123–124, 125–126, 132, 146, 150, 158, 158n, 159, 164, 197; postponement of marriage by, 157, 159, **160;** and social insurance, 168, 168n

baby bust, 3

Baltimore, Maryland, 29n

banks, 90

barbers, 31, 82, 83–84, 86

bathrooms, 154n

beauticians, 31, 33

Bedford Stuyvesant, 116

beef and veal consumption, 25, 51

Birth and Fortune (Easterlin), 80n

birthrates, 9, 10, **155;** among black unmarried teenagers, 158; declining, 69, 73, 103, 156–157, 190; middle class vs. poor, 11; and migration, 103, 103n, 112; in 1950s and 1960s, 50–51, 50n,